Nudes, prudes and attitudes

Issues in Social Policy

Antibody Politic: AIDS and society
Tamsin Wilton

Domestic Violence: Action for change
Gill Hague and Ellen Malos

Nudes, Prudes and Attitudes: Pornography and censorship
Avedon Carol

Nudes, prudes and attitudes
Pornography and censorship

Avedon Carol
with cartoons by Lee Kennedy

New Clarion Press

© Avedon Carol 1994

The right of Avedon Carol to be identified as the author of this work has been asserted in accordance with the Copyright Designs and Patents Act 1988.

First published 1994
Reprinted 1995

New Clarion Press
71 Pilley Crescent
Cheltenham
Glos GL53 9ES

New Clarion Press is a workers' co-operative.

All rights reserved. Except for the quotation of short passages for the purpose of criticism and review, no part of this publication may be reproduced, stored in a retrieval system or transmitted, in any form or by any means, electronic, mechanical, photocopying, recording or otherwise, without the prior consent of the publisher.

This book is sold subject to the condition that it shall not, by way of trade or otherwise, be lent, resold, hired out or otherwise circulated without the publisher's prior consent in any form of binding or cover other than that in which it is published and without a similar condition including this condition being imposed on the subsequent purchaser.

A catalogue record for this book is available from the British Library.

ISBN paperback 1 873797 13 3
      hardback   1 873797 14 1

Typeset in 10/12 Times by Jean Wilson – Typesetting

Printed in Great Britain by T. J. Press (Padstow) Ltd

This book is dedicated to Carol Pearson, Claire Moses, Melanie Martindale and Doris Beauchamp; and to every women's studies teacher who encourages her students to look around and think for themselves.

Contents

Preface	viii
Acknowledgements	x
1 Introduction: the function of censorship	1
2 Sex and censorship: a tradition of hostility	9
3 Pornography and its context	24
4 Feminism and pornography: the modern movement	38
5 The research	60
6 Perversion	89
7 Feminists versus feminists: the insult to women	120
8 A dangerous game	147
9 Men against pornography: a clouded mirror	171
10 Feminism and the future	190
References and further reading	202
Index	209

Preface

Pornography. It's almost a dirty word in itself. Is it really violence toward women, as some claim, or is it merely a scapegoat onto which we have projected our worst nightmares? Within the feminist movement, the debate over pornography has divided women who once worked and marched side by side. Out in the general culture, it has become the means by which feminism is represented as punitive, shrill, repressive, man-hating and anti-sex. Young women who believe in women's equality often shy away from being involved or associated with the feminist movement precisely because the debates within it over sexuality and pornography have seemed so puritanical, and long-time feminists doubt each other's commitment to making a genuine challenge to sexist culture. The debate has been characterized by polarization, mythology, name-calling and even violence – but what, exactly, should it really mean to women and men who long for an end to violence, discrimination, hostility between genders, and the institutionalization of heterosexism? How do those who feel they have been dropped into the middle of an acrimonious fight begin to separate myth from reality and make sense of the issues?

The anti-pornography view has been widely disseminated throughout the United Kingdom in recent years and has certainly had the strongest representation in the media. This book, on the other hand, attempts to illuminate the arguments from the viewpoint that has received much less in terms of the media spotlight, and I make no apology for the fact that I take a wholly anti-censorship position. Long experience of having to fight censorship first of black civil rights and Vietnam anti-war activism and then of the women's liberation movement has taught feminists such as myself that censorship is too dangerous in the hands of governments and cannot answer the questions posed by bigotry, misogyny and sexual violence. Some feminists have indeed taken the position that pornography must be banned and that no intelligent woman can possibly have come to an alternative conclusion on her own; I hope to show in this book that there are legitimate feminist concerns about censorship and the way that the present argument over pornography has been posed, and that we need not have been 'brainwashed' by men or paid off by the pornography industry to oppose censorship of sexual materials. The claim that we cannot think for ourselves and come to different conclusions is one of the most sexist assertions I have ever heard.

My contention is that anti-pornography activism is not merely a useless device for eliminating sexism and violence, but also a disaster for feminists, women in general, and society as a whole. As I will show, the movement for sexual censorship poses a clear and present danger to us on four primary points: it gives enormous and dangerous powers to the state; it promotes the very repression that is implicated in causing sexual violence; it derails honest and open feminist discussion of sexuality and related vital issues; and it further stigmatizes and disempowers women in the sex industry (as well as other sexually active women and sexual objectors), making it ever more difficult for them to take control of their (and our) lives and improve their (and our) conditions.

Being an old-fashioned women's liberationist, I sometimes use terminology that is no longer current, or is not widely used, but is more comfortable to my own beliefs. For example, as someone who is neither black nor Celtic/Aryan, I am happier with the phrases 'women of colour' and 'people of colour' than I am with 'black', as they are more inclusive of the rest of us than other terms are (although I still use the term 'black' when speaking specifically of those once known as 'negroes'); I reject negatives like 'non-white' that presume that the default human condition is white. I also insist on using the word 'gay' for bisexuals and homosexuals as a general term referring to all males and females who are not heterosexual, although I use 'lesbians' when I am referring only to homosexual women; 'gay and lesbian' and 'lesbian women' are both redundancies that make me twitchy.

As a feminist, I naturally refuse to use the male generic, which is not generic at all but really does denote maleness – as science fiction writer Joanna Russ suggested when she mentioned phrases like 'residents and their wives': those commuter marriages, she said, could be hell. (Canadian feminist Susan Wood used to remind people of a paper she'd seen called 'The uterus in rats and men', just to show how silly it really is.) And, as a feminist, I write as a woman rather than as an 'objective' outsider to real life; my use of the word 'we' when referring to women is not meant to exclude men, but merely to do my part in bringing women back into the English language as subjects rather than as bystanders. I also write as a feminist, as an activist, and as a member of Feminists Against Censorship. That is the viewpoint I begin and end with, and I have deliberately chosen to write in a way that reminds the reader that an individual with personal views and experience is responsible for the text; there are no 'objective' observers.

I am never happy with books that treat lesbianism and bisexuality as afterthoughts, a sort of 'non-ladies auxiliary' of 'real women'. Yet a difficulty is posed here in the discussion of pornography and sexuality, as the entire question is so often presented as a matter of male behaviour, and so much of the argument is based on our assumptions about heterosexual relations. This makes it necessary to examine that heterosexual context in some detail. Let me make my apologies now to anyone who feels that, once again, the presumption of heterosexuality appears to be too strong; unfortunately, the arguments about pornography and censorship are only necessary in the first place because our diversity has never been taken for granted.

Acknowledgements

I am grateful to those bright, witty, knowledgeable and brave women who make up the network that is Feminists Against Censorship, particularly Nettie Pollard and Niki Wolf for immediate help, Mandy Merck, Elizabeth Wilson and Mary McIntosh for useful historical background, and especially to Roz Kaveney and Linda Semple, who brought us all together.

Special thanks to Gayle Rubin, whose work provided a helpful reference. Thanks also to Abigail Frost, Owen Whiteoak and Dave Langford for the dictionaries, to Martin Barker, who offered unlimited permission to quote from his book, *The Video Nasties*, and to Nadine Strossen, who was similarly supportive.

I am profoundly grateful to Marcia Pally, who gave me permission to quote without limit her reference materials in *Sense & Censorship: The vanity of bonfires*. These were essential and irreplaceable, containing quotations from interviews that can be found nowhere else. Her dedication in pursuing so many rumours to find out what they refer to, and in consulting leading experts on her own, is admirable and inspiring.

And, as always, I can't thank Rob Hansen enough, for things too numerous to mention – but especially, in this case, for coming up with the title.

Parts of 'Don't get fooled again: assailed in Britain', written for the Sex Panics issue of *New York Law School Law Review*, 38, 1993, were cannibalized for the production of this book.

1
Introduction: the function of censorship

In each of us, there is a little fascist who fervently wishes to suppress any expression by others of beliefs we find threatening to our values. When ugly ideas spread around us as if carried by a plague virus, often leading to uglier acts, the urge to shut people up, stop their voices from conveying their thoughts, can become irresistible. In time, we may expect governments to take control of our neighbours' tongues, somehow believing that the powerful tool of censorship can never be directed against our own thoughts.

Governments, of course, love to be handed a device that can direct the type of thinking that is permitted in public. It takes little time before those in power recognize the flexibility of censorship in suppressing criticisms of themselves. Obscenity laws can be selectively enforced against social campaigners or critics of the government. A law that is made to suppress racist and sexist hate speech can be turned to stopping feminist and anti-racist activities because they are said to promote hatred of whites and men. Or if the powerful have no sympathy with the law, they can simply ignore it while instituting their own political censorship outright; anti-censorship arguments hold little sway in a society that has already accepted the premise that some thoughts must be stopped. Without a strong anti-censorship tradition in a culture, governments can get away with silencing all dissent.

All of these methods have been used – often with frightening success – in democratic western countries. In the early days of birth-control movements in Britain and America, the women who fought for reproductive control were jailed for their 'obscene' speech. In Canada, modern laws meant to protect blacks and women from hate speech and the alleged harm of pornography have been turned against the very people who fought to have those laws passed. The signers of the American Bill of Rights enacted a constitutional right to absolute freedom of speech and freedom of the press, and then promptly turned around and passed anti-sedition laws that blatantly violated it. Later, US federal, state and local governments used obscenity laws to suppress black music, anti-racist and anti-war activism, and finally feminist materials. And Hitler rose to power in Germany spouting anti-semitic propaganda despite long-standing legislation that specifically outlawed hate speech against any identifiable group.

Often, the decent people of a society will agitate for censorship they believe will protect its less powerful members, but such legislation has never been known to eliminate oppression. The truth is that governments and their powerful friends *always* have freedom of speech; one way or another, they will promote their values and make them seem acceptable to enough people to ensure that the programmes that follow from those values will be enacted, or continue, with little effective dissent. The most destructive and malicious beliefs can become so popular that no one cares to enforce censorship against them, even when such laws are so strongly worded that it seems impossible they can be ignored.

No legal restraints can ever stop even the most evil idea once people come to suspect that it is based on some subtle grain of truth. Silencing debate does not stop such a belief, but rather allows it to take root out of the public eye, underground. Racist ideas, for example, often gain their legitimacy not from overt, hateful promotions of violence against stigmatized groups, but from far less explosive discussions that may sound reasonable and unprejudiced at the time. Gay rights campaigners know that AIDS particularly affects the gay community, but saying so has been used as an excuse to violate the rights of gays. Code words and phrases can be used in place of racial slurs in order to circumvent laws as well as slipping racist beliefs past our built-in alarm systems before they are noticed – as terms like 'the poor' and 'welfare recipients' (or, often, 'welfare cheats') have been used in America to refer to blacks, despite the fact that most poor people and most welfare recipients are white.

Anti-hate-speech campaigns also tend to take a patronizing view of oppressed groups, and emphasis on a need to offer such groups special protections often creates resentment on both sides: the oppressed group is made to seem weak and unable to stand up for itself – indeed, may feel discouraged from doing so – while whites and men may feel that minorities and women are being given what amount to special privileges. It is far more appropriate to respect the ability of women and all people of colour to defend our positions intellectually by making sure we have the

Introduction: the function of censorship

opportunity to do so; preventing the opposition from voicing their own views to protect us only makes it appear that we have no strength or ability to face them down.

It is useful to make people more sensitive to other groups in their writings or representations, but speech codes and laws also have a chilling effect on media artists that can ultimately have negative consequences. Maria Reidelbach provided a rather ominous example from the comics industry in her *Completely Mad*:

> Soon after its institution in 1954, the Comics Code Authority had virtually eliminated representations of members of ethnic groups in comics; their restriction against 'ridicule or attack on any religious or racial group' had, as historian Pamela B. Nelson has pointed out, 'intimidated many cartoonists into avoiding ethnic images altogether.' But Joe Orlando sees a more insidious meaning behind the code. 'It reflected the society. Look at the advertising, the magazines like *Saturday Evening Post*, the kind of people they represented were certainly not a melting pot, they all looked liked WASPs, and they were hairless, and they didn't sweat, and the women all wore white gloves.'

With recent calls for similar codes in the recording, television and film industries, we could well be on the way to a similarly restrictive and homogenized state for modern media. For 1950s America, this meant a bland uniformity with grossly repressive consequences. Reidelbach quotes cartoonist Robert Crumb on just how bad it was: 'If you were growing up lonely and isolated in a small town, *Mad* was a revelation. Nothing I read anywhere else suggested there was any absurdity in the culture. *Mad* was like a shock, breaking you out.'

Censorship campaigns also serve governments when social unrest would rightly cause activists to target government policies themselves if a scapegoat – like blacks, comic books or pornography – were not found instead. When unemployment is high and governments are unresponsive, property crime, vandalism and domestic violence will always rise. Increases in criminal activity lead to calls for action, and if government is to avoid taking responsibility, it must find another 'culprit' – violent TV programmes being a current popular example. Using public fear of crime as an excuse to take more control of our right to expression is very convenient for those in power, and has the added bonus of giving the appearance of 'doing something' about crime when in fact it in no way reduces crime or addresses the problems that cause that crime.

The programmes and profits of the powerful depend on the maintenance of traditional values, no matter how oppressive they may be, and the

4 Nudes, prudes and attitudes

introduction of new ideas into such an environment poses a tremendous threat to their continuation. If values drift too far, the power structure can crumble; the best defence against social change is the suppression of any new ways of thinking that might arise. It is never an accident that, therefore, liberationist thought is prosecuted far more often than racist or fascist speech. For example, Galileo's belief – that the earth revolved around the sun – threatened the very power of the church, and he suffered for it; on the other hand, Hitler's speech was directed against those with little power, and was tolerated and accepted, despite being illegal. Similarly, Britain's Public Order Act 1936, which was intended to stop fascist demonstrations, has been used against anti-fascists, gays and other left-wing demonstrators, but the British National Party is still permitted to march through London.

Pornography, today, is a central focus of censorship efforts. Sexual material threatens to uproot the very foundation of our long tradition of silence and repression, which is why governments and religious moralists have always opposed free expression in this area. Explorations of sexuality and sexual diversity pose a serious threat to a social structure based on the centralization of reproduction and rigid adherence to sex roles. Suppression of female sexuality, in particular, is crucial to a structure in which women are seen as the linchpin of the family and society, the mechanism by which male irresponsibility and violence must be controlled. More ready access to sexual material has visibly led women to question those traditional roles, and the moral right has reacted with horror to this new openness.

Traditional anti-pornography campaigners from the religious right have, obviously, been the perennial foes of feminist activists; yet, ironically, some feminists have more recently jumped on the bandwagon of anti-pornography campaigns. Anti-porn feminists believe that their opposition to pornography rests on premises and principles that differ radically from those of the old social purity movements, and that they can harness anti-pornography feeling safely, avoiding the historical dangers of sexual censorship. Indeed, many of them maintain that what they propose is not censorship at all, but a new view of civil rights protections that would empower women.

Yet other feminists refuse to participate in anti-pornography activism, and many of us strongly oppose any measures that would further stigmatize recreational sexual material and the women who are involved in its production. Anti-censorship feminists cite a wide range of reasons why anti-porn feminism is, in the words of feminist activist Gayle Rubin,

Introduction: the function of censorship

misguided, dangerous and wrong. We have already seen the Canadian government use a 'feminist' anti-pornography law to prosecute a gay bookstore and a lesbian magazine. We have seen the right-wing Attorney General's Commission on Pornography (the Meese Commission) in the United States, under the Reagan administration, exploit feminist testimony to promote traditional censorship. We have seen half a century of intensive study of the causes of sexual violence and abuse – research that clearly demonstrates the harm of sexual repressiveness – go completely unnoticed, as if it never existed, while rape is blamed on women who pose or play in front of a camera. We have seen innocent women stigmatized and blamed for the evil that rapists and child abusers do. Most of all, we have seen a return of precisely the view of women and sexuality that was central to the traditional social purity campaigns: women as sexless, men as rapacious; women as victims, men as brutes; sexual pleasure as dangerous and anti-social, repression as necessary to social stability.

Women certainly have reason to fear a society in which sexual violence is promoted and accepted. The question is, why should what has historically been a widely acceptable view – women as the sexual property of men – be blamed on a marginal genre like pornography, when respectable institutions like the church and the state have promoted those same values unhindered for thousands of years? If religious scholars and judges have traditionally upheld the view that women must submit to their husbands, why pretend that such attitudes come from pornography? When the Bible – still the largest selling book in the world – is so consistently held up as proof that God requires us to be sexist and homophobic, how can anyone claim that pornography is the source of these practices?

Research on sexual offenders has confirmed that repressive religious upbringing and family abuse in childhood are the principal causes of sexual violence later in life against women, children and even some men. Serial rapists and rape-murderers, as well as child sexual abusers, almost invariably turn out to be people who have swallowed strict conservative sexual values. But banning the sources of those values – the clergy and the Bible – would not be acceptable to our society. Censoring religion is not a popular policy, both because the combined might of religious leaders constitutes a powerful political lobby and because repressive religion itself is a useful tool of social control. (Interestingly, freedom of worship is one of the few freedoms that most westerners can agree to support.) Pornography, on the other hand, is subversive – it privileges individual pleasure, it ignores social convention, it allows us to step out of our roles and play games that do nothing to advance profits or the state.

6 Nudes, prudes and attitudes

It seems strange, however, that feminists, who have spent the last two decades criticizing the family, religion and the state as sources of sexism, now count among their number some who are unwilling to recognize the contribution of these institutions to women's oppression, instead joining the traditional anti-pornography mainstream in citing pornography, a genre with only marginal influence on widely accepted social norms, as the vital ingredient in sexual violence.

Clearly, campaigns against pornography are more acceptable than campaigns against the Bible, but what is interesting is that anti-porn campaigns are always acceptable, completely in keeping with sexist social conventions that stigmatize individual pleasure, instrumental sex, and sexual exploration for women. Since feminists have long recognized the need to re-examine our sexuality and sex roles, it should be surprising that so many women have given their support to campaigns that would further suppress the availability of sexual material. But we have all been raised in a society that portrays sexual desire as male, violent and dangerous, and it is easy to be swayed by anti-pornography rhetoric when it speaks directly to fears that have become second nature to us.

The government and the moral right have been happy to exploit these fears of sexuality and violence in promoting the further erosion of our already limited freedoms of expression, despite the fact that the United Kingdom already has the strongest censorship in Europe and the English-speaking world. The success of these campaigns rests in large part on a number of falsehoods, ranging from the claim that science has proved a link between pornographic materials and violence to the constant refrain that violence has increased because our laws have become more permissive. History is rewritten, science is misrepresented and dissenting voices are suppressed in order to fuel the ever-increasing demands for yet more censorship. Abused women and children are dragged into the public eye and mercilessly exploited to evoke horror that will motivate us to demand more repression rather than question the speciousness of arguments for censorship. Blinded with the rage we feel upon hearing the stories of battering, rape and other abuse, we forget to ask who, in the end, will really be served by the new laws we have been manipulated into wanting.

It should always be remembered that censorship is a weapon of the powerful that they can use whenever they feel threatened by expressions from those who are not in power. Laws to suppress public expression will not be enforced by minority groups or by feminists; no matter how they are intended and how carefully worded, they will be interpreted, prosecuted and judged by the same police force and judges who for so long have been willing to harass gay venues, accord men the right to rape their wives, and look the other way when discrimination and violence are directed against women, gays, foreigners, people of colour and people with physical impairments. Freedom of expression is the only means that ordinary people – particularly members of oppressed and stigmatized groups – have for making our complaints known and raising the consciousnesses of those who would overlook our needs. If we are to retain the ability to campaign for relief from oppression, we must not keep handing the government powerful tools that would suppress our activism.

Censorship campaigns, then, serve the dual purpose of distracting the public from recognizing the genuine causes of crime, violence and oppression in society while simultaneously empowering the government to curtail further criticisms of the very causes of those crimes that have generated public outrage in the first place, many of which emanate from the policies of the government and the values it promotes.

It is certainly true that we seldom have to look far to find ideas that are thoroughly repellent to us, but censorship does not uproot those ideas or stop them from spreading. The best defence we have against racist, sexist or other oppressive beliefs is to debate them wherever they arise, holding them to the light and exposing their falseness and inherent dangers – what feminist lawyer Nadine Strossen, president of the American Civil Liberties Union, calls 'counterspeech'. As she pointed out in 'A feminist critique of "the" feminist critique of pornography', a central tenet of civil libertarian thought is that the best antidote to bad speech is *more* speech – speech that can counteract the falsehoods that are purveyed by racists, sexists and other proponents of oppression. Censorship only stops us from being able to refute bad ideas; rather than accept censorship, we should demand more thorough and open debate of misleading and dangerous ideas that may permeate our culture, so that we can show up their flaws.

Some people have tried to describe the debate between anti-pornography feminists and anti-censorship feminists as being polarized between 'pro-pornography' and 'anti-pornography' arguments. This is simplistic at best, and largely false. Although there are certainly pro-pornography arguments within the anti-censorship camp, pornography itself is by no means all there is to our argument. We do believe that women should – and must – be free to examine sexuality in whatever way we choose, and if pornographic writing or visual representations are a part of this, they pose no threat to us. Some anti-censorship feminists dislike pornography, but are far more worried about censorship. Others of us are concerned about the effect anti-pornography activism is having on feminist arts and about the dangers it poses to sex workers. Many of us simply doubt the potential of the anti-porn programme to do any good, and quite a few of us suspect that anti-porn activism will actually increase, rather than reduce, harm to women. It is not that we believe freedom of expression, or the availability of pornography, will in any way *guarantee* a more free, just, safe or equal society; it is merely that we are certain that the potential to build such a society is being diminished, and will be further diminished, by continuing and increasing censorship. If we grant the state the right to control what we can see and say, it will *never* return that right to us when we need to use it to improve our world.

The argument of this book

Given that censorship is so dangerous, it is frightening to see people court it so casually. Yet we hear few demands that the government support its moves for censorship with serious evidence for its claims that sexual or violent materials are known to cause anti-social acts. In the following chapters, I will try to show that there is no evidence for these claims, that the arguments against pornography and for censorship are not supported by any scientific or historical evidence, that anti-pornography activism is a distraction from the real needs of women, and that the very nature of the way the arguments are posed rests on sexist and repressive beliefs.

Chapter 2 traces the growth of anti-sexual attitudes in the UK and North America and describes how this tradition has been used to justify censorship. The context of pornography as a 'men's club' is given in Chapter 3, and the modern feminist movement's response to it is detailed in Chapter 4. Chapter 5 discusses the research and shows that it provides no support for the claims of the anti-porn campaigners. The attitude of the moral right to perversion – any sexuality that does not exist for the sake of reproduction – is analysed in Chapter 6. Chapters 7 and 8 show how the issue of pornography has divided the feminist movement and dangerously distracted attention from the real causes of women's poor position in society. Male anti-pornography activism is explored in Chapter 9. Chapter 10 considers the future, and especially the need for a more honest and open approach to sex if we are to reduce violence and oppression for every member of society, child, woman and man.

2
Sex and censorship: a tradition of hostility

Centuries ago, before it became corrupted by anti-sexual attitudes, the word 'whore' referred to a lover of either sex, but, as with other words having sexual content, it became debased until it took on its current meaning of 'prostitute'. (Similarly, 'tart' was once used as an endearment for males or females, in much the same way we now say 'sweetheart' or 'honey'.) There is a horrible logic to this, since women who were 'lovers' rather than wives were condemned by society; in fact, if a woman was known to have had non-marital sex, her reputation would be ruined, she would be considered unmarriageable or could be legitimately discarded by her husband, her 'character' would make her ineligible for domestic service, and her only likely survival option was indeed prostitution.

'Respectable' women often felt the precariousness of their own position. This was particularly acute in homes where the men earned enough money to pay for domestic services that took both housework and child-rearing out of the hands of their wives. Women were not expected to replace their 'womanly' duties with others considered more appropriate to men, and those who did were often considered to be mentally unstable, as Charlotte Perkins Gilman so ably illustrated in *The Yellow Wallpaper*. Wives in this position were left feeling that they had only one responsibility, and that was to provide sexual services to their husbands; in short, they felt like whores.

The industrial revolution changed things for many more women, particularly in areas where farming had been a principal family lifestyle. Previously, it had been common for women to play some role in the family business: doctors were sometimes assisted by their wives; farmers' wives and children were involved in farming themselves; and a shopkeeper's family would help stock the shelves, work at the counter, and sweep out the shop. Additionally, women were daily involved in some form or another of material contributions to the household, including production: a farmer couldn't afford to run his business without a wife to cooperate in both the work and the production of children who would also work; spinning, weaving and sewing generally took place inside the home and were most commonly done by wives and daughters or female domestics. The destruction of the cooperative family that had begun when the church split the clergy off from women began to cement as women's work moved to factories, where it was taken over by men. Whereas once children were expected to earn their own keep by the time they were six, both women and children eventually came to be seen as consumers who sapped family resources rather than as workers who made a vital material contribution. As women in middle-class households had fewer productive duties toward their families, their feelings of uselessness grew.

Where this syndrome is strongest, we tend to see the emergence of activism on the part of such 'respectable' women to eliminate prostitution. Many people have noted that charity work and activism were very much the occupations of otherwise idle, privileged women, but the relationship between their own circumstances and the focus on women who catered to men sexually outside of marriage is sometimes overlooked. It is true that these women were often disturbed by the possibility that their husbands were attracted to the offers of 'working girls' and that it has always been women's function in society to control male sexuality; however, it is also possible that the women who took money for sex directly made them uncomfortable with the similarity they were feeling to these 'fallen' women, and they preferred to take them out of the picture lest their resemblance become too obvious.

The desire for 'good' women (or 'ladies') to distinguish themselves from 'bad' women has always been a part of the dynamic between women in society. Pointing the finger elsewhere is, of course, a vital survival strategy for women who know that if they are perceived as falling into the latter category, their lives can be devalued by others. When 'bad' women are seen as fair game for rape, it is simply good sense that most women want to put as much distance as they can between themselves and those women who are treated like walking targets. That the price for this should be paid by those 'bad' women themselves is seldom questioned.

There have always been dissenting voices, however, some of which can be traced to the earliest activism on female equality and sexual freedom. In the earlier part of this century, the suffragist movement was split over the sexual freedom issue, and many feminist historians feel that it was this issue that destroyed the movement for feminism at the time. While people ranging from Marie Stopes and Margaret Sanger to H.G. Wells and Victoria Woodhull had emphasized a need to recognize women's sexual needs and power to control their own reproduction rather than to suppress sexuality, the slogan of British women's suffrage was 'Votes for women, chastity for men', and American suffragists eventually repudiated Woodhull, despite her previous success in having been able to address Congress on suffrage. Some feminists opposed the efforts of Stopes and Sanger to bring birth control to women, saying that without the danger of unwanted pregnancy, women would no longer have an excuse to refuse their husbands when they wanted sex. Stopes herself was clear that she intended her reforms for married women alone, and she broke with Sanger over the issue of abortion as a back-up method of birth control. Sex-positive attitudes were still largely seen as bringing 'decent ladies' down to the level of prostitutes.

With the growth of mass-produced pornography, the prostitute has been joined by the porn model or actress as a fit object for our contempt and opprobrium. Some of the language that is used to condemn such women has changed over the last century, but the sense that these women are simultaneously victims of society and the enemies of good women has not really dwindled. Women who wish to see themselves as more virtuous or more enlightened still see women in the sex industry as at once the agents of harm to other women and the puppets of men, and still put more stress on eliminating their trade than on eliminating the conditions that might have made them 'victims' in the first place.

But 'ladies' may be fearful of pornography for another reason that hits closer to home: the fact that men use it for sexual arousal. With a history that still leaves many of us feeling used rather than pleasured by sex, we may feel that any material that makes men feel desire may inspire the 'beastly urges' of the male and thus subject wives to ever more demands for sex.

For the Victorians, a good wife simply had to steel herself to 'do her duty'; most doctors took the view that female sexual response was in some way dysfunctional or destructive, if they acknowledged that women were sexual at all, and it was even claimed that only non-orgasmic women could avoid uterine disease. One or two rare doctors wrote positively about the capabilities of the clitoris – anonymously. Overall, most people had no idea that the clitoris existed, and the common assumption was that 'female sexuality', if you could call it that, was merely a matter of being a receptacle for male desire – the only kind that mattered. With the expectation that sex would be perfunctory at best, and even the possible fear for a woman's health if female desire should be satisfied, many wives were understandably less than enthusiastic about stimulating male desire.

These assumptions may be changing for some of us, but our society's distrust of male arousal is still very strong, and sex is not always satisfying to every woman. The personal experience of women for whom sex has been unpleasant, combined with our overall discomfort with sexual openness, still makes it easy for us to attack sexual expression.

Repression disguised as progressiveness

And so the pattern that began at least as far back as the 1850s with the Female Mission on the Fallen distributing leaflets against prostitution, and of course the original Obscene Publication Act 1857, has continued: the Obscene Publications Act 1959 was followed by the Obscene Publications Act 1964, covering even more material. In 1964, Mary Whitehouse formed the National Viewers and Listeners Association to oppose what they viewed as too much permissiveness, particularly on television (a point they keep making, although many of us have to wonder where all this televised sex *is* and how we keep missing it), and they have been fairly effective in influencing the government and introducing the television watershed for 'adult' viewing, and other restrictions. (Indeed, they now argue that, since some children stay up all night, and since late-night material can be videotaped, there should be *no* material on television that is not 'suitable' for children. They already seem to have convinced some authorities that the watershed itself is not actually a watershed, but that the *real* watershed should come at least half an hour after the 'official' watershed begins, as people might not turn the set off straight away.) Though quite a few people assume that the law has always become increasingly more permissive, the reverse is actually true: stronger restrictions have continued to be introduced over the last few decades, with more types of material being considered illegal and more invasive types of enforcement becoming accepted.

What most people remember is a small number of obscenity trials during the 1950s and 1960s that demonstrated to the censors that it wasn't so easy to get juries to agree that sexual representation was, by itself, 'obscene' – that seeing such images would 'deprave or corrupt'. Most members of the British public have trouble believing that there is any real harm in showing movies in which people are naked or involved in the more common sexual activities in a consensual context. Although images of violent sexual assault and degradation or of paraphilias ('perversions' such as sadomasochism – SM – or urination fantasies) tend to disturb many people, most pornography does not fall into this category to begin with, and certainly not most of the works that were being prosecuted at this time. In fact, the most notorious censored works had been books like D.H. Lawrence's *Lady Chatterley's Lover*, which contained neither photographs nor depictions of unusual sexual acts. (An obscenity ruling against Radclyffe Hall's lesbian classic, *The Well of Loneliness*, had made it unavailable to the public until 1948.) In particular, *Lady Chatterley's Lover* had been 'offensive' because of values that no longer held in society: the once scandalous suggestion of a sexual relationship between a working-class man and a woman of higher status. But attempts to revive the book later met with other objections – the explicit sexual language was considered by some to be unacceptable (particularly if seen by 'your' wife or servants). Nevertheless, it was generally felt that the inclusion of explicit sexual descriptions was not by itself sufficient reason to ban a book that had other literary merit, and this exception was written into the 1959 Act, although that otherwise strengthened the law and made seizures by the police much easier.

The 1960s are remembered as a time of growing permissiveness, and this is certainly true in terms of some changes that occurred toward the end of that decade, particularly with the 1967 legislation that made it easier for women to get abortions and decriminalized homosexual acts between males over 21. The abolition of the death penalty seemed to mark a turning away from the violence and barbarity of the past. It was a time when women were at last permitted to explore our sexuality to some extent without being cast out of society or incarcerated in mental institutions, and the children of unmarried women no longer received birth certificates stamped 'illegitimate'. However, as Feminists Against Censorship explained in *Pornography and Feminism*:

> The 1964 Obscene Publications Act further tightened the law by closing various loopholes about evidence and extending it to cover photographic negatives as well as material for sale. This last point is interesting, because it was the first time that the law recognized, and sought to regulate, the production as well as the distribution of pornography. It was a recognition that obscenity was no longer just a category of harmful materials but an increasingly separate branch of publishing with its own technology, entrepreneurs and outlets.

And 'liberalizing' the law, however defined, can't really be said to have eliminated the threat of censorship – particularly where radical political material was concerned. During the period remembered as 'the Sixties', sexual expression was very much a part of the political milieu, and it was no accident that a prosecution was launched against the counterculture magazine, *Oz*. Most commentators agree that the attack on *Oz* was itself political censorship. Ironically, it was the issue known as *Schoolkids' Oz*, put together entirely by people under 18, that inspired the charges; material by minors was apparently corrupting adults. A conviction was originally secured, but since the judge had misdirected the jury, it was quashed on appeal in 1972.

An equally disturbing case of the same period involved charges of conspiracy to corrupt public morals and to outrage public decency against a counterculture newspaper, *International Times*, for printing gay contact ads. Since homosexuality was no longer a crime, this was especially disturbing to civil libertarians – and it was hardly as if gay advertisers were marching down the street soliciting partners with bullhorns. Nevertheless, *International Times* was convicted on both counts, and this is only one of a series of cases of the period in which the courts extended the scope of the law.

Governments of western European and English-speaking countries have tended to launch inquiries, commission reports or hold hearings before pursuing further censorship, and often this is done in the hope of discovering supporting evidence that can be cited to justify the new laws, although sometimes it is merely a delaying tactic. There are strong parallels between the use of these methods in both Britain and America, as well as in the fact that the reports issued generally fail to support censorship. (Often the general public ends up remembering the publicity about the reports better than it remembers the changes in law.) Both the 1957 Wolfenden Report on homosexuality and prostitution and the 1979 Williams Committee on Obscenity and Film Censorship took the view that legislation from the British government should look to harm, rather than merely morality, and this was seen as a liberal position at the time. Similarly, commissions in America tend to make reports that exonerate pornography. However, the parallels are not so strong when it comes to legislation. In contrast with the US, where the First Amendment makes it much more difficult to legislate censorship, the Thatcher government ignored the Williams Committee report and instead enacted the Indecent Displays (Control) Act 1981 to restrict the display of indecent material, and brought in local authority licensing for sex shops in the form of the Local Government (Miscellaneous Provisions) Act 1982.

Even so, the Reagan administration's tactics were in many ways similar to those of the Thatcher government and its agents in the sense that both concentrated heavily on using economic means to enforce suppression of sexual materials. In Britain, licensing laws make it punitively expensive to open any shop dealing principally in sex aids or sex toys and sexual materials. In America, the Justice Department launches repeated, multi-jurisdiction suits against publishers; juries may not convict defendants of 'obscenity', but publishers and distributors, even if found not guilty, may still be forced out of business by the enormous costs of defending themselves in court. Most British book dealers and publishers already know that fighting a winning case can still be financial suicide.

The Festival of Light

In the face of 'Sixties permissiveness', the moral right took up the banner to fight the good fight against sexual expression and licence. The evils of abortion, homosexuality, pornography and sexual activity in general had to be confronted; the wild, licentious children of the 1960s could not be permitted to deprave society with their perverted morality. One weekday evening in 1971, a coalition of anti-sex moralists launched their Festival of Light Campaign at Central Hall, Westminster, with speakers and folk groups heralding the restoration of Christian values. Malcolm Muggeridge, Mary Whitehouse and Cliff Richard are well-remembered figureheads. Anti-apartheid bishop Trevor Huddleston had originally been announced as a supporter, but the Gay Liberation Front (GLF) wrote to him about his involvement and he met with them; he later withdrew from the Festival of Light, but it is not known whether the GLF intervention was directly responsible.

GLF fiercely opposed the Festival and organized some 60 of its members and supporters to attend the packed-out launch at Westminster. GLF's Nettie Pollard later told me that while anti-gay, anti-drug, anti-abortion and anti-sex rhetoric poured from the podium:

> A woman in the audience stood up and exclaimed, 'I'm saved! I'm saved! Praise Jesus!' She then threw her handbag, her hair, her dress and her breasts into the air, leaving a heavily made-up young man. Scandal swept the audience and Christian women went up to a group of nuns saying, 'Pray for calm, sisters.' Unfortunately, at that moment the nuns stormed the stage doing Indian whoops. The 'nuns' were both male and female.
> Chaos ensued, many others in the audience unfurled banners and shouted slogans, and Christian heavies started dragging protesters out. We got

16 Nudes, prudes and attitudes

The 'nuns' were both male and female

together again outside among some respectably dressed GLFers who were trying to make their points to people leaving the meeting. One long-haired man was pushed by a police officer and responded by kissing him. The officer tried to arrest him. Then the policeman looked round at a sea of GLF faces, muttered, 'Don't do it again', and slunk off.

The next event was held around a month later in Hyde Park after a march by a sizeable number of Festival of Lighters. This time GLF was joined by a number of people from the women's movement as well as anarchists and libertarians. We both disrupted the rally and held an alternative 'Festival of Life' nearby.

A few years later they changed their name to the one they use today, Christian Action Research and Education (CARE). They still target abortion, sex education, homosexuality and pornography!

The voices of freedom may have felt they won a moral victory, but the effect of highly visible and vocal right-wing activism has been to give the appearance that the likes of Mary Whitehouse represent the will of the majority. One survey after another has shown that most people, when specifically asked whether they believe sexual depictions in magazines or on (paid) satellite television should be banned, say it should not. The Independent Television Commission's 1993 survey of viewer attitudes toward material on television showed that more than 70 per cent of the public were not offended by anything on the four main channels (72 per cent for both ITV and Channel 4, 74 per cent for BBC1 and 80 per cent for BBC2), and far fewer than 15 per cent had complaints about sex on television on any channel (12 per cent for Channel 4, 11 per cent for ITV, 10 per cent for BBC1 and 7 per cent for BBC2); yet the government persists in speaking as if there is a huge public outcry favouring more censorship. While many people say they believe in censorship of some materials they find particularly awful, or believe some materials should only be available to adults, few believe that the law should forbid all representations of common sexual behaviour. Most would be surprised to know just how much is banned in Britain: erections, penetration and genital contact are all forbidden in visual representations made for erotic purposes, for example. The law as it is written and practised in no way serves the beliefs of the vast majority of the residents of the United Kingdom; it is far more consistent with the will of a small, vocal and repressive lobby of moralists.

Lies, damned lies and censorship

Today, the argument that pornography (or violent material) causes harm is the principal point made by pro-censorship campaigners from every camp. The enforcement of Victorian morality is no longer generally regarded as a credible justification for banning pornography, and even those who campaign against sexual material on fundamentalist Christian grounds tend to stick to the 'harm' argument rather than talk about morality.

The assumption that certain material causes harm was used to justify extensions of censorship during the campaign against 'video nasties' that resulted in the Video Recordings Act 1984. Although there has never been research to justify the claim, anti-video-nasty activists spoke *as if* it were known, obvious and proven that children watching horror films would in some way be damaged or become damaging to others as a result of seeing such films. The Thatcher government at the time at first resisted the push for legislation, but the rise in the crime rate that resulted from their policies had created an outcry against increasing violence that could not be answered by the government honestly, and in this case a law against video nasties must have seemed like a good scapegoat. In his 1984 book *The Video Nasties*, Martin Barker notes that the prime minister made her first reference to a need for legislation on videos just prior to discussion of whether a Central Policy Review Staff report on unemployment had predicted riots in Liverpool. Barker quotes Thatcher from Hansard:

> That report did not predict the Toxteth riots. It did, however, take the view that if high unemployment persisted and if the entire region became one of concentrated disadvantage, the existing supporting services and income redistribution mechanisms would be inadequate to prevent social unrest.

It must have been difficult for Margaret Thatcher to admit, even in such careful words, that the very government that had pretended to provide a more stable and controlled society had enacted policies that were actually leading to greater 'social unrest'. The police, who had at first been given a great deal of new funding by Thatcher's government and had therefore been very supportive of her, were eventually forced to admit that the economic conditions that resulted from Conservative policies actually led to rises in the crime rate. It is certainly no accident that Thatcher changed her tune to one more supportive of censorship at this time, nor is it an accident that Prime Minister John Major began publicly worrying about violent television just at the time that new concerns about rising crime – particularly car-jacking and joy-riding – hit the news with growing intensity.

The concern with 'video nasties' concentrated on the presumed harm that came from viewing 'slasher'-style horror movies such as *I Spit On Your Grave* and *Driller Killer* (see Chapter 5). It is interesting to note that the 'harmful effects' of these movies that seemed to generate such concern included the possibility that children would have nightmares, on the one hand, and an implied tendency to commit violent crime, on the other. Moreover, the fact that children might indeed have nightmares about horror movies was considered to be proof enough that the movies had 'effects', and that, therefore, it was obvious that the more anti-social effects of active violence must also be a genuine risk of viewing such movies.

Yet when the Video Recordings Bill was written, it did not confine itself to censoring mere violence. Indeed, the Bill was written in such a way that it could be used to censor political material as well as pornography. Out of a spurious claim that the violence in horror videos was dangerous and must be banned, the government was able to pass legislation that made materials not under discussion illegal. The general public had voiced neither a desire to see portrayals of common sexual acts banned, nor a need to limit the political impact of ideas in video; yet this is what, ultimately, the Video Recordings Bill did. Even educational depictions of human genitals and sexual activity are covered by the Bill.

The Bill is also breathtaking in the scope of powers it gives to a single office. As Barker points out:

> It requires that all videos should be classified along the same lines as films for cinema are currently classified by the British Board of Film Censors (BBFC). That is the surface. Scratch at the veneer and it looks very different. First, it is written into the bill that the criteria for classification are to be much tougher than for the cinema: clause 4(1) requires that classification must 'have special regard to the likelihood of video works ... being viewed in the home.' ... the bill empowers the Home Secretary to designate a body (known to be a revised BBFC) to classify videos. He can require annual reports from them on any matter he chooses and, if unhappy with their work, can remove their designation (clauses 4–6). In addition, the DPP [Director of Public Prosecutions] will still have the power to prosecute any classified video it does not like under the Obscene Publications Act. That would be a great embarrassment to the BBFC. To avoid this, it has already been announced that the BBFC have been issued with secret guidelines by the DPP. In effect, they tell the BBFC how they must do their classifying. In reality, therefore, *the DPP* will determine what is acceptable or unacceptable for classification.

So the Director of Public Prosecutions, an unelected official, makes the decision as to what sort of movie can be given a certificate, and this will be based on what materials are considered appropriate 'in the home' – for children, in other words. Most ominously, the requirements for the legality of the work are secret – we cannot know before we make a film whether it can be passed for certification – and even after the video has been certificated, a dealer can still be arrested for distributing it if the DPP decides he doesn't like it anyway. We, the public, have no guidelines to tell us what we can produce, nor can we as viewers know what materials are being kept from us. We cannot, for example, write to the DPP or the BBFC and ask for the list of guidelines – no doubt so that we can be kept in the dark about how many things that we wish to see are being censored without our consent.

With more recent promises of greater openness in the 1990s, it has become slightly easier to get information on guidelines. However, the tendency to pass odious laws of this nature in the wake of manufactured social panics has not abated. Whenever a particular criminal outrage captures public imagination and leads to calls to 'do something', our legislators can generally be trusted to do something stupid. Following the conviction in late 1993 of two emotionally disturbed boys for the murder of two-year-old James Bulger, an all-party group of MPs demanded greater restraints on 'violent videos' and pornography, although there was no reason to think such media had any relationship to the murder, as the police have said over and over. Yet the judge in the case included blame for violent videos in his remarks, and the press ran with this story.

The two boys who killed Jamie Bulger had a known history of serious problems; government cuts have been implicated in the neglect of those problems, but of course conservatives are not free to say so. The moral bankruptcy of our leadership is so great that any distraction will do if it takes our attention from the real social problems that lead children to evolve into killers. 'Video nasties' and sexually explicit materials already having been made unlawful, there is little left to ban, but it is easier to goad the public into fears of problems that do not exist than it is to cope with the problems we already have.

'Protecting' children

The same kind of sleight of hand has been used to condemn pornography since the 'video nasty' scare. Claims that harm has been proven as an effect of pornographic materials are widely disseminated, despite the fact that considerable research has been unable to demonstrate such harm. Moreover, pornography is persistently described as containing dangerous depictions of violence and perversion, although most pornography has no such content. Wild statements are made to the effect that there is widespread dissemination of child pornography – films and photographs made by sexually abusing children before the camera – when in fact child pornography is altogether very rare and little of the child pornography that does exist would fit this description. (Much of it is written and involves no real children at all; most pictorial material used by paedophiles is still photography of children playing or posing, often clothed, sometimes naked, but not involving any sexual contact with another person. Violence is not a common theme in written child pornography.) It is fraudulently claimed that it is necessary to enact new laws to make this terrible child pornography illegal, when in truth sexual material involving children is already wholly criminalized and no new legislation could make it more so. Indeed, if the police raid your house and find your own baby pictures, you could be arrested for possession of child porn. Photographs of children do not have to be sexual in any way to suit the legal classification of 'child porn'. Yet anti-pornography activists carried out an aggressive campaign in London during the late 1980s and early 1990s in which they asked people to sign petitions to ban child pornography, not encouraging them to read the text of these petitions, which asked for a ban on *all* pornography.

Recent campaigns by Michael Hames, the head of the Obscene Publications Squad, have also concentrated on the portrayal of pornography as nothing but a record of child abuse and perversion. This is a gross misrepresentation of the content of most pornographic materials, but it is meant to convince the populace that new laws must be enacted in order to eliminate the irredeemable filth we are to assume is flooding into the United Kingdom from the rest of Europe. On 27 August 1993, an edition of *The Cook Report* was broadcast on ITV in which Hames campaigned to extend the current law to apply specifically to computer-generated sexual materials. As usual, Hames spoke as if he were merely trying to stop an enormous influx of child porn films from entering Britain over the telephone wires and being received by children on their home computers; the truth is that the technology to do this is not widely available to children, and even if it were, there is little sexual material being sent via modems – or any other media – that would offend a reasonable adult in Britain.

But what offends reasonable adults and what worries them in terms of what their children see are different things altogether. We may feel no concern about the idea that those over 21 are viewing movies of other adults having sex with each other, but we get nervous at the suggestion that our children might see those same movies. This fear has been mercilessly exploited by anti-pornography campaigners who wish us to believe that nothing that can be seen by adults will be kept from children. Even if this is true, is it such a tragedy? We are meant to believe that it is, but there is no evidence that children are harmed by viewing pornographic materials. Indeed, existing research on sex offenders found that sex criminals see porn later in life than other men, and they see less of it; it also shows that such men are likely to come from homes where sex is not talked about, attitudes towards sex are repressive and restrictive, and sex education is limited or non-existent (see Chapter 5). Yet those who support censorship of sexual materials continually reiterate their belief that children will be harmed by exposure to pornography, as if it were a demonstrated fact.

On the contrary, there is plenty of evidence to suggest that repressive attitudes about pornography could be harmful and may actually play a role in the creation of sex offenders. The Child Sexual Abuse Treatment Program (CSATP) in Santa Clara, California, is the oldest such programme, and has long-standing experience with the exploration of the causes of child abuse. In her resource supplement to *Sense & Censorship*, Marcia Pally quoted this statement from Dr Henry Giaretto, CSATP's founder and executive director:

> Our program has not been designed to include collection of data on the use of pornography because the literature and our own clinical experience showed no link between the commission of child sexual abuse and sexually explicit material. While it has been clinically noted that some perpetrators read and/or view sexually explicit material, many others express their feeling that pornography is immoral. In contrast to common belief, a great number of men who turn to their children for sexual purposes are highly religious or morally rigid individuals who feel that this is 'less of a sin' than masturbation or seeking sexual liaisons in an outside affair.

Pally also tracked down the source of a claim by the American Family Association that the Michigan police had reported a finding that pornography is used or imitated in 41 per cent of the sex crimes they investigate – a claim that turns out to be entirely false. She describes her interview with Michigan's criminal profiler, Detective Sergeant David Minzey:

> Michigan has the oldest sex-motivated crime data base in the country, dating to the 1950s, with 70,000 cases recorded. Minzey's department has found no causal link between sexually explicit material and sex crimes. 'We have gone into our data base,' Minzey said, 'and have never been able to pull out such a causal relationship.'
>
> The 41 percent statistic, Minzey explained, apparently comes from a master thesis by Darrell Pope at Michigan State University (1977). 'There is a strong religious strain in Pope's work,' Minzey said. 'Pope was trying to establish causality, but as you know, you cannot establish causality between sexually explicit materials and sex crimes. We'd make a better causality case for alcohol.'

Another 'harm' that is claimed to come from seeing pornography is the possibility that people will become 'perverted' by watching depictions of paraphiliac acts; that is, a person who looks at sadomasochistic materials might become a sadomasochist, or a person who looks at child pornography might become a paedophile. A similar claim is made with regard to an 'addiction' theory of pornography that says that people who look at pornography will both 'need' to continue looking at porn and will also need the equivalent of larger doses – that is, more hard core and 'perverted' porn. Thus, it is believed, a man might start off looking at movies of people having missionary-position intercourse and then discover he needs 'the harder stuff', like SM materials, to achieve arousal; he might then become acclimatized to the SM porn and need to go on to child porn.

These beliefs have been pretty effectively disproved over and over, and no evidence exists to support them. People tend to look at materials that represent sexualities that already turn them on, and stick to those. The only reason a person progresses to 'the harder stuff' is that the soft stuff didn't really represent what appealed in the first place. People do get ideas for some positions or places that they might not have thought of previously, and may be more likely to accept that such acts might be possible or at least not 'disgusting', but if the act doesn't already appeal to their established sexuality, it will have no effect in terms of arousal. Peterson, Moore and Furstenburg found that exposure to pornography had no effect on later sexual practice. Or, as Barry Lynn said, 'While exposure to sexually explicit depictions of oral sex may increase the chances that a couple will try it, the same cannot be said for sex with chickens, coprophilia or actual sadism.' All evidence shows that children's basic sexuality is established early in life and will not suddenly be changed by later exposure to sexual materials.

What pornography may do – and this is what disturbs the moral right – is help people feel more at ease both with their own sexuality and with variation in that of other people. Many gay men have reported that viewing gay porn made them feel less isolated and more accepting of their sexuality. Some researchers have said that male students at American universities were more tolerant of homosexuality after viewing porn. Ironically, the researchers who reported this finding, Dolf Zillmann and Jennings Bryant, said that this was a demonstration of greater 'callousness' towards women. That should tell feminists just exactly how much we can trust anti-pornography researchers; we have known for a long time that men who are intolerant of homosexuals have problems relating to women and are particularly intolerant of women who stand up for themselves.

But our historical traditions of fearing sex and sexual representation make it difficult for us to admit even that pornography may not be so harmful, let alone that it has possible positive effects.

3
Pornography and its context

1. writings, pictures, films, etc., designed to stimulate sexual excitement. 2. the production of such material. – Sometimes (informal) shortened to **porn** or **porno**. [C19: from Greek *pornographos* writing of harlots, from *porne* a harlot + *graphein* to write]
(Collins English Dictionary, 1986)

writings, pictures, etc. intended primarily to arouse sexual desire
(Webster's New World Dictionary of the American Language, 1973)

1. (see quote) **1857** DUNGLISON med. dict. pornography, a description of prostitutes or of prostitution, as a matter of public hygiene. 2. description of the life, manners, etc. of prostitutes and their patrons; hence, the expression or suggestion of obscene or unchaste subjects in literature or art; pornographic literature or art. **1864** WEBSTER, *pornography*, licentious painting employed to decorate the walls of rooms sacred to bacchanalian orgies, examples of which exist in Pompeii
(Oxford English Dictionary, 1928)

1. the explicit description or exhibition of sexual activity in literature, films, etc., intended to stimulate erotic rather than aesthetic or emotional feelings. 2. literature etc. characterized by this.
(Concise Oxford English Dictionary, 1991)

The word 'pornography' came into English usage almost simultaneously with the desire to regulate it. 'Bawdy' art, jokes, verse and literature had existed before, but categorization was a passion in the nineteenth century, and it is understandable that a specific term was sought to identify this genre. But the Victorians also had a powerful dislike of sex, and their prejudices are reflected in the very construction they chose. Walter Kendrick, in *The Secret Museum*, traces the common use of the word to the Victorians' effort to classify the erotic works that were found in historic Greece; 'pornography' would define the kind of material that women, children and the lower classes could not be allowed to see: material with sexual content that might tend, according to Lord Justice Cockburn's interpretation of the Obscene Publications Act 1857, to 'deprave and corrupt'. Although 'obscenity' was the legal term for what would be banned, it was understood that 'pornography' could automatically be consigned to this category. Repressive campaigners whose view of sex was strongly negative saw instrumental sex as the behaviour of prostitutes, and thus the Greek root *'porne'* was used to achieve the word that now refers, generally, to all recreational sexual material intended to arouse. While there is some evidence that the word was actually used once or twice by at least one Greek writer in discussion of the lifestyles of the lower classes, including common commercial prostitutes, it does not appear that the Greeks themselves made much use of this term.

By the mid-twentieth century, 'pornography' was a universally recognized catch-all term for illegal recreational sexual media, particularly as it became possible to mass-produce photographic images and, consequently, visual representations of sex became accessible to the less wealthy members of society. Erotic images had been produced by artists at the behest of rich patrons; often these were images of a patron's mistress. As it became possible for the common man to acquire his own collection of sexual images, a distinction came to be made between the 'art' of the preceding generations and the erotic materials that were able to appeal to a larger audience. The class basis of the line drawn between high-culture 'erotica' and low-culture 'pornography' was fairly explicit from the very beginning.

At the end of World War II, the pin-up photographs that had been popular with soldiers solidified into a genre of their own, eventually giving rise to publications such as *Razzle* in Britain and *Playboy* in the United States. The women portrayed in these pin-ups and magazines all fit the common standard of female attractiveness at the time, and to a certain degree it can be said that these particular portrayals have retained some popularity as an artefact of this period's pornography even though the fuller-figured actress or model of that day has long since been superseded by the slimmer, smaller-breasted women who were later popularized in film with Audrey Hepburn and in fashion with Twiggy. By the end of the 1960s, it was already the case that middle-class tastes tended to see voluptuousness in women – particularly larger breasts – as a sign of 'excess', emblematic of tasteless, 'tacky' preferences in the lower classes. Although the models in modern 'top-shelf' magazines would have been too skinny for post-war pin-up magazines, an interest in more voluptuous women does seem to have been retained by working-class men to a much greater degree than in the middle and upper classes, and the magazines do reflect that; the women are not always as thin as those found in fashion and film. (It would be interesting to know whether the uproar over 'page 3' photos would be as great if the women pictured did not occasionally deviate from the middle-class standard of slim, small-breasted beauty.)

Again, this distinction in class difference does play an important role in the stigmatization of popular soft-core materials in contrast to the classier 'erotica' that is less often the target of modern anti-pornography campaigns. In addition, 'erotica' is expected to have higher production values – that is, to have been produced at greater expense – and to be less frank about its intentions and content. Or, as a lesbian nurse told me on the train to Scotland: 'Erotica – that's pornography where people drink wine afterwards.'

The split between high art and mass culture is an interesting point for feminists in particular to examine, as we have long recognized that many art forms and crafts that are associated with women have been devalued and trivialized in our society: men are interested in news, but women gossip; men are logical, women are emotional; men read novels, women read 'genre fiction'; men create important things, women do 'housework'. But even some things that are associated with male interest are trivialized in similar ways. In her introduction to Gibson and Gibson's *Dirty Looks*, Carol J. Clover may have put her finger on just exactly why pornography and other 'low-culture' materials do not receive our highest approval:

> Pornography's shame lies in the fact that it has one simple, unequivocal intention: to excite its consumer. We are in general suspicious of forms (including music and dance forms) that aim themselves so directly at the body, and it is no surprise that the other two film genres that do so (horror, which is meant to speed the pulse and promote screams, and melodrama, which is meant to jerk tears) are also consigned to the lower reaches of the status scale. ... What is erotica (that favoured category of pro-censorship feminism) but a category that moves us less, a form that, as [Lynda] Nead says, 'allows the viewer to be aroused but within the purified, contemplative mode of high culture'?

The 'men's club'

Historically, pornography was a genre aimed principally at men. One reason for this was the simple assumption that women, who were not supposed to be very sexual, could not be interested in sexual materials, and thus there was no point in treating us as part of pornography's audience. Yet another reason was that women had little discretionary income – indeed, for a long time we were not permitted to have our own money – and thus it was unlikely that we would be given money that might be spent on women's sexual materials if such things existed. (Women have used romantic fiction for this purpose all along, but denial of that process is remarkably common.) Of course, even many of the men who produced pornography would have been threatened by the idea that women were viewing pictures of nude men and sex for the purposes of arousal, if such an idea should have occurred to them. It would certainly have been considered highly inappropriate behaviour for any woman who did.

But most things were marketed to men, even when they were products – like the family car – that women played a strong role in choosing. For a very long time, advertisers tended to assume that all buyers were men, even when women had begun buying cars for themselves and were a strong part of the market. In fact, even fiction and magazines for general audiences tended to operate on the assumption that the readers were male, despite the fact that market research had shown that women buy more reading materials than men do.

When the modern women's liberation movement emerged in the late 1960s, one of its earliest demands was that such androcentric assumptions should be thrown on the scrap-heap where they so obviously belonged. Feminists could see that the consistent viewpoint from which only men are protagonists (subjects) and women never more than the trimmings or prizes (objects) created a false view of life and made oppressive attitudes about women all too acceptable. By investing art and science with a female viewpoint, our very perception of those things – and their inherent 'truths' – underwent a visible metamorphosis: our understanding of human beings and the world began to change dramatically.

Perhaps the best primer on the re-examination of culture from a feminist perspective is Robin Morgan's book from 1970, *Sisterhood is Powerful*, a wide-ranging collection of essays by women who put sexist culture and science under a microscope, and found it wanting. Psychology, said Naomi Weisstein, had constructed the female in an image that did not really resemble her; great writers, said Kate Millett, had presented a picture of women that misrepresented and insulted us; the Catholic church, said Mary Daly, oppresses women. Even secretarial work and housework were looked at in a new light. Men's excuses for keeping women out of the professions and on low pay scales, as well as their remarkable ability to avoid getting their hands dirty in the kitchen, were wiped away by women who were taking no prisoners.

Make no mistake: women were horrified even back then at the astonishingly offensive and dangerous sexism we found buried not just in banks and law firms but even in medical texts – and it had been going on for centuries. This generation had been raised to believe that women had gained 'equality' with the vote, but then we discovered that our continued inability to get the good jobs, the money, or even some reasonable sense of safety in law was all-pervasive, systematic and not even illegal. It should sicken us all that after more than 25 years of feminist campaigning, marital rape was not criminalized in England and Wales until 1991 – and then only by case law, not by Parliament; on the books, women are still deemed to have consented to rape by getting married. It seems strange that more energy has been directed at banning telephone sex (the government and British Telecom have both reacted noisily and quickly to restrict advertising and access to the 'premium' 0898 numbers that give suggestive but non-explicit recorded messages) than at legally confirming, once and for all, that no one, ever, has the right to sexually assault another person.

But women's liberation had a programme: we would openly and loudly criticize sexist media; we would demand admission into the professions and particularly into the universities where values were taught; we would break the ceiling on women's progress through the upper ranks of both business and public service institutions (schools, hospitals, etc.); perhaps most importantly, we would write the books, the magazine articles, the television shows and films and we would be allowed to make our own viewpoint known. And to a very great extent, we did exactly that; we now see women winning awards, writing textbooks and heading university departments, where once there were only men.

Feminists, at least on the surface, never gave any appearance of wanting to have anything to do with pornography. Whatever the common assumptions had been about the maleness of the general media audience, women were still expected to see most television, general release film, books and magazines. In the case of pornography, however, it was always assumed that we would have no interest – and more, that we *should* have no interest. Surely no single genre ever made women feel more excluded, and our resentment about that feeling of exclusion should surprise no one. Moreover, if we were not meant to see pornography, we could have no comment on it, no quarrel with its sexism, and no criticism of its internal values. Indeed, it was the one area where it was unthinkable that we could demand that we be allowed to participate in order to improve it.

Could this be why so many feminists have automatically taken the position that pornography should be banned rather than reformed in the way we have been reforming other genres and media? Have we simply accepted the assumption that women cannot participate as consumers and creators of pornography, and decided that if we can't play, then the boys can't play either? Is this sense of exclusion instrumental in making it easy for us to believe that the sexual fantasies men have while reading pornography are really about something much nastier than sex?

The idea that women are and should be excluded from sexual discourse is an old one, and although it has become considerably weakened in the last few decades, it is clearly still exerting its influence on the argument over the presence of sexual materials in our society. Assumptions abound that the very nature of sexual desire makes it an unpalatable subject for recreational consumption by women and children. To a significant number of people, sex remains a dark and unsavoury aspect of our existence, too sordid and bestial to be appreciated by any but the most (equally) bestial members of our society: men.

Pornography, then, was emblematic of all that was wrong with men; their very desire to look at pictures of strange women in order to achieve arousal and orgasm seemed to be at the crux of their failure to make women feel fully recognized. One 'feminist' criticism of pornography has been that by allowing themselves to become aroused while looking at pictures of women they do not know, men are able to project their own idealized view of sex and relationships onto women in their fantasies, and thus, it could be said, they learn only to love that image they have invented and find convenient, and not real women. The suggestion here is that women do not have fantasies about men they do not know.

Of course, young girls certainly do have erotic fantasies about strange men. Most often these are actors or pop stars, but perhaps women only kid ourselves about the degree to which these young gods are invested with more personality than soft core models are given by their fans. Beatles fans in the 1960s, raised in unconscionable sexual ignorance, had little appreciation of the sexual appetites and possibilities that might pertain among their heroes, let alone of their individual personalities, values and interests. Some women arouse themselves by reading romance novels about people who do not exist at all. Nor is it uncommon to find that some women fall 'in love' with men whose behaviour is not at all what they want in a partner, and simply hope that once these men are hooked by love or marriage, they can be changed into people who behave more manageably. Both females and males start off with idealized fantasies; we learn about the difficulties of dealing with real people as we enter relationships and are forced to confront those difficulties.

Perhaps the biggest problem we have in understanding how to accept the variations and practicalities of those dealings is that we tend to look at 'women' and 'men' as if we are talking about only two personalities – the 'male' personality and the 'female' personality – rather than at a lot of different individuals with widely varied quirks, tastes, experience and interests. Historically, authorities have discussed what 'men' are and what 'women' are – or at least what men and women should want – without acknowledging that we all have differing styles, tastes and desires, and must be dealt with one at a time. If textbooks continue to describe a single ideal of 'the female' – as they did for so long – men are bound to be confused when they are faced with real women who aren't much like that ideal. The generations of women who were taught that we should want only one thing – marriage – were equally confused by the fact that we also wanted other things.

It is true that girls seem less likely to have explicit sexual fantasies, or specific interest in the genitalia of their imagined partners, than boys do. But males are much more aware of their own organs from an earlier age; from the very beginning, they can see their genitals, and they often have to handle them during the course of the day – when they dress, and when they urinate. Females, on the other hand, never have to touch ourselves except through great wads of toilet paper; our genitals are largely invisible to us, tucked up inside where they don't get in the way, don't have to be arranged and aren't seen. Indeed, generations of women have gone to their graves without ever knowing the existence of the clitoris. It is hard to imagine men remaining so ignorant of their sex organs.

With the invention of the tampon, women finally had a legitimate reason to touch themselves in that hidden 'inside' area. But this contact was brief, was unrelated to arousal, and bypassed the clitoris, and it did not require looking at the organs in question. Without sex education, and with censorship effectively keeping sexual materials far from the mainstream, those of us who were raised in the 1950s and 1960s had little knowledge of sexual function and pleasure.

Women have generally been discouraged from childhood from making too much of the male body, and it is probably also true that the social emphasis on female physical appearance makes us feel strong resentment – and therefore resistance – to the idea of emulating what we perceive as a male obsession with the physical appearance of a potential partner. Thirty years ago, social scientists insisted that women were not influenced by the way men looked – we liked them for their minds rather than their bodies – but those social scientists turned out to have an inaccurate idea of what their subjects should find attractive in men. Male sociologists thought the women they studied would be looking at broad shoulders and big biceps; later studies found that what heterosexual women looked at were men's eyes and backsides. But we had already learned that looking – viewing with appreciation – was a male trait, and one that was used to find us lacking. We often felt some pride that we were not reputed to share this trait with men.

Seeing sex, speaking sex

In her book on pornographic film, *Hard Core*, Linda Williams discusses at some length the fact that sexualized images of women were a part of motion-picture technology from the very beginning. It is almost as if a desire to 'see' sex is at the heart of our artistic endeavours. But the moment we move into the visual arena, we are faced with a conundrum: while male arousal and orgasm can be revealed to the camera's eye, female response can only be hinted at. How can we expose the sexuality of the female if we cannot see it?

Anti-pornography rhetoric makes much of the fact that pornography is 'for' men and makes the female body the object of the camera – and certainly this appears to be the case in 'top-shelf'-type pornographic magazines, since little else can be shown. Yet in motion-picture pornography, the visibility of male response has made it an important focus of the camera's eye, and thus male organs, erection and ejaculation are crucial factors in pornographic film. It is illegal to show these things in Britain, but in most of the pornography seen elsewhere, male sexuality is portrayed heavily precisely because of its visible 'truth'.

For much of our history, then, sexual representation of women was forced to rely on facial expressions and voluntary body movements – all things that can be easily faked. In contrast, we knew men were aroused because we could see their erections, and knew they had achieved sexual satisfaction because we saw ejaculation – a common convention of pornographic film (the 'money shot'), although during actual coition we would not normally see this.

This same difficulty in knowing female response no doubt plays an even more vital role in creating confusion between males and females in their individual sexual interactions. Belief in female sexual response has not always been strong in our society – indeed, there are large parts of our culture in which it is still assumed that women do not lust in the ordinary sense, but rather respond in purely emotional ways, to love. But even where it is understood that women can feel sexual desire and pleasure in the same way men do, how are men to know whether women are truly responsive or are merely going through the motions?

If individuals are in a long-term sexual relationship, a woman's lover may come to recognize her response patterns – the sound of her breathing, the particular movements her body makes in the course of arousal and orgasm – but women vary so widely in these responses that it would be difficult to take such cues for granted in the first sexual encounter with a woman. The problem for heterosexuals is compounded by a plethora of social facts as well: many women were raised to believe that men 'know' what to do, and therefore it would be a grievous insult to try to instruct them; telling a man to change his technique might deflate his ego; women who know too much about sex are tramps, slags or sluts. Discussing the practical facts of sex between lovers is often very intimidating for people, and, as a result, many are afraid to use direct verbal cues that would help a lover know what to do. In addition, we don't grow up using sexual language in direct, positive ways, and it is difficult even to find a vocabulary for conveying our thoughts and desires.

The problem of vocabulary is particularly tricky since 'acceptable' words like 'penis' and 'vagina' have deliberately been used in very clinical, non-sexual ways, while the original English words referring to sexuality – like 'cunt' and 'fuck' – have been pushed so far down into the realms of that which is seen as unsavoury that they have come to have secondary meanings that are highly negative and in some cases appear to have become the primary meanings. Thus, as 'fucking' has become a negative adjective (as in 'my fucking tax bill' – although it is also possible to have 'a fucking good time') and 'cunt' a nasty noun ('you stupid cunt'), many people have come to see 'fuck' as a negative version of intercourse in love-making, and many women feel that referring to their genitals as 'cunt' is to insult them. The English word for the male organ, 'pintle', was stigmatized early on and has disappeared from use completely, already having been replaced in common parlance by the euphemism for another item that liquid may spew from: 'cock', from watercock. And if there is a convenient old English word – or even a euphemism in modern use – for the clitoris, even our lexicographers of obscenity have not been able to find it.

But many of us feel just as queasy about saying 'penis' and 'vagina'. Their use in dry, medical-sounding descriptions gives them a terribly unerotic feel that makes them seem contrived and out of place in erotic contexts. Moreover, they are not very attractive words, and sound as alien to many of us as they are to our language; once again, these euphemisms are from the Latin. Many people use 'sword in sheath' as a metaphor describing heterosexual relations. If we use language that tries to make sexual organs analogous to lethal weaponry and cutting instruments, it is difficult to approach sex as a more cooperative activity. Much of our discussion of heterosexual intercourse rests on this perception that the entry of the male organ between the folds of the labia is a forceful insult to the flesh of the woman, as if it cuts and tears in every instance of copulation. The philosopher Eric Newmann said that the penis invades the vagina, the sperm invades the ovum, and thus the natural relationship between men and women was one of rape. But this is a gross misrepresentation both of our sexual experience and of biology: some male writers have described a feeling of falling, rather than pushing, into a woman's body, while others have actually revealed a fearful experience of being surrounded, or of drowning, inside a woman; both male and female erotic writers have talked of the male being 'welcomed' into the woman; and observation of conception suggests that the ovum may actually do something very like 'deciding' when to open to a sperm, even 'grabbing' at the organism for implantation. Yet much of our language for sexual activity treats it like a military invasion of the female by the male.

Pornography, of course, relies more heavily on the vernacular. In addition to 'cunt' and 'cock', we have other common terms such as 'pussy', 'dick' and 'prick', along with some usually found these days only in porn: 'quiff', 'quim', 'muff', 'bush', 'quail', 'snatch'. It is no accident that lesbians looking for a name for the first British lesbian sex magazine chose *Quim* as their title; it is one of the few words for the female genitals that have no other meaning, as either a euphemism (like 'muff') or an insult (like 'cunt'). Many women use 'pussy' to refer to their organs, but even this has meanings that make us ambivalent about the word: we are not always comfortable with terms that equate us with small, cute animals, and 'pussy' is also used to insult men for being weak or cowardly. It may be very useful for feminists seeking a non-loaded word with erotic content to adopt the term 'quim' from pornography and claim it as our own.

'Fuck' is also a highly problematic word throughout society. Many people insist on referring to sexual intercourse as 'love-making', although this is misleading, since we make love in many ways that do not necessarily centralize, or even involve, sexual intercourse. Is kissing love-making? Is it sex? It is also true that we may experience sexual intercourse that is not specifically about love, but rather specifically 'about' sexual pleasure. The idea that sex can occur outside of loving relationships is highly stigmatized in our society, and our use of sexual language often reflects the belief that there is something tawdry, callous or even evil about sexual acts undertaken purely for the fun of it without committed love being the context or at least the goal.

In our attempts to recognize this, we may sometimes try to use less loaded language, saying we have 'had sex', but even this creates a distortion, since intercourse does not define all that sex is; fellatio, cunnilingus, 'mutual masturbation' and even nipple manipulation are surely 'sex', as indeed are private masturbation and any other activities undertaken to arouse or enhance sexual desire and lead to orgasm. It is perfectly reasonable to say that we have sex with ourselves when we masturbate, although no penetration may be involved. On the other hand, words like 'intercourse', 'copulation' and 'coition' are devoid of the lustiness many of us would like to express in our personal sexual language.

Seen in this way, the word 'fuck' suddenly takes on a certain practicality, but it may be difficult to overcome our feelings that 'fucking' is something less than a mutual, cooperative activity between partners when we live in a world in which many women feel abused in sexual relationships with men who do not seem to care at all about the women they are with. People often feel that 'fucking' is something vaguely nasty that men do *to* rather than *with* women, although it must be said that, regardless of which word is used, society has long tended to assume this about heterosexual intercourse. There is a conflation here of two unfortunate social facts: first of all, the presumption in society that women never willingly engage in instrumental sexual activities; secondly, the recognition that many men do tend to approach sex as something they 'get' from women, and thus make no effort to secure the pleasure of their partners. (And, as mentioned above, there has been a long historical association with the negative impact of instrumental sex on women; non-marital sex could 'ruin' a woman, and society extracted a high price from women who were discovered to have engaged in sexual acts with partners who were not their husbands.) Our culture's specific focus on intercourse as 'real' sex often encourages people to overlook other sexual activities that many women may find necessary to facilitate arousal and satisfaction, which has made it difficult for some women to enjoy intercourse at all. Since the word 'fuck' already had negative connotations simply because of its specific reference to sex, it has become easy for us to use it to mean a kind of *bad* sex, a sex without respect, emotion or mutual pleasure. Still, it is easier to picture lovers saying, 'Let's fuck', to each other than to imagine them saying, 'Let's copulate.'

Our persistence in looking for euphemisms to underline moral perceptions of sexuality or disguise the truth of what we really do actually warps our ability to discuss and understand our sexuality. It doesn't seem likely that we will be able to have true, honest discussion of sexual issues, either in the public arena or between lovers, if we continue to be so hesitant to use more honest and precise terminology. The very vagueness of terms like 'have sex' or 'make love' does more to obscure than illuminate. Yet it will be difficult to reclaim words like 'fuck' and 'cunt' unless we insist on using them openly as specific sexual, rather than hostile, words, and persistently challenge the insulting uses of those words. (Personally, I tend to respond to negative uses of 'cunt' by saying, 'Why do you talk about cunt as if it's something bad? It's the best thing that ever happens to most people.')

Unfortunately, even pornography is of little use as we search for a better word than 'clitoris'. The short-hand 'clit' is usually found, but, except for the occasional use of made-up phrases like 'love button', there is no evidence of a word we might comfortably use with affection. The truth is that we have a scandalously meagre vocabulary of female sexuality because women, historically, weren't really supposed to *have* a sexuality, and censorship has made it even easier for us to overlook both female response and the organs involved.

Changing the socio-political landscape

As pornography became more visible to the general population, a dialogue did start to enter the public discourse about women's sexual dissatisfaction. Unfortunately, some of this was misunderstood in the context of already-existing mythologies about sex; for example, when women complained that men did not 'take enough time', some men assumed this solely referred to the time involved in copulation itself – that is, that they didn't last long enough. This may have been a genuine concern for some women, but in many cases women were talking about the period before copulation when women need to build up desire before intercourse; without sufficient prior arousal, penetration can be painful rather than pleasurable. Yet men were being given advice to do the multiplication tables in their heads in order to stave off their own orgasms. Generally, this visible lack of passion did not enhance the sexual experience for women.

Pornography may not have been explicitly educational in helping people see where they could improve their technique, but it certainly helped to put sexuality on the public agenda of issues that could be taken seriously. (And there were some useful portrayals in pornography; for example, it is the only place that female self-stimulation during intercourse is depicted.) Some women even became involved in the production side of creating pornographic materials (see Chapter 7 for an example). As porn films aimed at a mixed audience began to be shown, men and women started to talk to each other – sometimes in the form of critiques of the films – about what they saw as useful questions or inaccurate portrayals of our sexuality. Until this time, it had been deemed inappropriate for women to participate publicly in discussions of sex *at all*. The new input from women into the sexual discourse was a radical departure from the generations of silence we had endured before, and it completely altered the way sex was perceived and portrayed within the more progressive parts of society.

These very discussions of sex led, ultimately, to discussions of sexual violence, and it is in this context that the value of pornography came to be questioned by feminists. The history of the demonization of pornography by some members of the women's liberation movement is a curious one; as the discussion of rape and domestic battering arose in the wake of a more open policy on pornography, some people seemed to feel that it was sexual violence itself, rather than merely the public recognition of it, that had emerged with the advent of the sexual revolution. Anti-rape activists frequently cited the current statistics on rape as a way to make people aware that sexual assault was not just something that happened to a few bad women, but a common type of violence that had a pervasive effect on the lives of many women. This was a stark contrast to the decades before in which rape was rarely mentioned and was treated as an uncommon outrage. Suddenly, for the first time in our history, women were publicly describing our own experiences of being raped, whereas previously it had been something we hadn't told our best friends.

As women began to accept that we needn't feel shamed by being raped, and as laws and social policies changed so that women were no longer being locked away for the rest of our lives, or at least forced to move, when it became known that we had been raped, we also went public, one result being that the number of rapes that were being reported to the police increased dramatically. Many people mistakenly assumed that this meant there were actually more rapes taking place, but household surveys have found no such increase in the number of women who say they have been raped. For example, Marcia Pally notes that the rate of rape remained static from 1973 to 1987, at 0.06 per thousand women in the population, according to the US Bureau of Justice Statistics. Nevertheless, the belief that rape has been increasing as sexual portrayals and discussions have become more acceptable (what the moral right calls 'Sixties permissiveness') seems to have a strong hold on the population.

In the meantime, pornography itself has changed remarkably: much of it is intended to be enjoyed by both women and men, and some women have begun making pornography aimed at a principally or entirely female audience – for heterosexual women who are dissatisfied with the sort of porn that men have traditionally made, and for lesbians who have had quite enough of phony 'lesbian' scenes in heterosexual porn. Although explicit pornographic films and videos are illegal in Britain, experience in the rest of Europe and the English-speaking world shows that women are now looking at motion-picture porn at roughly the same rate as men. It is no longer a men's club.

4
Feminism and pornography: the modern movement

Modern anti-pornography feminism can trace its roots back to two prongs of the women's liberation movement: on the one hand, the image analysis that was being done by feminists with regard to television, film and literature; on the other hand, the anti-rape, anti-violence activism led by Women Against Violence Against Women (WAVAW) that generated the Take Back the Night (TBTN) marches. This came to be known as Reclaim the Night when it came to Britain.

Take Back the Night

Take Back the Night began in the US with a demand that a woman's right to travel safely on the streets at night be acknowledged. Historically, it had been considered inappropriate for women to travel unaccompanied after sundown, and the common assumption was that only loose women – principally prostitutes – would ever do so. This often resulted in the claim that women who had been raped in the streets after dark had been 'asking for it' by being out alone in the evening. 'What was she doing out there?' was the common question; 'What did she expect?'

But women should not expect to be raped at night (and indeed, those who do go out at night find it is not a usual experience), and we want and need free access to our cities and towns at any hour in the same way men are already presumed to have it. The women who came of age during the sexual revolution were unwilling to be prisoners in their homes after the sun went down, and wanted to participate in the emerging youth culture – a culture whose activities frequently took place late at night – as freely as men could. Both the real dangers of campus rape or other sexual violence in public places, and the perception that women should stay at home rather than risk those dangers, were intolerable. Women's liberation had placed that desire to have our freedom accepted into a political context, and thus a feminist campaign for women's access to the night streets was born. TBTN marches were frequently held on university campuses, with hoards of women, often holding candles, walking together in areas where women might feel in danger when alone. Eventually, these marches spread to other no-go areas of the cities, including that most threatening of all, the 'red-light' district.

Unlike Britain, where sex shop licences might (theoretically) be granted in any commercial district, America has a welter of zoning laws that prohibit porn shops and sex shows in some areas and shunt them off to parts of town that are already considered to be less attractive – often the commercial areas of the poorest districts. These neighbourhoods will already have the highest crime rates and the worst policing; the addition of a strong and easily recognized trade in stigmatized goods and services, attracting transient and anonymous customers who feel no responsibility to the people in that industry or the surrounding neighbourhood, further erodes the stability and safety of such an area. These blocks will become known as places to procure not just sexual material and services, but also drugs and other contraband (including untraceable guns). The knowledge that violent acts against prostitutes are less likely to be prosecuted than crimes against others only adds to the feeling that the most anti-social acts are permitted in red-light zones – anything goes. The police seldom patrol such areas, and they do not answer calls for assistance there with any great diligence; middle-class women generally take for granted that these places are closed to them.

It was inevitable that TBTN would eventually target red-light districts as the areas where women felt the least safety. Women often feel insulted even when propositioned – mistaken for prostitutes – in adjacent neighbourhoods, and this can also make us feel our safety is threatened. If one man can mistake you for a hooker, so can another (a police officer, perhaps), and there is a certain threat that, both legally and socially, there is no way to distinguish yourself from the 'bad' women in society – a particular worry in America, where all prostitution is illegal in most states. Moreover, if a woman is assaulted in such an area, it is easy to suspect that her presence there will be questioned and will be seen to mitigate her assailant's culpability – 'What was she doing there?' Red-light districts, in effect, are a strong statement to women that there are still parts of society where we are both unwelcome and unprotected, and where rape is socially tolerated.

Early image analysis

Just as the movement against rape and domestic violence was beginning to focus on the parts of town where the sex trade was most visible, the image analysis that had been part of feminism from the beginning – most notably with Kate Millett's *Sexual Politics* – had fixed its eye on a specific analysis of pornography. This, too, was inevitable; women's discomfort with pornography, together with society's tendency to treat it as utterly base, had already led to a frequent use of the term 'pornography' to refer to other, non-sexual representations that were indisputably odious. As Gayle Rubin explained in 'Misguided, dangerous and wrong':

> Due to the stigma historically associated with sexually explicit materials, we already use the words 'obscene' and 'pornographic' to express many kinds of intense revulsion. For example, war may be 'obscene' and Reagan's policies 'pornographic.' However, neither is customarily found in adult bookstores. Since the terms are commonly used to convey profound and extreme disapproval, it is all too easy to utilize them to invoke anxiety, disgust, and repulsion.

Feminists who were examining and exposing the sexist depictions of women in popular culture used pornography as an example of the far extremes of sexist representations of women. Many of us were citing its mere existence as proof that the standard, 'acceptable' images of women in mainstream media led ultimately to a violent and degraded perception of women (but not, it should be noted, that pornography was the source of those images and perceptions). It must be understood, however, that at this time no one was treating pornography itself as much more than a metaphor; we talked about it, but we did not examine it. By the time feminist theory actually addressed pornography directly, it was without reference to the real content of pornographic materials; that is, we had developed an analysis of the violent and degrading male dominance that was conveyed by pornography to its users without actually looking to see how much violence, degradation and male dominance of women could in fact be found in 'adult' media. When some of us did finally study the subject, we were more than a little surprised.

Pornography, we had thought, was the repository of all the worst evils of male imagination in regard to women; we expected that all of the violence, all of the anger and jealousy men expressed in other media would be as naked as the models in porn, stripped of any subtlety or mask of respectability. Psychologists and philosophers had long insisted that male sexuality was composed of dominance and sadism, and thus we assumed hard core pornography to be a catalogue of all the most abusive fantasies, where women performed as nothing but doll-like slaves to the whims of every male. It was easy for us to make this assumption; women had spent little time actually looking at hard core pornography, and men had been spending an embarrassing amount of time publicly defending all-male domains on the grounds that there were so many things they wouldn't be able to say in the presence of women. We couldn't help but conclude that what men had to say to each other in our absence or fantasized in private could only reveal an approach to us that would rival our worst nightmares.

Soon slide shows of pornography, accompanied by lectures explaining that men fantasize violence against women when they masturbate, were proliferating throughout the feminist movement. Often these presentations were filled with highly unrepresentative and sometimes gory images that would be difficult to find in pornographic materials. I remember seeing such a slide show in one of my women's studies classes at the University of Maryland, where one photograph, it was explained, was of a transsexual, using a razor blade to slice little cuts into her thighs.

Looking for the violence in porn

Shortly thereafter, I undertook my own overview research on pornography, delving through porn shops in America and thoroughly examining every magazine I found on sale, and never saw a single picture like that. How anti-porn feminists find these rarities I do not know, but they are certainly uncommon to most porn and most male fantasy. Throughout the late 1970s and early 1980s, I pored over images of women in stockings, women in basques, women in corsets and women in nothing at all, but I did not find the images of torture and blood that have been described by anti-porn feminists as being representative of pornography. Even when I began to focus specifically on magazines aimed at the sadomasochistic (SM) audience, I found nothing that fitted these descriptions.

I certainly did see whole magazines with photos of nothing but women in lacy underwear tied up, but pictures of dominant males were rare and there were no images involving blood or cuts, and when I turned to the back of those magazines I found one personal ad after another from men who were seeking women who would tie them up. At this point I was forced to acknowledge something that had never occurred to me before: that men were looking at these pictures and identifying with the women in them. That is, the women were *not* the objects of their fantasies, but the protagonists of their fantasies – themselves.

There were indeed magazines where dominance was portrayed, but the majority of these depicted female dominants. In some cases these women were posed alone, but often the women were dominating other women. Photographs in general tended to be of women, but in many written stories males were forced to submit to women, and these greatly outnumbered stories in which the principal dominant was a man. Even where male dominance was portrayed, the men, rather than acting independently, were often accompanied by a stronger woman who played a greater role in dominating the 'victim'. Sometimes the dominatrix turned the tables and dominated her accomplice as well. Frankly, I was seeing more strong women in the pornography than I had ever seen in mainstream media.

Although I looked at many SM materials, I found few portrayals that could honestly be called 'violence'. Indeed, even magazines that emphasized spanking and caning generally showed photos where someone was about to be struck, rather than any contact between the hand or paddle and the 'victim'. I never saw a single drop of blood in the magazines I looked at and even marks on the skin were very rare. I later discovered that this was consistent with other overview research that has been done on pornography, where depictions of violence were rated in some as low as less than 2 per cent of content. This hardly supports the view that pornography in general is a 'catalogue of violence'. Yet some claim that pornography is not only violent, but increasingly so as times have become more permissive. On the contrary, researchers consistently find that violent portrayals are rare and have continued to decline in pornography since 1977. For example, Ted Palys, in 1986, studied XXX videos (the triple X is used to denote real porn) and found that violence there had decreased. We see the same in other research, such as Scott and Cuvelier in 1987, and Donnerstein and Linz in 1986, among others. *Soft-core*, a study of porn magazines in Britain by Thompson and Annetts, and *Hard Core*, a study of porn films in the US by Linda Williams, confirmed it again in 1990.

I doubt if I would ever have advocated censorship, regardless of what I had found – my experiences with censorship of feminist materials would have been enough by themselves for me to doubt the usefulness of such measures and to fear the consequences. But I did have a lot of assumptions about pornography and male sexuality that were exploded when I was forced to look at these materials and see for myself that violence against women is not a very popular sexual fantasy for males.

Like many other women, I had assumed that hard core pornography – which most of us never saw unless we went out of our way to look into porn shops' stock (and which is legally unavailable in the United Kingdom) – would expose the ugliness of the real male fantasies I thought were only being coyly hinted at in the more common soft core magazines like *Playboy* and *Penthouse*. Instead, I found those things that were really missing from both soft core magazines and mainstream media: assertive women who were unconcerned about whether they would be thought 'unladylike'; women who did not look like the glamorized Hollywood blonde; women in different shapes and sizes; women of different colours and racial features; women who were older, more mature, than those portrayed by Hollywood; women who didn't shave their bodies, as well as those who shaved everything. The visual variety of women in hard core much more closely resembled the real women I knew than anything I had seen on television or in general-release film.

And the behaviour of the women! These were women who went out to get what *they* wanted, rather than waited around for some man who was the real 'star' of the story, or of their lives. And more importantly, no one seemed to mind; it was the first time I had seen an entire genre in which women were not condemned for being sexual, pursuing their own needs, and getting what they wanted. In mainstream media, women who had careers were usually portrayed as being emotionally disturbed, evil, or 'afraid to be a woman'; in pornography, women could have careers and still have sex lives.

We had been told that pornography was the template for common acts of violence against women, and yet, I never saw in pornography anything that resembled one of the most common (and most acceptable) kinds of violence against women: the beating or killing of a woman for infidelity. The courts are usually harsh on women who kill their boyfriends or husbands for taking up with another woman (or even for threatening their children), but men experience astonishing leniency for murdering women who did not give them their full attention. Indeed, many men have avoided jail altogether for killing wives or girlfriends who were seen with other men (or believed to be seeing other men), tried to break up with their partners, or were (it was said) guilty of 'nagging'. (On the other hand, even when a woman is known to have been the victim of serious physical battering from her partner, women who kill such partners usually go to jail on substantial sentences; women who kill for any lesser reason, such as infidelity, can expect to spend even more time in jail.) It is not uncommon to hear of men insisting that if they find out their female partners are seeing other men, 'I'll kill the bitch.'

I've never seen or read a pornographic story where a woman was murdered for any reason. And if a man should walk in and find his partner in bed with another man, the preferred scenario in porn is that he either watches and enjoys it or climbs in and joins them. Even in SM materials, infidelity is at worst treated as an excuse for more SM games, but never as a justification for killing.

I won't say that I didn't see sexist portrayals in pornography, nor will I pretend that there were *no* glamorous Hollywood blonde types in hard core. But I saw that everywhere, and still do. It was the fact that I also saw contrasting representations – including many that completely contradicted the standard sexism of 'respectable' culture – that interested me. I have now come to feel that it would be mightily refreshing to see movies coming out of Hollywood that are no more sexist or racist than hard core pornography.

Redefining terms

But Robin Morgan had said, 'Pornography is the theory, rape is the practice', and several other feminists, including American anti-porn analyst Diana Russell, were developing the theory of a relationship between sexual material and women's oppression. The claim that men were directly caused to rape by seeing pornography, or that their attitudes toward women were changed sufficiently for them to be more likely to rape after being in an environment that contained pornography, was being repeated throughout the English-speaking world. Researchers at universities were now doing experiments that attempted to prove this relationship in the laboratory, and there were increasing reports that the evidence supported the claim. Anti-pornography feminism became the most vocal and visible part of the movement, and in Britain it came to be seen as the only possible feminist position. In America, the premier feminist magazine, *Ms.*, has taken a wholly anti-pornography position, as has its founder, Gloria Steinhem, and of course the editor who took over when it was revived in its current format, Robin Morgan.

By the mid-1980s, Andrea Dworkin had distinguished herself as the leading feminist anti-pornography campaigner in the world. Her book *Pornography: Men possessing women* is often cited as a source for facts, figures and theories in support of the belief that pornography is central to woman's oppression. Later, in *Intercourse*, she outlined the view that copulation itself – fucking – is the basis for the oppression of women. Dworkin suggests that women do not, cannot and should not enjoy sexual intercourse; this position is at the foundation of many anti-pornography feminists' theories that recreational sexual materials misrepresent women because they portray women as enjoying sexual acts – acts which we are presumed to detest.

On several occasions, Dworkin has been invited to speak in Britain on pornography, and her analysis is the basis for much of the rhetoric that is heard in both Britain and America. An entire episode of BBC television's *Omnibus* in 1991 was dedicated to Dworkin and her view, with no dissent from an opposing voice. Together with feminist lawyer Catharine MacKinnon, Dworkin has promoted a new definition of pornography and designed a law for America that would bypass the First Amendment's guarantee of free expression; pornography, according to Dworkin and her supporters, is violence against women, and should be treated as a violation of our civil liberties.

In Britain, Bristol MP Dawn Primarolo introduced her own Location of Pornographic Material Bill in July 1989 to ban the sale of 'pornographic' media anywhere but in porn shops, using the new 'feminist' definition:

(1) Pornographic material means film and video and any printed matter which, for the purposes of sexual arousal or titillation, depicts women, or parts of women's bodies, as objects, things or commodities, or in sexually humiliating or degrading poses or being subject to violence.

(2) The reference to women in sub-section (1) above includes men.

Many gay rights activists and other feminists were horrified by this language, which is so vague and general that it would include virtually any recreational sexual material. Obscenity laws have often been used to harass gay bookshops and publications, and the specification in section (2) of the Primarolo definition seemed to be a deliberate inclusion of gay male materials as well as those aimed at heterosexual women.

Another problem with the bill is that it forbids the sale of 'pornography' as so defined where *any other goods or services are sold*. Since Britain's sex shops also sell sex toys and lingerie, that would mean pornography could not be sold there; a new form of licensing for porn shops, rather than sex shops, is presented in the bill. Interpretation would be by Trading Standards officers, who are ill-equipped to make such a judgement. Moreover, dealers in other materials that may have erotic content (such as most bookshops) would be at a loss to determine whether they could sell any materials at all that depict sex.

But the main difficulty is in redefining pornography in this way to begin with. Most people, when they talk about pornography, know that they mean sexual material, and although the feminist definition seeks to avoid this common understanding with references to humiliation and violence, the explicitly sexually arousing nature of pornography is used in feminist anti-porn definitions as well; we are meant to think that recreational sexual material in general is not being censored – only the 'nasty' bits – but this can hardly be the case. Any item or person in a photograph is the 'object' of the camera's lens and of the viewer, for example, and thus any depiction, whether sexually explicit or not, can be said to treat those pictured as 'objects, things or commodities'. Moreover, our definitions of what may be 'sexually humiliating or degrading poses' vary widely; some anti-pornography campaigners have specifically cited fellatio as uniformly degrading, particularly when performed from a kneeling position, and it is sometimes claimed that intercourse itself degrades women. Indeed, some anti-pornography campaigners have explicitly stated that *any* sexual depiction of a woman is degrading to women. What would be left for the remaining category, 'erotica'?

And who is going to define and enforce this law? Certainly not the same feminists who may have worked to pass such legislation. Experience has already made clear that a law of this nature is just another tool for the police and courts to curtail the distribution of material that contradicts the centralization of heterosexual, reproductive intercourse. The Canadian courts agreed to such a 'feminist' interpretation in law in 1992, and the first victims were a lesbian magazine, *Bad Attitude*, and Glad Day Bookshop, the gay bookstore in Toronto where it was sold. In a subsequent issue of *Bad Attitude*, editor-publisher Jasmine Sterling wrote:

> I support the law because it does provide some protection for women and children. However, the law was written without an understanding of SM or lesbian sexuality. It was written solely in terms of heterosexuality. And for this it should be protested.

Bad Attitude has become a political cause for freedom of the press, sexual freedom and the right of homosexuals and lesbians to express their sexuality. But the government is not the only one who would like to see freedom of sexual expression repressed. Recently I attended a New Year's brunch and was saddened to hear, later, how upset some of the women were that a 'pornographer' was in their midst. It's funny I don't feel like a pornographer. One of the reasons I do *Bad Attitude* is I love erotica and pushing the limits of sexuality. Is it pornography to enjoy and express your desires?

Jasmine Sterling thought she could support a law against 'pornography' without placing herself in the line of fire, despite the fact that she publishes a lesbian sex magazine with sadomasochistic content that has already been attacked by feminist anti-pornography campaigners, because she somehow thought that lesbian sexual materials couldn't be 'pornography', whatever that is. Many women are willing to agree that 'pornography' is bad, degrading, and should be banned – as long as they think 'pornography' is something enjoyed only by people who are unlike themselves, expressing a sexuality they do not share. We would do well to remember that each of us has a sexuality that someone, somewhere, disapproves of.

Heating up the feminist porn wars

Although the rhetoric of anti-pornography feminism had been in Britain for many years, many people date the emergence of a coherent and highly visible 'feminist' anti-pornography campaign in Britain to Clare Short's 1986 introduction in Parliament of a Ten Minute Rule bill that would have banned the appearance of pin-up nudes in the popular press – 'page 3 girls' as they are usually known, due to their placement on that page in some of the nation's tabloids. Some of Short's male opponents publicly responded with a barrage of offensive sexist comments, appearing to underline a relationship between misogyny and these newspaper photos, and perhaps pornography in general. Numerous women wrote to Short in order to express both their shared discomfort with page 3 pictures and their outrage at the appalling treatment she had received from her colleagues. In the introduction to her book collecting these letters, *Dear Clare*, Short described how she and others were galvanized by this response from women to form the Campaign Against Pornography (CAP), now probably Britain's best-known feminist-oriented anti-pornography group. Later, CAP launched a campaign against the distribution of soft core men's magazines in newsagents' shops, called Off the Shelf.

Sheila Jeffreys and Catherine Itzin both, separately, were already more closely aligned to the feminist movement in Britain. Jeffreys was notorious for her involvement in promoting political lesbianism as exemplified in her book *Anticlimax*, in which she makes her case that, men being unsatisfactory, women should turn to other women for our sexual and emotional partnerships. Like Dworkin, Jeffreys sees heterosexual intercourse as being less than pleasurable for women. She denies that anti-censorship feminism, heterosexual feminism or bisexual feminism can exist, and refers to all those who disagree with her position as 'sexologists'. Unfortunately, since Jeffreys' entire argument seems to rest on the negative qualities of men, there is little in her book about lesbianism based on love of women, and thus she gives every impression of advocating that women use other women as substitutes for men.

Itzin, on the other hand, claims civil libertarian credentials, and formed Campaign Against Pornography and Censorship (CPC) to promote activism against pornography, and to promote anti-pornography laws, from what she claimed to be an anti-censorship position. Nevertheless, like Dworkin and MacKinnon, she suggests that freedom of expression is a trivial concern in the face of the harm she alleges pornography does to women. Pornography itself, she says, silences women by misrepresenting us and making us look less important, less worth taking seriously, in the eyes of men and society. Like a number of anti-pornography campaigners, Itzin cites laboratory research at US universities in support of her belief that pornography is a cause of male sexual violence against women. For Itzin, then, it is a question of which of us is to be censored: women or pornographers.

CPC has supported the introduction in Britain of laws similar to the Dworkin–MacKinnon legislation that would create civil liability against pornographers if women who are sexually assaulted can prove in court that the pornography was responsible for the actions of their assailants. Doubtless many rapists will be happy to make alliances with their victims in order to pass the blame along to others and possibly reduce their own sentences or support arguments for early parole, but it seems unlikely that such cases will bring in verdicts that will be satisfactory to the women who pursue them; women will be forced to negotiate with the men who raped them to get them to testify as chief witnesses in court, but juries may not be so willing to pretend that *Playboy*, rather than the rapist, is responsible for the crime.

While CPC has promoted the Dworkin law, CAP speakers have promoted the Dworkin analysis in Britain. One of CAP's more prominent members, Sam Chugg, told the TV programme *The Time/The Place* that pornography was the cause of sexism. This ahistorical view flies in the face of over 20 years of documentation and analysis by feminist historians, anthropologists and sociologists who recognize that the lower status of women and sexual violence exist even in societies that have never had prostitution or pornography, and that, although broad access to pornography is a very recent phenomenon, rape has been with us throughout known history, as has sexism. We can document the existence of societies that had sexism without pornography; we can find no evidence of sexism having emerged *from* pornography.

In fact, despite Itzin's insistence that seeing pornography causes members of society to treat women badly, at no time in history has women's position been better than it has become in the west during the same period that pornography has been widely available. We have gone from a world in which women were offered little (if any) opportunity to expand their experience beyond home and church (certainly in peacetime) to one in which women are authorities in every field; from a world where women had no right to keep their own money to one where women have the same legal rights as men; from a world where only men were the authorities on women's lives to one where women speak for ourselves. Before there was mass-produced pornography, women were not expected to discuss sex or sexually related issues in public at all, and even the experts on pregnancy, child-rearing and lesbianism were men. In her biography of Marie Stopes, June Rose noted that the vice-chancellor at Oxford had tried to scuttle a public appearance by Stopes, saying he would not consent to 'any public meeting of undergraduates addressed by a lady on any problems connected with sex or the birth-rate'. Today the recognized experts on these issues are women – all within the period that sex magazines, pornographic films and porn videos have become accessible. Although women have certainly not achieved equality, we have at least made a beginning that once seemed well out of sight.

Anti-censorship feminism

There were other feminists who had always looked at pornography because it gave them pleasure, and they were not so easily fooled by the claim that pornography was violent and that women could not enjoy it. Some of these women ultimately felt driven out of the feminist movement because they could not agree with anti-pornography feminism. Others remained in the movement and campaigned against the anti-pornography position within feminism. And, perhaps most interesting of them all, there were the feminist lesbians who, as Jasmine Sterling did with *Bad Attitude*, chose to try to devise their own erotic materials for the enjoyment of other women. These were joined by numerous other feminists who had no interest in pornography but who had serious concerns about censorship and were particularly annoyed that more than two decades' analysis of the social causes of sexism and sexual violence were being thrown away and replaced with anti-pornography rhetoric.

Feminist anti-censorship activism had been a part of the women's movement all along – indeed, it is fair to say that in the early days, feminists were so uniformly anti-censorship that it was generally presumed to be a part of the feminist position. Many feminists, bearing the scars of earlier censorship battles in the civil rights movement and the anti-war movement, principally in the US, had been unsurprised when feminist materials had themselves generated charges of obscenity and moves to suppress them. Women's poetry, so often about sex, childbirth, lesbianism and anger, was seen as obscenity too, and there were numerous actions aimed at keeping such materials off the shelves of libraries and bookshops. *Ms.* magazine, although it contained no erotic writing or pictures, was a popular target of the moral right. *Our Bodies, Ourselves*, the women's health-care handbook, was also attacked. Gay materials were natural targets, too – *Gay News* had no nudes, as the singer Tom Robinson observed, but it was also called 'obscene'. And *Spare Rib*, of course, was banned in the Republic of Ireland because it contained information about reproductive control.

For most veterans of the fight to prevent censorship of women's materials, the idea of feminists jumping on the anti-pornography bandwagon now meant giving away our most effective tool for fighting *against* sexism. Whatever offences we expected pornographers to be committing, we could see no point in letting the state decide where to draw the line – and certainly not while the state was becoming increasingly more repressive, more sexist and more vocally misogynistic than it had been in a long time. When avowed feminists like Dworkin and MacKinnon worked hand in hand with right-wing legislators in Indianapolis and on the 1986 Meese Commission, whose report recommended traditional censorship, the majority of American feminists saw the women's movement being exploited and co-opted by the most virulently sexist men in America, and all for purposes that were meant to harm, rather than help women (see Chapters 5 and 8). The 'new right' activists who had supported the Reagan administration's most repressive actions were already making it clear that they were specifically opposed to women's liberation; they were not our friends.

When the right-wing legislators who invited Catharine MacKinnon (and most emphatically *not* Andrea Dworkin, whose uncompromising style of personal presentation was far less 'professional' and acceptable – and less 'feminine' – than MacKinnon's) to introduce the Dworkin–MacKinnon legislation to an inquiry in Indianapolis, held in 1984 to promote anti-porn legislation, it was no accident that they made no effort at all to involve the local feminist community. They knew they would get no support from that quarter. Indeed, when local feminists got wind of attempts to bring the ordinance to Indiana, they were furious, and actively opposed it.

American feminists formed the Feminist Anti-Censorship Taskforce (FACT) in order to defeat the Dworkin–MacKinnon ordinance and to defend the anti-censorship view within the movement. Groups of this nature were of vital importance if women who opposed censorship were not to be driven from the feminist community. A number of FACT women, calling themselves the Caught Looking Collective, produced the book *Caught Looking*, containing essays critical of the anti-pornography position, along with photographs illustrating the subject matter. Feminist conferences were held about pornography and censorship in which one speaker after another identified anti-pornography feminism as a dead end, and more, as a danger to feminist goals. After the 1982 Scholar and Feminist IX Conference at Barnard College, New York, the papers, edited by Carole S. Vance, were published as *Pleasure and Danger*, perhaps one of the most comprehensive books on the theory and politics of women's sexuality. The contributor pages of this book read like a *Who's Who* of the feminist movement, including Kate Millett, perhaps the first great feminist media analyst; Dorothy Allison, editor of *Quest: A Feminist Quarterly*; Mary S. Calderone of Planned Parenthood; and a host of women's studies teachers, social workers, Latina writers, anthropologists and other feminist activists.

Feminists Against Censorship

In Britain, anti-pornography feminism was getting a free ride from the media. The feminist movement as a whole was already in disarray from one campaign after another to stigmatize alternative approaches to sexuality within the feminist and gay communities. Political lesbians and lesbian separatists had virtually driven heterosexual and bisexual women out of the feminist movement, and even sex-positive lesbians were fleeing in droves. The common image of feminists portrayed in the media throughout the country was the stereotype of man-hating lesbianism. The older, more established feminists who understood the dangers of censorship had little time for the highly personalized and explosive in-fighting that had come to characterize the debate.

In this milieu, it became possible for anti-porn women to walk into the 1989 annual general meeting of the National Council for Civil Liberties (NCCL, sometimes known as 'Liberty') and voice emotive support for their resolution to consider laws against pornography – a once unthinkable move. NCCL had a long tradition of opposing state censorship, and in any other context it would have been reasonable to expect these speakers to be laughed out of the room. Indeed, some people tried, but the response from the anti-porn women was that they were being laughed at merely because they were women, and such attitudes about women came solely from pornography. If NCCL cared about women, they said, the AGM would have to vote for their resolution. Their combination of guilt-tripping, misrepresentations of scientific research, and exploitation of the strong emotions evoked by images of rape and child abuse managed to get them just enough votes to push their resolution through.

That NCCL had overturned its history of supporting free expression was the final straw that, at long last, galvanized feminists in Britain to realize that the job had to be done and no one else was going to do it for us. Almost immediately after the NCCL annual meeting in the spring, women began to meet to plot strategy for representing the anti-censorship view. We chose the name Feminists Against Censorship to make clear precisely who we were and what we stood for. A short leaflet was written and produced by group members, paid for by a quick whip-round at a meeting, and we began making appearances in public.

The response from the anti-pornography cadre was fierce and immediate. Our members were shouted down and called 'pornographers' where we appeared in public. Barbara Rogers, then editor of *Everywoman*, noted there that some of the FAC women present at our first appearance had North American accents (two were Canadian, and one was a student from the United States), and implied that there were no British women present. At the launch itself, the presence of 'Americans' was taken as evidence of a relationship to 'the multi-million dollar American porn industry'. Coupled with this astonishing bit of bigotry, it was noted that our leaflet was attractive, which was treated as evidence that vast sums of money had gone into creating it, so clearly we were funded by the pornographers. (Feminists apparently are not capable of designing an attractive leaflet without the help of pornographers.) The 'fact' that we are 'heavily funded' by pornographers has circulated throughout the left since our beginning, as a result.

That we are actually feminists continues to be disputed, despite the fact that FAC has, since its first day, included some of the most noted long-time feminists in Britain, women who in many cases date back to – and even before – the famous 1970 Ruskin Hall conference that is still considered a major landmark in the early days of British feminism. The meetings where we workshopped our first leaflet were held in the home of Mary McIntosh, whose credentials can be traced to the earliest moments of the women's liberation movement in Britain, when merely suggesting that there could be more to a woman's life than taking care of her husband was a scandalous, radical statement. Elizabeth Wilson, who did some of the first public speaking on FAC's behalf, may be one of the best-known feminist writers in Britain – the strength and intelligence of her work has brought her a following in America, as well. Nettie Pollard, one of our most active organizers, has feminist roots that go back to the Gay Liberation Front, Women on Ireland and the feminist *Red Rag* collective. Sheila Rowbotham, also once a member of the *Red Rag* collective and still one of Britain's most high-profile feminists, voiced early support for FAC. Members such as Lynne Segal, Sue O'Sullivan, Gillian Rodgerson and Mandy Merck all have long, impressive records with the feminist and gay communities. How were these women suddenly 'not feminists'?

Feminists for Free Expression

In the United States, the Dworkin–MacKinnon legislation was going nowhere on a locality-by-locality basis. Although it passed in Minneapolis, the Supreme Court declared it unconstitutional. Anti-pornography activists ranging from the Christian right to supporters of Andrea Dworkin began promoting a federal bill to suppress pornography. But, as anti-censorship women had warned from the beginning, the bill that was eventually presented to the Senate in 1992, while relying on the 'feminist' condemnation of pornography as a civil rights violation, ignored the so-called feminist definition of porn and retained the traditional, specifically anti-sexual approach to pornography using the definition that can be found in any dictionary. In other words, feminist rhetoric was being used to justify suits against *all* recreational sexual materials, which anti-porn feminists at the Meese hearings had said was exactly what they did *not* want.

The introduction of Senate Bill 1521 was enough to motivate even those US feminists who had so far continued in their habitual private projects and left the anti-censorship work to others. Active feminists all over the country reacted with outrage, and chapters of the National Organization for Women (NOW) launched specific letter-writing campaigns against S. 1521. The negative response of the feminist community to the bill actually slowed its progress through the Senate – it was the first time some senators had realized that the anti-pornography position was by no means supported by the entire feminist movement. Indeed not, as *Billboard Magazine* (7 March 1992) reported:

> More than 180 businesswomen, authors, artists, teachers and home-makers have formed the Ad Hoc Committee of Feminists for Free Expression to oppose the bill. The signees include activist Betty Friedan and writers Judy Blume, Erica Jong, Susan Isaacs and Jamaica Kincaid.
>
> The committee joins the two largest chapters of NOW – California and New York State – plus the New York City chapter in a letter-writing campaign.

Other signers included: feminist poet and writer Adrienne Rich; women's studies academics like Wendy Brown; reproductive rights activists Kelli Conlin and Lynn M. Paltrow; Judith Levin of the Women's Rights Litigation Clinic; lesbian authors Phyllis Lyon and Del Martin; president of the American Civil Liberties Union (ACLU) Nadine Strossen and her then personal assistant Catherine Siemann; Isabelle Katz Pinzler of the ACLU Women's Rights Project; Barbara Ehrenreich, Karen De Crow, Nora Ephron, Nancy Friday, and numerous other authors, academics, journalists and even – despite the hostility they had been feeling from feminists – sex workers.

When, in summer 1992, the Pornography Victims' Compensation Act was passed by the Senate Judiciary Committee on a 7–6 majority, Feminists for Free Expression (FFE) sent out a sample letter to be signed by others who wished to see the bill fail.

> Dear Senator;
>
> I am writing as a feminist to oppose the misnamed Pornography Victims' Compensation Act. Though the original bill has been amended, it remains

a powerful danger to feminism and freedom of expression. The premise of S. 1521 – that violence is caused by words and images – is false. Violence against women and children flourished for thousands of years before the printing press and camera, and continues today in countries like Saudi Arabia and Iran where no commercial sexual material is available. Correlation studies in this country, Europe and Asia find no rise in sexual violence with the availability of sexual material. No reputable research shows a causal link between 'obscenity' or 'child pornography' and violence.

While messages of sexism pervade our country in many forms, sexual and nonsexual, *suppression* of such material will neither reduce violence nor further women's goals. S. 1521 diverts attention from the economic, political and psychological causes of harm. Address these, and you will gain the confidence and votes of millions of Americans.

S. 1521 merely reinforces the 'porn made me do it' excuse for rapists and batterers, and it is book banning by bankruptcy. Feminist women are especially keen to the harms of censorship, legislative or monetary. Historically, information about birth control and female sexuality has been banned under the guise of morality and the 'protection' of women. Such censorship has never stopped violence.

The most likely outcome of S. 1521 is that crime victims will in no way benefit while book, movie and magazine producers and distributors are put out of business. I urge you to give S. 1521 the speedy death it deserves and turn your attention to constructive laws that will reduce violence.

The FFE draft letter presents perhaps the best short review of the essential, specific anti-censorship position that can be found among most women throughout the movement: that the drive for censorship is based on a falsehood (the harm of porn); that it will be used to suppress *feminist* work, as such programmes have in the past; that it will also endanger any other media producer who deals with sex in any way; that sexist content is by no means specific to sexual media; that anti-porn feminism 'diverts attention from the economic, political and psychological causes of harm' that truly endanger us; and that it offers an excuse to rapists and batterers while protecting women not at all.

Women and sexual materials

Feminists Against Censorship, however, went further, pointing out that the creation of sexually explicit material, including pornographic works or works that might be called pornographic, was actually a needed part of the feminist programme. Our sexuality, long suppressed and distorted by censorship and sexism, was still something we needed to understand for ourselves; freedom to do so in print and pictures was not something we were willing to give up. Although not all of us have an erotic interest in commercial pornography, we are certainly interested to know what women, left to our own devices, might choose to portray. In our first leaflet, 'Ask yourself ... Do you really want more censorship?', we said:

> Women need open and safe communication about sexual matters, including the power relations of sex. ... We need sexually explicit material produced by and for women, freed from the control of right wingers and misogynists, whether they sit on the board of directors or the board of censors.

And far from attempting to separate ourselves from sex workers and victimize them, we treated the sex industry as just one of many industries where women might find themselves exploited in their work: 'We need a safe, legal working environment for sex workers, not repressive laws or an atmosphere of social stigma that empowers police and punters to brutalize them.' We also pointed out the contradictions in anti-pornography feminism:

> Suddenly the feminist movement that once fought for freedom and sexual self-determination is advocating giving power over our lives to judges and the police; suddenly what it says about our freedom and our sexual desires sounds like the ravings of the Right. Suddenly feminism is about censorship rather than about opening possibilities.
> There is a place for sexually explicit material in our lives. We need a feminism and a society which respects sexual variety and sexual choice.

The result has been a continuous stream of letters and phone calls from women who have re-entered the feminist movement upon learning that they would once again be accepted without having to advocate repression, and many others who had retired but felt censorship was such a vital issue that they wanted to get involved again in order to fight it. Although the amount of media coverage we receive has not been enough to balance the high-profile play that the anti-porn position has been given, our message has begun to circulate, and many people no longer take it for granted that all feminists would agree with further censorship of sexual materials. By 1990, the combined efforts of Feminists Against Censorship and the more established, traditionally civil libertarian Campaign Against Censorship were barely enough to overturn the CPC resolution of the year before at the next NCCL annual general meeting; in 1991, a FAC motion opposing all sexual censorship passed overwhelmingly.

Most of the women who originally formed Feminists Against Censorship were established feminists with jobs, families and other commitments that left them little time and energy for high-profile campaigning. Quite a few had started from a relatively conservative position as regards pornography: that they didn't like it and considered it wholly sexist, but still opposed censorship. Some women had specific concerns about the way lesbian materials were being hampered by censorship, and most of us were all too well aware that gay materials in general were prime targets for prosecutions and seizures. We all knew that laws against pornography generally affected reproductive information, safer sex and feminist materials. The more radical among us wanted to broaden the discourse on sexuality and were adamantly in favour of improving pornography with input directly from women. Additionally, we had arguments early on about how much we should be responding to CAP's and CPC's hysteria about illusory bogeymen like 'snuff' and the 'deluge' of child porn – whether we would be letting them set the agenda on their terms.

We also recognized a serious need for income and had lengthy discussions of whether we could accept money from pornographers if it was offered. One or two women said we needed the money so desperately that we couldn't turn any donation down. Others pointed out that whether we took money from pornographers or not, we were already being accused of having funding from them, so it made no difference. Most of us, however, were not enthusiastic about being involved with mainstream pornographers, who did not strike us as having particularly feminist attitudes (or genuinely pro-sex attitudes, in some cases) to begin with. In the end, this turned out to be a moot question, since we were never offered any such funding, and the pornographers weren't interested in our programme. (A few individual women who worked for sex magazines did eventually join the group, but they did so without any support from their employers.)

PUSSY

One younger member of FAC, Anna Marie Smith, had little patience with what she saw as a conservative, slow-moving group of establishment feminists who were mired in arguments about policy. She wanted to be doing something more direct and radical – so she went over to the gay activist group OutRage! and started her own anti-censorship action group, Perverts Undermining State ScrutinY (PUSSY). Smith's approach was to draw gay men and women together for direct action on specific issues as they arose. She maintained her ties to FAC, and several FAC members became involved in both groups. (Smith's own account of the formation of PUSSY appears in *Pleasure Principles*.)

When, in 1991, Gay's the Word and the women's bookshop Sisterwrite both declined to carry Della Grace's book of lesbian photography, *Love Bites*, PUSSY and FAC acted together to attempt an intervention. A regular FAC meeting was to take place just as the word came out, and FAC's Roz Kaveney hastily organized a larger meeting (Smith found the venue) and made sure interested parties in the gay and feminist communities – male and female – could attend.

It turned out that Gay's the Word, the sole gay bookshop in England, would carry neither *Love Bites* nor the lesbian sex magazine *Quim*, and Sisterwrite also declined to carry them. Silver Moon, the other women's shop, had originally planned a window display of *Love Bites*, but now said they were worried about a prosecution because of one of the pictures. In fact, of all London's major alternative bookshops, only Housman's and Compendium would carry both *Love Bites* and *Quim*, and Compendium refused to sell them to men. FAC and PUSSY jointly arranged another meeting, at the London Lesbian and Gay Centre, that included representatives of the bookshops and other activists, but little was resolved. (We did receive a letter of support from West and Wilde, Britain's other gay bookshop, in Edinburgh, who said they were too busy selling *Love Bites* and *Quim* to attend in person.) In June 1991, FAC and PUSSY sponsored a bookshop walk to Sisterwrite, Silver Moon and Gay's the Word, where we handed out leaflets and encouraged the customers (and passers-by) to engage with the shops and the community about censorship of lesbian materials.

The Pink Paper reported this action as a call for a boycott, although in fact we encouraged people to take their custom to these shops. The last thing we wanted was to create economic distress for community enterprises. What we did want was to see the feminist and gay communities rethink their positions and show greater support for lesbians who were investigating their own sexuality without the resources that go to more traditional (and sexist) sexual materials. But while *Love Bites* received a cover story in *Time Out* and was carried by most major bookshops, gay and feminist shops failed to support it.

PUSSY

Smith's energy and charisma proved to have been the essential ingredient in PUSSY; when she finished her studies and left Britain to take a job in the United States, there was one further large meeting organized jointly by FAC and PUSSY, but after that the group seemed to fade away. In the interim, however, FAC had developed a more informed and radical approach to pornography and censorship, and was independently beginning to organize more independent public events and active campaigning.

The debate within the feminist and gay communities has broadened greatly since FAC was formed, and recently we have even had quiet contact and support from a few female MPs, as well as other feminists who had felt silenced and excluded by the 'feminist' anti-pornography campaigns.

Yet interviewers still ask, 'But wouldn't feminists disagree with you?' If Betty Friedan, Lynne Segal, Kate Millett, Elizabeth Wilson, Adrienne Rich, Sue O'Sullivan, Nettie Pollard and Gillian Rodgerson are not feminists, who on earth is? Certainly not women who would take away the rights of women to express our diversity and make our own choices.

5
The research

The laboratory and its effects

Many claims about scientific evidence proving a link between pornography and violence have been repeated endlessly in support of censorship. Most of the research in question comes from the United States, where universities have research programmes in place all the time. The majority of these studies are done in psychology departments and use psychology students as their subjects – a point that should be carefully borne in mind, as much of this research is actually designed to be performed on 'naive subjects': people who have no idea what the meaning of their behaviour is or how much of what they experience during the experiment is genuine. For example, a common method is to test subjects' willingness to 'aggress' against a research confederate by asking them to deliver electrical shocks to the confederate; but the subjects do not know that their 'victim' is a research 'stooge', and the shocks are not real. One problem arises straight away: how do we know that the subjects in the experiment are not aware of this?

Shocks

Research using faked electrical shocks and confederates who would pretend to be shocked became well known during the 1960s after Stanley Milgram released the results of a particularly famous study in which he demonstrated that subjects could successfully be encouraged to give apparently lethal shocks to stooges merely because they had been told to. At the time this work was done, this method was not so widely known, but the results gained a great deal of media attention and are now frequently cited in much psychological and sociological literature, as well as newspaper stories and other contexts that are not specifically academic.

Many people who are interested in the social sciences will have heard about this research long before they have reached college age. It is not unreasonable to expect that psychology students may have become familiar with the idea of giving faked shocks prior to entering the university.

At American universities, psychology students are usually told that they will be given course credit for participating in psychology experiments being conducted in the department. It will generally be the case that these students have been spending a great deal of time reading about the experiments performed by researchers, and Stanley Milgram's work will probably be referred to more than once. (Milgram's work was discussed in the first chapter of the text for my first psychology class at the University of Maryland. I couldn't begin to detail the number of times I saw his work mentioned in my later coursework. Milgram was also discussed in some of my sociology texts, and I had previously encountered him in feminist works as well as my general reading. By the first time I participated in a psychological experiment, I had already thought more than once about how I would respond to an instruction to give 'electric shocks'.) Indeed, this method has also been used in some pornography effects experiments for many years now, and students who are asked to give shocks after seeing pornography may actually have read similar studies before participating in the experiments.

Environment

Students may often be aware that particular kinds of research are done at their university. For example, the University of Wisconsin at Madison is known to be a site of research on pornography effects. Do the subjects of those experiments already know that they may be taking part in such research? Additionally, this particular campus has a highly regarded women's studies department in a small town that is dramatically influenced by its student population. (Even the local science fiction convention is noted for its feminism.) Does that fact influence the attitudes that will be found on campus? Does it make the research subjects more aware of what kinds of reaction the researcher is hoping to demonstrate? Milgram himself is often cited as evidence that student responses are strongly influenced by the demands of the researchers.

It is important to remain concerned about questions like this, as some people claim that pornography effects research has suggested that males who are shown pornography are more likely to deliver these faked shocks than are men who have not been shown pornography. It might be useful to ask what it means when a man is more likely, after seeing pornography, to deliver a 'shock' he *knows* to be fake. Giving the shock is interpreted as 'aggression', a willingness to do harm, but if the subject knows he is not doing harm, could it mean something else – something positive, perhaps? In 1970, D.L. Mosher thought he found 'aggression' in pre-angered subjects who were shown pornography – but what if the subjects were not showing aggression, and instead merely intended to use what they considered to be a symbol, in order to express their discomfort with the research confederate who had angered them? The effect Mosher found may have been, simply, a greater desire to communicate. This could even be interpreted to mean that pornography had shown a positive effect.

Even keeping these considerations in mind, the effects of the laboratory should not be underestimated – every time one researcher seems to have found an effect, another researcher discovers that it is difficult to duplicate the results. Often, studies using the same methods get opposite results. Despite Mosher's finding, most of the major researchers – Baron, Bell, Donnerstein, White, Frodi, Zillmann, Sapolsky and so on – have found that men show no more aggression after seeing pornography than after being shown non-sexual images, and their studies on pre-angered subjects have often shown that subjects show less aggression after seeing pornography.

Controlled effects

Another reservation about laboratory research is that experiments are set up to show only the desired effect – that is, a subject may be willing to do any of a number of things after seeing the materials under study, but given only one behaviour option. Your urge after seeing a particular film may be to play pinball, change your motor oil, walk in the park or help a neighbour move furniture, but the only option the researcher gives you is to deliver a shock or fill out a questionnaire – could this be the cause of frustration you express in your subsequent behaviour or answers?

Perhaps most importantly when we are talking about pornography effects, the likelihood is that many research subjects would prefer to masturbate after viewing pornography, yet they are not allowed to do that. The behaviour that is encouraged in the laboratory is itself entirely artificial, but even if it were not, it is hard to believe the average young male wouldn't prefer better options than filling out questionnaires and pushing buttons after being aroused by pornography.

The researchers themselves have often stated that it is important to remember that what the research shows is laboratory effects, and that there is no evidence that these effects have any relationship to behaviour outside the lab. For example, some researchers have found that they can show increased 'aggression' after viewing violent material in the laboratory, and from this people tend to assume that violent television or film causes higher violence in society. But there is no evidence that such a relationship exists outside of the laboratory environment, and there is some evidence that quite the reverse may be true: when the Palm Beach County Jail in Florida started showing 'slasher' movies to the prisoners in 1987 as part of their routine entertainment, the rate of prison fights dropped dramatically – by more than 50 per cent – as Marcia Pally pointed out.

Another problem with pornography effects research is that, although our desire has been to look at causes of sexual aggression, none of the aggression shown in the lab was sexual in any way. There is certainly no analogy between pressing a button to give electrical shocks and committing an act of rape. The environment of the laboratory setting is completely unlike the contexts in which men commit acts of real sexual violence.

It is also noteworthy that the effects of the materials are contingent on how shocking or otherwise emotionally arousing they are to the viewer. The strongest arousal responses were found when the material viewed was a film of eye surgery. Audiences that are particularly shocked by pornography may be showing a strong arousal response from shock – that is, sex guilt – rather than sexual stimulation. It is not always clear what the reactions of research subjects are to; even in the case of pornography, our responses may arise from different attitudes and values. In addition, anything that increases the heart rate or skin temperature may create this 'aggression' response; in Edward Donnerstein's words: 'And yes, there are studies where males bicycle ride and then are more aggressive when they are angered.' How can we eliminate all stimuli from the environment – and is there really any reason we should want to?

Laboratory results

Even given all of these reservations about the artificiality of the laboratory and the methodological problems that come with it, the research by no means supports the belief that negative effects of pornography have been shown in the lab. In 1987, Edward Donnerstein, Daniel Linz and Stephen Penrod reported in *The Question of Pornography* that subjects shown non-violent pornography:

exhibited no significant increases in the tendency to (1) hold calloused attitudes about rape, (2) view women as sexual objects, (3) judge the victim of a reenacted rape trial as more responsible for her own assault, or (4) view the defendant as less responsible for the victim's assault.

By and large, researchers have tended to find that responses to sexual material are less aggressive than responses to non-sexual material. In some cases, the suggestion was that violent material, rather than sexual material, caused aggression. Some studies compared non-violent sexual material to violent sexual material and found more effects of aggression in the latter case; others compared violent sexual, non-violent sexual, and non-sexual violent materials, always finding that the more violent and less sexual the material, the greater the aggressive response. It may be, however, that it was less a case of violent content causing aggression and more a case of sexual material causing less aggression; that is, the more violence there was, the less sex, and the less sex, the more aggressive the response. It may also be the case that the violent (as opposed to neutral) content is more likely to distract the viewer and thus negate any positive effects from the sexual content. Or it may simply be that people were more shocked by the violence than by the other content.

Pro-social effects

Research by D.P. Przybyla in 1985 and K. Kelley in 1989 demonstrated what are called 'pro-social' effects of pornography when their subjects were shown to be more helpful after viewing sexually explicit materials. Mueller and Donnerstein had already found in 1981 that subjects' pro-social behaviour would be increased by an arousal stimulus. This suggests there is a great deal more to the question of pornography effects than has been implied by anti-pornography campaigners. Overall, it seems fair to say that a person in a stimulated state, regardless of the stimulus, is more likely to be expressive, whether what they wish to express is positive or negative – not something we needed research to tell us.

Definitions and likelihood to rape

It is generally the case that we have no means to interpret what actually caused the responses that were found in the laboratory experiments. The same problem applies when we look at studies that asked subjects questions rather than trying to encourage specific behaviour.

In a well-known 1984 study by Neil Malamuth, male students were asked how likely they would be to rape if they knew they could get away with it. At no time was the word 'rape' ever defined for the students, although numerous differing definitions seem to be circulating in society. Many people perceive some acts of forcible sex as not being rape if they fulfil certain other criteria: a married woman is seen by some as having agreed to sex on demand from her husband in perpetuity, and her lack of immediate consent and his use of force therefore become irrelevant; some people believe that rape laws are only meant to protect chastity, and a woman who has had more partners than are deemed appropriate no longer has any chastity to protect; it is sometimes felt that women who have had many partners cannot possibly mind one more who just didn't happen to be invited; rape by 'friends' is seen as being 'not so bad' and therefore pressing rape charges would be seen as churlish; having been in any way flirtatious (or apparently so) before the rape took place may be seen as a promise of sex and thus it may be concluded that sex was not rape but consensual; and so on. On the other hand, some feminists have promoted a view of rape that does appear to include consensual acts – seduction is sometimes equated with rape, for example. In fact, some feminists have gone so far as to say that there is no difference between rape and consensual intercourse. On many American university campuses, rape discussions have seen the use of the term 'rape' to be highly inclusive, and many students may have come to equate the word with any intercourse undertaken without specific verbal discussion. How do we know how many definitions of rape – or even which definition of rape – the men in Malamuth's study were using? Whatever definitions were in use, most of those men expressed no likelihood to rape.

It is worth emphasizing Malamuth's results, since this study is often cited as proving both that most men would rape if they could get away with it and that they were more likely to say they would rape after seeing porn. In fact, Malamuth divided his subjects into three groups – one that was shown pornography, one that saw a video of a woman discussing her experience of being raped, and one that saw nothing – and found no difference between the responses of the three groups. And, despite the qualifier that this was a case in which a rapist knew he would not be caught and punished, 65 per cent of the men reported no likelihood at all to rape, and most of the others said they were not very likely to rape, even in this rare, safe circumstance. Yet even in the case of those who expressed *some* likelihood to rape, we have no way of knowing how they were interpreting the question.

The varying definitions of rape that are present on a university campus in America create an enormous amount of confusion in research. A good example of this can be found in the *Ms.* magazine Campus Project on Sexual Assault, a study at the University of Arizona by Mary Koss that 'found' that 27 per cent of female students had been raped an average of twice in the period between ages 14 and 21 – although 73 per cent of those 'victims' said that they disagreed that they had been raped. In other words, the subjects in this study were using a very different definition of rape from that used by the researcher.

Other research has not shown any heightened likelihood to rape or perceive women in a degrading way, even when subjects are shown 'degrading' sexual material. Again, there was a definitional problem, of course; the researchers do not always agree on what images are degrading. Many feel that any representation of women enjoying sex is degrading, and some researchers as well as some feminists have defined fellatio as degrading. Many of us do not, however, feel degraded by such acts or their representations. The same problem even applies to SM materials: the people most likely to view them, sadomasochists, do not perceive them as degrading, although many other people interpret them that way. Christian members of some of the panels that heard testimony in American anti-pornography hearings expressed the belief that lesbianism degraded women; even the most adamantly heterosexual feminist would have trouble buying that interpretation.

Some might call it cheating

Anti-pornography activists often cite government reports as 'evidence' that western countries recognize how dangerous pornography really is. Some of the government-sponsored commissions never bothered to review the scientific research at all; for example, the Australian parliament came to the conclusion that anti-social and violent effects could be attributed to pornography, but they never even brought in an expert review of the evidence.

The American Meese Commission did ask for a review by Dr Edna Einsiedel, who found no support for a link between pornography and anti-social behaviour. A study was commissioned to show that modern popular men's magazines were increasingly violent, but instead it found that only 0.6 per cent of the imagery could be said to include violence, force or weaponry of any kind. A report was also commissioned from the Surgeon General, C. Everett Koop, that found no support for a belief in harm from pornography. But the final report by the commission simply ignored Einsiedel's findings and never mentioned the magazine overview, and the Surgeon General's report was suppressed; instead, the claim was made that the evidence of harm from pornography was proven. Nevertheless, two women on the panel, experts themselves, wrote a minority report disputing the Meese Commission's official report. They were not much pleased by the suggestion that vibrators should be banned, either.

Similarly, we can see that suspicious means were used in Canada by the Metropolitan Toronto Task Force on Violence Against Women. In 1983, they asked feminist Thelma McCormack (who is often credited with having brought women's studies to Canada) to report on the possible links between pornography and sexual aggression. As normally happens when knowledgeable social scientists examine the research, McCormack's report, 'Making sense of the research on pornography', said there was no evidence of such a link. The Task Force dismissed and suppressed her work, and then hired another researcher, this time one who was already committed to an anti-pornography position. This was David Scott, by no means a feminist supporter, who claimed to have found a clear and compelling relationship between pornography and sexual aggression.

In fact, most studies and reviews commissioned by governments in Europe and the English-speaking world have not been able to find scientific support for the much-touted link between pornography and violence.

Can pornography change men's minds?

Callousness toward women

Along with the belief that pornography increases men's likelihood to rape, another frequent claim is that research proves it makes males more prone to believe in rape myths (such as that women enjoy being raped) or have worse attitudes towards women. The research most often cited for this is from Dolf Zillmann and Jennings Bryant, who did studies to show that men became more 'callous' towards women after viewing pornography. Some anti-pornography campaigners often refer to the 'callousness' research as demonstrating the harm that pornography does, but a careful

68 Nudes, prudes and attitudes

look at Zillmann's prejudices is in order before we even begin to accept his data. Zillmann thought men were 'callous', for example, if they believed a woman was capable of initiating instrumental sex. Feminists have also said that women are capable of initiating instrumental sex, of course, without looking at pornography. As noted earlier, Zillmann also listed a greater tolerance for homosexuality as a 'callous' attitude. This already suggests that Zillmann's attitudes are diametrically opposed to those held by feminists; what he calls callous, we often call non-sexist.

Daniel Linz and Neil Malamuth class this position as moral/authoritarian. In *Communication Concepts 5: Pornography*, they note that Zillmann and Bryant meant to test:

> the moralist assumption that pornography fosters a lack of respect for, and belief in, traditional institutions such as marriage, traditional relations between the sexes, and traditional roles for women. They hypothesize that the use of pornographic material may lead to general acceptance of sex crimes, alter perceptions of evaluations of marriage, spawn distrust among intimate partners, inspire claims for sexual freedom, and even diminish the desire to have children. In effect, these researchers have turned their attention to the moralist contention that pornography is causally related to the general decline of basic values in American society.

Generally, only one of the 'callous' attitudes Ziilmann and Bryant listed is mentioned by feminist anti-pornography campaigners: that men were more likely to express dissatisfaction with their current sexual relationships. We are apparently meant to fear from this that if our male partners (or potential partners) have access to pornography, they will be disappointed in our own appearance or sexual performance and either start making demands for more sex (or 'kinkier' sex) or leave us for more satisfactory partners. Or at least 'cheat' on us.

I remind you once again that the subjects of this study were primarily male college students – most of whom probably did not have secure long-term relationships to begin with. And while it may be perfectly normal for a macho stud to hide the fact that his sex life is less than perfect, it is hardly a desirable trait. So why do we assume it is a bad thing if a young man is more willing to admit that he may very well be lonely, or confused, or otherwise dissatisfied with his sexual relationships? And in view of the fact that feminists have for quite some time now been complaining that sex between men and women isn't as good as it should be, isn't it about time that something made men admit that this is, in fact, the case? If so many women are unhappy with the general run of their sexual relationships, it is certainly not desirable that men say they are happy with them just the way they are. Nothing is likely to change until we all admit that our lives can be made better.

Having noted the varied interpretability of Zillmann and Bryant's findings, the Surgeon General's report said that the only reliable finding of the research that supposedly proved men were more callous towards women after looking at pornography was this: the group that saw pornography estimated more accurately the prevalence of sexual practices in society. The control group, which did not see the material, tended to underestimate grossly how common certain sexual acts were.

But even this result may be less reliable than it appears, due to methodological problems. Zillmann and Bryant had tried to include non-students in their research, but many of them left the study group when they discovered they would be asked to look at pornography. This meant that the control group contained a different population – older, perhaps more settled married men, for example – and thus the differences in the answers the groups gave to the questions might only reflect different attitudes among the different groups, and not pornography effects at all. The study was no longer controlled. In the end, the research may only mean that older, married men are less critical of their partners than young, single psychology students, and that such young, educated men have more liberal attitudes about women's roles and homosexuality, and more realistic knowledge of sexual practices in society.

Desensitization

The claim is often made that viewing pornography will 'desensitize' men to violence – that is, that men will be less likely to find sexual violence disturbing after seeing pornography. Aside from Zillmann, the research most often cited to support this is a study by J.B. Weaver, made in 1987. However, Weaver didn't use pornographic materials at all, but rather American network television and general-release film. Even naked breasts cannot be shown on US network television. There were no X-rated materials in the study, let alone XXX materials. (An X rating is given to a film, including a general-release film with only minor sexual content, that contains sexual material deemed unsuitable for viewers under 18. More recently, the NC17 rating has been introduced to allow film-makers to produce materials that contain sex but are not intended to be pornography and do not follow porn's conventions; however, this is being treated just like an X rating, and has quickly come to be considered the kiss of death. Triple X is used – principally by pornographers – to denote actual pornography.)

But what do we mean by 'desensitization', anyway, and why would seeing pornography desensitize men to *violence*? It must be remembered that pornography itself contains far less violence than most media, and that there is no logical reason why men should become more casual about violence just because they have seen pictures of sex.

The word 'desensitize' seems to have connotations of becoming less human, less caring; but this is an over-valuation. In fact, the real 'desensitization' that comes from viewing pornography is that many people often become bored by it once their curiosity is satisfied. Some people also find that porn ceases to be exciting to them once they stop thinking of it as 'dirty'. Those who are not very responsive to visual pornography may be eager to see it at first, just to find out what it really is like and whether it will appeal to them, but once they learn that it does not stimulate them and is not as shocking as they expected, they may find it very dull. It should also be kept in mind that the very idea of being shown pornography in the research lab – which in this case is often an ordinary classroom – carries its own excitement. College students, who have just reached the age where Americans can legally see material which shows naked breasts, may think that being shown pornography will be an interesting departure from the normal run of activities they ordinarily experience in the academic environment; but after a few hours or even weeks of exposure, it is all routine. The students in Weaver's study may have been excited by the prospect of participating in a media study that might show them material they would not ordinarily see, but soon have become disappointed when they realized it was just the same old stuff that was available on the television at home.

Those of us who have worked in clinical environments must also learn to be 'desensitized' to experiences that at first overwhelmed us. As a women's health counsellor, I had to learn that I was no use to the women who came to me for advice if I kept getting too upset about their circumstances; they needed me to be able to think clearly and advise them dispassionately, not to get so worked up that I couldn't do my job. I was desensitized, but I never stopped caring, and I never stopped getting angry about a society that often put women in positions that we should never have to confront. At the same time, I was becoming *more* sensitive to subtler issues that might be the less obvious causes of the problems my clients were facing. Similarly, many medical students faint when they first see surgery; if they did not become desensitized, they would never be able to perform as doctors. Once they get over the shock of seeing people cut open and bleeding, they are able to become more discerning of other medical details. Being 'desensitized' does not mean becoming insensitive.

Many people need to learn to overcome their embarrassment about sex and sexual imagery, genitals and members of the other sex, before they can learn to deal honestly with these issues and other people. Until they are 'desensitized', they are not always competent to show the openness, natural curiosity and sensitivity that are essential to good, honest sexual interactions. If seeing an endless stream of pornography is necessary to teach boys to stop giggling at the mention of sexual acts and organs, pornography may be a very good thing indeed.

Attitudes and rape

It would be impossible – and a bit boring – to review every single piece of research on pornography or sex crime here, and it is never easy to find out enough information about how the research is actually done – what questions were asked, what the assumptions of the researchers were, and so on. Sociologist Alison King, in 'Mystery and imagination', has gone over some of the research in more detail, asking similar questions. One point she makes is that we must look further into the attitudes that men have prior to committing sex crimes – and prior to seeing pornography. Even Zillmann's work suggests that conservative sexual attitudes are implicated in rape, King points out; and, further:

> the vast majority of studies seeking to determine rapists' motivations uncover similar attitudes and motives without realizing their importance. Professor Kelley has long recognized that it is men with 'conservative and stereotypical' attitudes towards women who demonstrate aggressive and callous tendencies towards women.

Of course, some people have tried to claim that pornography itself accounts for those attitudes, but it is unlikely that people with highly conservative values would be those who were receiving the most exposure to pornography in early life. In fact, in 1990, when Dr Larry Baron compared the amount of pornography in an area with gender equality in the environment, he found that the greatest degree of gender equality was in areas with the highest circulation of pornography. Baron said that the best predictor of inequality in an area was the number of religious fundamentalists there.

Here we begin to see what might be behind the real causes of rape: conservative, repressive sexual attitudes that emanate not from pornography, but from religious sources. All the research indicates that rapists are more likely to think unchaste women deserve to be punished; this is obviously an attitude that more closely resembles those found in some religious teachings than anything in pornography.

Where do rapists come from?

Many researchers have found repeatedly that the worst sex offenders come from homes where sexual information ranged from non-existent to highly negative. H.S. Kant and M.J. Goldstein found in 1978 that the homes of sex offenders were those where conservative and traditional values were enforced by proscriptions, and Goldstein had already found in a 1973 study that all of the rapists in his sample had been punished for reading pornography, although only 7 per cent of men in a control sample had been. The implication is clear that children will be less likely to grow up to be offenders if they have honest and open sex education as early as possible (and that they shouldn't be punished for looking at pornography). Children currently rely on friends and family for most of their sex education, but if parents are not forthcoming with information, they can easily be misled. The workshop on pornography held in 1986 by Ronald Reagan's Surgeon General, C. Everett Koop, found that children rarely see sexually explicit materials, despite the fact that what would be considered hard core pornography in Britain is freely on sale to adults in the United States. Rather, children whose parents try to prevent exposure to sexual information will probably pick it up from friends. Suzanne Ageton found in her 1983 study of women and real-life aggression that the most consistently powerful factor in violence was a delinquent peer group; the other important factor was attitudes about women and violence.

Rape myths

James Check, one of the few researchers who still supports the anti-pornography cause, said on an episode of *Dispatches* in autumn 1992 that research where 12-year-old boys are asked to name their principal source of sexual information showed that boys who gave 'pornography' as their source were more likely to believe rape myths. Check interprets this to mean that the boys are picking up rape myths from the pornography, but it is unlikely that North American boys would have read any pornography that portrays rape myths in any way at this age; it is more likely that the boys are saying 'pornography' because they have no other source to cite, or because they don't want to admit that they had to learn things from their friends or parents. Boys who believe rape myths at 12 are unlikely to have had sources of sexual information besides the usual word-of-mouth mythology – 'boy talk' and conservative 'family values'. Most pornography does not portray rape, and a North American 12-year-old, if he has seen pornography of any kind, is most likely to have seen pin-up magazines like *Playboy* in which material referring to rape is very rare and certainly does not portray rape as stimulating. (Indeed, most of the writing in *Playboy* is of a more intellectual bent, and even the fiction is not very sexually oriented; editorially, *Playboy* is as hostile to rape as any feminist.) There is also no evidence that the boys who did not believe in rape myths had seen less pornography than the boys who did; rather, they simply had a better source, such as informative parents, friends or sex education, that they could cite. Other research by Kant and Goldstein has shown that rapists have seen pornography later and less often than other boys. The same conservative parents who might convey rape myths to their children are also those most likely to prevent their children from attending sex education classes if they are available, as they can easily do in America. Unfortunately, the Major government announced plans in 1994 to make it easier for parents in Britain to prevent their children from attending sex education classes, as well.

It would seem clear from research of this nature that sex education, rather than censorship, is our best defence against young males growing up believing in rape myths or becoming rapists themselves. There is certainly no evidence that rape declines or disappears when pornography is not present.

Other correlations

The claim continues to be made that areas in which sexual materials are available are areas where rape rates are high. Even before we look more closely at those studies, it is worth bearing in mind that correlations are not necessarily helpful; for example, the rate of breast cancer has risen since smoking has been banned in more and more offices, though no one takes this as evidence that smoking (or 'passive smoking') had been preventing breast cancer. The same applies to those correlations between rape rates and pornography. But, as Marcia Pally says, 'Baron, Strauss and others found this correlation to be spurious; it appears because both rape rates and pornography sales correlate with other facts, such as the number of young men living in a given locale and presence of a macho ethic in that area.' In other words, men between the ages of around 15 and 35 are those most likely to commit violent crime, and areas with a high population of men in that age group will have more rapes. But of course, young men are also most likely to buy pornography. The relationship is to age, rather than directly between pornography and rape. Joseph Scott and Loretta Schwalm found much the same thing in their 1988 study, and also that there was no correlation between rape rates in an area and the presence of pornographic movie houses. They did find a stronger association between rape rates and the sales of outdoor sports magazines like *The American Hunter*, *Guns and Ammo* and *Field and Stream*, suggesting once again that the macho ethic is a related factor. In 1991, Cynthia Gentry found that rape rates were highest in areas with a high number of male residents between the ages of 18 and 34.

Even so, the relationship is not so clear. For example, the US state with the lowest circulation of pornographic magazines is Utah, but it ranks 25th (out of 50) in the number of rapes. Utah, of course, is a state well known for its high Mormon population; it is possible that religious attitudes, rather than pornography, account for the higher rape rates, as well as for greater restrictions on pornography. New Hampshire, on the other hand, has a very high circulation of pornographic magazines, and yet is only 44th in rape rates, well down the list.

Berl Kutchinsky, of the Institute of Criminal Science at the University of Copenhagen, looked at sex crimes in Denmark over the period between 1965, after hard pornography had been decriminalized, and 1982. Kutchinsky found that rates of rape did not rise in this period. Some people have tried to dispute Kutchinsky's evidence on the grounds that he had pointed out that sex crime in general had declined but that this would naturally have happened since some acts had been decriminalized, and it would merely be a statistical fact that they were no longer reportable crimes. However, forcible rape itself had not been decriminalized. Kutchinsky also noted that rates of rape in West Germany had declined slightly since the pornography bans had been lifted in 1973, although other violent crime had risen.

John Court, a Christian psychologist who was once a leader of the Festival of Light, published several papers attempting to discredit Kutchinsky, and also claimed to have demonstrated that rape rates in Hawaii had declined in a two-year period during which sexual material had been restricted there. However, most researchers have recognized the lack of reliability in Court's work, and the Williams Committee on Obscenity and Film Censorship (see Chapter 2) was scathing in its dismissal of him. Even so, Court was forced to admit, when pressed by the 1990 New Zealand Indecent Publications Tribunal, that there was no proven link between sex crime and pornography. As Pally notes, he told the Tribunal, 'What I am saying is that we do not have evidence that there is such a causal link. I cannot sustain it from my data and I don't know anybody who can.'

Debriefing

A particularly interesting question about pornography – and about censorship – is raised by Edward Donnerstein's 1982 experiments in what he calls 'debriefing', in which, after seeing particularly misogynistic pornography, male students were shown materials that contradicted rape myths. What Donnerstein found was that men who were 'debriefed' about rape myths after massive exposure to violent and misogynistic films were far less likely to hold discriminatory and stereotypical attitudes about women than they had been before seeing the pornography. Most impressively, the men showed a much stronger positive effect from 'debriefing' after seeing anti-rape-myth materials when they saw the violent material first than they did if they saw the 'debriefing' materials alone.

What this suggests is that massive exposure to misogynistic materials can actually make men more disposed to absorb feminist-oriented anti-rape-myth arguments. This is consistent with much feminist experience from the 1970s, where it was clear that women who had less exposure to *overt* misogyny were more likely to find feminist complaints about sexism 'unrealistic' than women who had been exposed to more direct sexism themselves. For example, analysts like Kate Millett who were personally familiar with the blatant misogyny that could be found in respected books had no trouble understanding feminist anger at the respectability of anti-women attitudes, whereas women who had not read such books themselves were unaware that men were receiving awards for writing basically sexist materials. Women who may have been passed over for promotions or refused jobs because they were female may be unaware of this and not feel that sexist discrimination has affected them; women who were told point blank that they were losing career options because they were women are more likely to understand, having seen for themselves, that sexism is a real problem.

Much feminist writing is, in effect, a combination of offensive material followed by 'debriefing'. Most feminist writers will often present examples of sexism first before going on to explain where the viewpoint of the quoted passages falls short. By first demonstrating the degree to which sexism pervades popular culture, the theorist prepares the ground for further exploration of the failures of society. Dworkin herself used such methods in her first book, *Woman Hating*, and again in *Pornography* and *Intercourse*. Her novel *Mercy* is usually described as containing continuous portrayals of rape and degradation – and yet was written in condemnation of social violence. Indeed, Women Against Pornography (WAP) and Feminists Fighting Pornography campaign against sexual materials in America by making slide shows of porn and displaying pornographic images. Catherine Itzin also uses slide shows and porn magazines to campaign against porn. And Feminists Against Censorship, of course, uses the works and statements of Dworkin, Itzin, CPC, WAP and CAP when we campaign against their point of view – as I have in this book.

With or without pornographic materials, however, it is apparent that men can be disabused of rape myths by being educated – 'debriefed'. If this is so, it is incumbent upon feminists to make sex education, rather than censorship, a priority.

Rapists, killers and pornography

Many anti-pornography campaigners have made the claim that the most serious sex offenders were readers of pornography. There is no evidence to support this, but since the advent of anti-pornography 'feminism' it has become convenient for violent sex criminals to claim that pornography caused them to commit their crimes.

The Moors Murders and de Sade

Anti-pornography campaigner Moyra Bremner, who has been active in trying to instigate a ban on the Marquis de Sade's *Juliette* since it was released in English translation in Britain, frequently cites the fact that a de Sade book, *Justine*, was found on the premises of Ian Brady's home after he was arrested in 1965 for the horrific crimes he and Myra Hindley, the notorious 'Moors Murderers', committed. The idea that this one book made the man into a killer is ludicrous, of course, especially when one considers that thousands of other people have read de Sade without ever committing an act of violence. In fact, it has been suggested that Brady never read the book, and merely possessed it because he thought it 'cool'. Brady obviously already had the kind of problems that most researchers on violent offenders cite as being a part of their background; such people commit crimes without ever seeing a single word by de Sade.

Of all the people I have spoken to who have read de Sade, Bremner is the only one I know to claim he 'advocated' murder and torture. Others point out that de Sade, who was so strongly opposed to the death penalty that he faced the guillotine himself rather than sentence others to it, wrote his works, while in the Bastille waiting to die (for having refused to invoke the death penalty as a sitting judge), about his philosophical approach to free will. Disgusting as his descriptions of the horrible acts we might commit under free will may have been, they were no worse than much of what was going on in the streets of France during the Terror. The book is a difficult read and not popular for use as pornography. Yet on the basis of one doubtful claim of a relationship between *Justine* and the Moors Murders, and the misreading of de Sade by one woman who obviously did not understand what she read, a Bill was introduced in the House of Commons to ban *Juliette*, and Bremner has continued to use this sort of reasoning to advocate bans on pornography in general.

Video nasties

In 1983, Mark Austin claimed that 'video nasties' had made him rape two women – he had seen *I Spit On Your Grave* (the only movie ever mentioned in the reports about his video-watching habits), and enacted a fantasy which he alleged was based on such movies. Martin Barker quotes the *Sun*: 'The nasties usually included violent rape scenes which ended with the victim enjoying the assault.' As Barker points out, there is nothing of the kind in *I Spit On Your Grave*; the victim is clearly terrorized, and must take time to recover enough to go back out and take her revenge – Brian de Palma meets Thelma and Louise.

Most so-called 'video nasties' are slasher movies, and many of these revolve around a device which Carol J. Clover, in her book *Men, Women and Chainsaws*, calls 'the final girl'. Clover points out that in these stories, although they may begin with a male viewpoint character (usually the killer), the viewpoint shifts to that of 'the final girl' who will ultimately triumph and be the sole survivor of the killer's massacre. She suggests that this viewpoint shift may serve two purposes: first, that the (young male) viewer is forced now to identify with the person who is on the receiving end of the brutality and thus experience the consequences of the killer's spree as a victim; second, that the viewpoint shift also creates a gender identification shift, where the viewer switches from identifying with a male to identifying with a female character.

Until *I Spit On Your Grave* came out, slasher films tended to emphasize more traditional values, like most mainstream media, and the female survivor was often the most chaste of the girls portrayed; *I Spit On Your Grave* turned that around by portraying an unchaste girl as the victor. The value of this cannot be underestimated; tradition tells us that sexually active women are 'bad' and that violence against them is justified, but most young women today are sexually active, and thus Jennifer Hills, the protagonist of *I Spit On Your Grave*, can much more authentically carry the standard for the rest of us. (Interestingly, Hills almost literally dismembers the myths about women 'deserving' rape, as part of her revenge.)

But in Barker's analysis, we are never *quite* allowed to get close to Jennifer. Although she recovers and rebuilds her life, she also involves herself in a cold-blooded revenge that requires her to get painfully close to her attackers. The film places her at a distance from the viewer; we can understand her fury, but we can never be one with her violence as she becomes the slasher.

Barker suggests that it is not the content of these films themselves, but rather the absence of heroic resolution that really horrifies the pro-censorship moralists. Unlike traditional action films, he says, these movies give us no answers and no viewpoint character that we can harmonize and ultimately share victory with. 'In these,' he says, 'there are rarely any heroes at all – and certainly not in the filmic sense. We are denied a centre from which to view things.' They are, in a sense, more complex than typical action films, where good is directly pitted against evil, and good ultimately wins. In the 'nasties', the viewer is robbed of the simple, pat ending where a hero triumphs against corruption. As a result, the films do not enclose the violent acts within the fictive frame, but force us to think about them, in the audience, off the screen. The films are not 'safe' for us; they make us too aware of the uncertainties of real violence, without happy endings, in real life.

In the build-up to the debate on Graham Bright's 1984 Video Control Bill, a scientific study was commissioned from researchers at Oxford Polytechnic to demonstrate whether children were viewing 'video nasties' in large numbers. However, before the work could be completed, a pro-censorship member of the parliamentary committee removed the research materials from the premises in Oxford. In far less time than it could have taken to evaluate these materials, a report was released claiming that an enormous number of young children were seeing 'video nasties'. According to the researchers themselves, the claims made by the pro-censorship faction's report are contradicted by what they know of the results they had collected so far; Brian Brown, who led the research, has repudiated the study entirely in 'Exactly what we wanted':

> My name was attached to the report as associate director of the enquiry; my research unit at Oxford Polytechnic was named as the place where it was based. This created a problem for us, as *a week earlier we had repudiated the framework, context and conclusions of the entire document.* We issued a brief statement distancing ourselves from the report, making it clear we neither wrote the report nor took responsibility for it. We made it equally clear that the report was the work of Dr Clifford Hill, that he was not a member of the staff of Oxford Polytechnic and that he had used a good deal of material whose source was unknown to us and for which he alone was responsible.

This is the research that was said to justify passage of the Bill. The fact that it had purportedly been performed under proper research conditions by respectable social scientists at a trustworthy academic institution was meant to convey the report's reliability. But the alleged researchers for the report, Brown and his team in Oxford, have made clear that the conclusions released by Clifford Hill are based on no foundation that they know of.

Snuff

The most odious of all 'video nasties' or pornographic films that is used to justify censorship is the 'snuff' movie. In these films, it is rumoured, women are actually killed. Of course, if this happened, it would be a matter of murder, not pornography.

The legend of 'snuff' started sometime in the mid-1970s, and eventually it was exploited by film-makers who hoped to use it to repackage a failed horror film, *Slaughterhouse*, to make it more saleable. The final version, released in 1976, was called *Snuff* and a new ending was added in which two members of the set crew appear to engage in spontaneous sex that ends with the murder of the 'script girl' by the 'producer'. Documentary methods are used to convey verisimilitude, although the characters are in fact actors working to a script. The 'killer' slices off the fingers of his victim and then disembowels her. When the film was released in New York, people thought they were seeing a real killing on screen, and this resulted in a media circus that eventually led to calls for the 'dead' woman to be found; she was, and testified for the authorities and the media that she was still alive. (It should be noted here that the gory special effects that are so convincing to viewers with no medical background are actually entirely unrealistic; fingers cannot simply be sliced off like butter with a stage knife, or even a real knife.) The ending of this movie is cited virtually every time anti-pornography feminists claim to have seen a real snuff movie. They have apparently said it so often that they think it is true, and continue to maintain that the murder of women is what men really want from their sexual fantasies.

In 1993, Trading Standards officers in Birmingham seized non-certificated videos from a dealer at a comic mart, claiming that they had finally found a real snuff movie. Despite the widespread publicity about this seizure, the truth is that they found an old horror film, *Cannibal Holocaust*, considered a classic of the slasher genre. No one died to make this movie, but the guardians of our morals cannot tell the difference between special effects and real life. The newspapers that report these pseudo-scandals never see fit to point out that, once again, we are being misled by the authorities.

No actual 'snuff' film has ever been found, although police worldwide have certainly looked hard for them. There is no evidence whatsoever to confirm the existence of 'snuff'. (This is discussed at greater length in *Bad Girls and Dirty Pictures*, edited by Alison Assiter and myself; Linda Williams also gives much more detail on the snuff phenomenon in *Hard Core*.)

Which leaves us with the same old gory horror films, and it is unlikely that males watching slasher movies will be influenced to become killers. It would be virtually impossible to assume from a movie like *I Spit On Your Grave* that women could enjoy rape; the woman in the film certainly does not.

In any event, although 'video nasties' are often equated with, and mentioned together with, pornography, they are not the same genre at all. Most genres these days have some sexual content in them, and some horror films use 'sexploitation' techniques, but they are not pornography and they are not sold as pornography. Buyers of pornography expect to see sex, not blood and gore.

Ted Bundy and pornography

Ted Bundy was a serial murderer who was finally caught in Florida in 1978 and sentenced to death. He had tried to have himself declared insane (and therefore not eligible for the death penalty) but had failed, when a right-wing member of the Meese Commission contacted Bundy and, it has been rumoured, offered to help get his sentence reduced if he would discuss the relationship between pornography and his crimes. Bundy, who had never blamed pornography for what he did before, converted to born-again Christianity and began condemning pornography for arousing desire in men for women who were not their wives. Dr James Dobson, a right-wing, anti-porn, anti-abortion, anti-gay campaigner who is president of a group called Focus on the Family, has made much capital out of his interview with Bundy condemning porn, which he has on sale in America. (Bundy did not specify *which* pornography had turned him into a killer.) CAP, Moyra Bremner and Mary Whitehouse often cite Bundy's final porn-blaming interview before his execution as 'proof' that pornography caused Bundy to kill. Yet when the police arrested Bundy, they did not find pornography in his home, and there was no evidence that pornography had been in any way involved; they did find cheerleading magazines. Pally reports:

> In his final interview, Bundy said, 'The FBI's own study on serial homicide shows that the most common interest among serial killers is pornography.'
> In response, an FBI spokesperson said, 'The FBI knows nothing about pornography.' Its study contains two sentences on it. Dr. Ann Burgess, one of the authors of the FBI study, told the press that the FBI wasn't looking at pornography. 'We never quantified it,' she said.

Research has consistently shown there is no relationship between pornography and serial killers, but the moral right frequently and spuriously cites non-existent reports by the FBI, the Michigan police and others that allegedly show such a relationship. It is not surprising that Bundy had heard these same false claims if he was meeting born-again Christians who were anti-pornography campaigners. This does not, however, lend any credence to his claim that pornography made him commit his crimes. If anyone aside from Bundy is responsible for his murders, investigators might hypothesize that it was someone in his family who taught him to be fascinated with brutality and violence. Numerous interviews with Ted Bundy and his family were conducted by Dr Dorothy Lewis, clinical professor at Yale University Child Study Center and professor of psychiatry at New York University. She found that Bundy and his mother, when he was just three years old, had lived with Bundy's grandfather, an extremely violent man who tortured animals and behaved brutally to family members. The little boy who would become a serial murderer began sticking butcher's knives into his bed and demonstrating other behaviour that worried some family members enough for them to think he should be removed from the environment. This, surely, is the cause of what the psychiatrist who interviewed him after his arrest, Emanuel Tanay, called 'the severe deformity of personality that he had'.

Yet Bundy had insisted in his final interview that killers like himself are 'normal' until they encounter pornography. 'We are your sons, and we are your husbands', he told Dobson. 'And we grew up in regular families. And pornography can reach out and snatch a kid out of any house today. And we had a wonderful Christian home ...'

In any case, it is bizarre to suggest that we should make the opinions of seriously disturbed individuals like Ted Bundy our instructions when designing social policies. It might be more interesting to ask why the most popular reading material cited by sex killers as inspiring their crimes is never mentioned by pro-censorship activists; that is, of course, the Bible.

So, as with all of the other accusations levelled at pornography, we again come up short. Whether the claim is made about popular music, violent television and film, or pornography, we always find that the real causes of violence go deep into the family backgrounds of the perpetrators, and not to violent or sexual materials they may have seen later.

Overall, there is no scientific basis for the belief that men become rapists or learn to accept sexual violence against women because of pornography, or that men experience any other negative effects from sexually explicit materials. When the Home Office report on pornography was released in 1990, perhaps its most important conclusion was that, although many claims are made about how men read pornography and the effects it has on them, no one has ever done any research to determine how men actually interpret and understand the sexual material they see. It is, at best, premature to pretend we know what men are learning from pornography.

Pornography and women's self-image

But what about women? Another claim made about pornography is that women experience a loss of self-esteem and are more likely to stereotype other women if we see pornography. Carol Krafka examined precisely that issue for her 1985 doctoral dissertation, and found that women did not show greater dissatisfaction with body image, lower self-esteem, more sex-role stereotyping or greater acceptance of violence towards women after seeing pornography that was deemed degrading and dehumanizing. Donnerstein had come to the same conclusion in 1984, and again in the work of Donnerstein, Linz and Penrod, we see the same results. In fact, T.L. Cash had found in 1983 that women had lower self-esteem after looking at ordinary fashion magazines. These results do appear to be more realistic than the anti-pornography claims; women are more likely to diet in pursuit of thinness than they are to try to eat their way to voluptuousness.

Victim testimony

Nevertheless, some women do claim that they have accepted abusive relationships because of pornography. In 1983, the Minneapolis City Council held hearings on pornography prior to passing the Dworkin–MacKinnon 'feminist' anti-pornography law. There was some (usually anonymous) personal testimony from women who said they had been abused because of pornography. (The complete text of those hearings was published in Britain by *Everywoman* in 1988.) The Meese Commission also heard personal testimony from women who said they had experienced violence or tolerated abuse that involved pornography or seemed acceptable because of it. Similarly, late-night chat shows in Britain often use the testimony of women who say their husbands began forcing them to commit perverted sex acts after using pornography. High-profile television programmes like *Omnibus*, *Dispatches* and *The Cook Report* have also done anti-pornography shows in which victim testimony of this sort was cruelly exploited in campaigns against pornographic materials. The victim's experiences were certainly horrifying, and some of them seemed to feel that, without pornography, these events would never have occurred.

Stories of this type evoke strong emotions. Many of us have been in abusive relationships ourselves and cannot help but identify with the pain that the speaker has gone through. As a result, the statements and opinions of the woman who tells such a story gain enormous credibility, and it is hard to look at them dispassionately, separate the very real pain from the opinion, and ask how much of the latter is useful. The women who tell these stories have obviously been in abusive relationships, but did they – or their partners – really learn to accept violence in relationships from looking at pin-up magazines? Why don't we ask why they had no other, better sources of information that could have told them that the violence was not normal? And how many other aspects of their upbringing are we not being told about – abusive family relationships in childhood, ignorance about sexual matters, male classmates who 'talk big', female friends and relatives who accept being treated as doormats – that might have been far more important factors in making them feel they had to accept coercion and violence themselves?

Many feminist anti-pornography campaigners say that personal testimony of this type is the *real* 'evidence' against pornography, that our actual experiences are more meaningful than mere statistics, and that, therefore, this anecdotal evidence tells the true story that the laboratory research misses out. But these stories don't really tell us what the causes of violence are unless we are prepared to read between the lines. In a society in which we are kept in the dark about sex during most of our early lives, it is not difficult for an abusive man to try to make us think that his violent world view is 'normal' – after all, what else do we have to compare it to? If your only sexual experience is with a partner who is violent and abusive, how do you know it is unusual unless you have been given a firm understanding that this is not something you should have to accept? Ignorance makes us especially vulnerable to people who would take advantage of our lack of knowledge. Suppressing pornography will not eliminate that danger for us.

Female socialization

Let's not forget that there are already many messages in society that tell women we are expected to please our husbands a great deal more than they are expected to please us. Women are expected to work to make and maintain relationships in a way that men aren't – there are plenty of magazine articles advising women of how to keep the interest of their husbands, but how many articles give the same sort of advice to men? Christian teaching says that a wife is a 'helpmeet' to her husband, not the other way around. It is the job of women to suit our husbands; the hand-in-glove partnership between men and women is one where the man is the 'hand', and the woman – the glove – might be replaced if she doesn't fit. Which means it's up to us to make sure we fit, since the size and shape of the hand cannot be changed. And some religions don't even make a pretence of believing in a 'partnership' between men and women; women are here to suit men, and what we want or need doesn't even count. Customs like suttee, foot-binding and female genital mutilation were not invented to suit the needs of women – but they weren't invented by pornographers, either. In fact, the message of clitoridectomy is quite the opposite of pornography: in porn, half the fun is in the idea that the woman is acting out of desire and for pleasure; genital mutilation exists to see to it that she won't. It is frankly embarrassing to see feminists spend more time trying to eliminate images of female pleasure than campaigning against the brutal destruction of women's ability to feel sexual pleasure.

But domestic violence and abuse are not limited to the sexual arena. It is woman's role to serve and satisfy her family members in every aspect of the home; this includes housekeeping and cooking, planning and arranging, and some husbands abuse their wives over these issues in much the same way that is claimed over pornography. Abuse consists of many factors: sexual demands when the wife is uninterested, or demands for sexual acts that do not appeal to her; shouting, belittling and violence when her cooking or housekeeping is not seen to measure up, along with demands for more intensive household efforts; anger when the woman is seen to have 'too many' friends, speak too often to men at parties, receive visitors – even girlfriends from school or the old neighbourhood – when her husband is out, or otherwise show too much social independence; undermining her self-respect about other interests she has, trivializing her job, dismissing her outside accomplishments, deriding her friends and family; separating her from those things she values, particularly if they are things that help give her some independence; never admitting that what she does is good enough; and, if she is sexually expressive, making her feel dirty.

Worse still, non-sexual abuse that is largely verbal has more acceptability in society; if you avoid a few friends because your husband doesn't like them, or stay home when you would have gone to a club meeting because your hubby wants you at home, well, that isn't 'abuse', is it? If your husband expects you to devote more time to cooking and cleaning, well, that's what a wife is supposed to do, isn't it? When you run home to mother saying your husband brought home perverted pornography and wanted you to perform degrading acts, she might give you some sympathy; will she be so sympathetic when you complain that he wanted you to cook supper every night? Men who wish to demean their partners and exert control over them sometimes use sexual issues and pornography, it's true; but many men find it far more effective to go after the household skills that are much more acceptable to push women into. For one thing, women who are shocked enough to object to kinky sex acts are not necessarily so shocked by 'requests' for more labour-intensive cooking. Methods of abuse that are more subtle often get the best – that is, the most destructive – results.

Yet we do not blame cooking, or cleaning, for abuse of this nature. We do not say that our husbands have no right at all to express opinions of our friends, nor do we say that housework and women's magazines should be made unlawful because men might make us cook and clean. If men try to coerce us into anything – whether it is housework or sex acts they have seen in pornography – it is obviously the coercion and the attitudes that allow them to think they may do it that make these things a problem. Some women may say that their husbands brought home pornographic magazines or videos and demanded they perform the acts in those magazines or movies; by the same token, some women can tell stories of partners who brought home cookbooks and demanded they cook, from scratch, according to the recipes in those books. We would not demand that *The Joy of Cooking* be banned; why should we believe that banning *Mayfair*, *Playboy* or *Brute* would solve our problems? There is obviously something more insidious at work than pornography when men feel free to put pressure on their wives or lovers to change their lifestyles in ways the women do not like.

The simple fact is that there is no sexual act, and no source of information about that act, that makes force or coercion acceptable. As Feminists Against Censorship said in our leaflet 'Pornography: there's no simple answer', even being kissed against your will is disgusting; it is irrelevant whether you were shown a picture of it first. If men think there are acts it is all right to force on us, *that* is the idea we should be attacking; it is actually a hindrance to suggest that the pornography, or the specific acts, are the problem. With or without pornography, we may suggest certain acts, or ways of performing them, to each other – kissing, cunnilingus, fellatio, a lighter or stronger caress, sexual intercourse, anal sex, SM, whatever. If we all understand that we have the absolute right to refuse undesired acts, none of this should be a problem. No matter how common a sexual practice is, no one is required to do it; some of us will refuse 'tongue kissing' or 'French kissing', even though it is very common and acceptable. We need not base our acceptance of these acts in our personal lives on whether we have seen pictures of them or whether other people do them. Some people will wish to be involved in lesbianism, SM, heterosexuality or other behaviour that is not to everyone's taste; people feel such urges, and discuss their interest in them, even when they have never seen pictures of them. If we recognize that we do not all have identical sexualities, and that our bodies belong to ourselves, and not to others, we begin to understand that we cannot make demands on each other, and we can't have the same expectations of every partner or hoped-for partner. Otherwise, we are merely stereotyping.

Trivializing sexual violence

This entire analysis seems to be completely overlooked in the 'victim testimony' approach to pornography. By suggesting that men abuse their partners because of pornography, and that it is the pornography that makes the abuse degrading, we trivialize the degradation and pain of the majority of rape and abuse victims for whom pornography has been irrelevant. I was recently told by an anti-porn rape crisis worker that being raped in a circumstance involving pornography is 'more degrading'. With all due respect, there was no pornography involved when I was raped, but I don't recall it being a barrel of laughs. How do we measure the degree of degradation women like me have experienced when we were raped, as compared with that of women who were raped when pornography was involved? We can't. But it might be worth considering that there is plenty of degradation to go around for women who have been made to feel that what happened to them is 'their fault' because they had nothing else to blame it on.

Many of the women in Feminists Against Censorship know that pornography had nothing to do with any of the sexual assaults or abuse we have suffered; yet *our* victim testimony is forbidden at meetings held by anti-pornography campaigners. At such meetings, women are encouraged to stand up and say how they have been hurt by pornography, and how much they would like to eliminate porn, but the testimony of women like me, or women who have had positive experiences of pornography, is not permitted. Gayle Rubin described her own experience of such meetings in 'Misguided, dangerous and wrong':

> I have attended many educational presentations by WAVPM [Women Against Violence in Pornography and Media] and WAP [Women Against Pornography], and in none of them was any questioning of their basic assumptions permitted. Questions were restricted to inquiries about implementing their programme, and those who tried to raise other issues were ignored or dismissed.

Paula Webster tells a similar story in the sex issue of *Heresies*. When Chicago Law School held their Speech, Equality and Harm Conference in 1993, with representation from no anti-censorship women, they silenced one prostitute, Carol Leigh, who had bravely stood up in the audience to attempt a dialogue, saying that Leigh didn't know that she was a victim.

Carole Vance, who actually went to the hearings held by the US Attorney General's Commission on Pornography (the Meese Commission), reported that speakers from the anti-pornography side were allowed to give victim testimony unhindered, while those who had positive experiences of pornography to report were treated with hostility and abusive questions in much the same way as rape victims are treated by defence attorneys in rape trials, and their testimony was cut short. That is something every feminist would do well to remember: women who 'admit to' positive sexual experiences are dismissed as tramps, both in rape trials and in 'feminist'-supported anti-pornography hearings. This is one reason why rapists get away with their crimes; what does it mean when women who call themselves feminists conspire in the same tactics? Vance's extraordinary tale of the hearings can be found in Lynne Segal and Mary McIntosh's *Sex Exposed*.

When 'feminist' anti-porn campaigners hold similar meetings in Britain, the audience is told that there will be time for comments later – but before questioning begins, they are instructed that statements or questions that contradict the presentation will not be welcomed. FAC's Alison Assiter reported that, at such a meeting in 1992 at Conway Hall, the justification given for this was that, 'Space must be allowed for women who have been harmed by pornography.' So anti-pornography campaigners claim they are interested in 'women's testimony', but they are clearly interested only in the testimony that supports their conclusions. They never hear our testimony, or if we somehow manage to get a word in edgewise, we are simply dismissed. Those of us who disagree and have different stories to tell are apparently not real women, and the rapes and abuse we have suffered aren't worthy of note.

Under the circumstances, it is dishonest to claim that the victim testimony used against pornography tells the whole story of women's experience and pornography's effects. Most rapes and abuse occur under circumstances that do not involve pornography, but these are never mentioned. Most male users of pornography do not become rapists, and most female users of pornography have positive experiences to report, but we are not allowed to hear from them. One sex worker who has horror stories to tell is believed; ten porn models who enjoy their work are not. In other words, victim testimony against pornography is one-sided and gives a wholly inaccurate picture. This is not 'evidence' in any honest respect.

Women who blithely ignore the many methods society uses to keep women down are distracting us from pursuing the real causes of violence. Women who dismiss the violence and brutality we suffer that is not related to pornography, and who refuse to accept the word of women who have had positive experiences of recreational sexual materials, are silencing us, harming us, and stereotyping us. This is not feminism.

6

Perversion

Thomas Aquinas once explained that masturbation was wrong because it perverted the proper use of our reproductive organs. Those organs, he said, were able to come to arousal and orgasm for the specific purpose of procreation, and any other use was an interference with what they were supposed to be used for. Perversion, then, is any sexuality that does not exist for the purposes of reproduction. The moral right still maintains those values; they say that those among us who use contraception are sinners who have sex for the wrong reasons, just as surely as homosexuals and sadomasochists are. Fellatio is a deliberate waste of sperm, of course, so any oral sex or mutual manipulation to male orgasm outside of a woman's vaginal tract also fits into the category of perversion.

Society has so long been organized around reproduction that many people still see any non-reproductive sex as perversion, and it isn't just born-again Christians who get up on their high horse whenever we veer too far from that old procreative imperative; we also have most of our judges, our legislators, and a host of parents and teachers who become virtually hysterical at the idea of making birth control available to teenagers who we know perfectly well are having sex, or permitting homosexuality to be discussed openly, or letting people do things for sexual purposes that we do not even object to when they are done for non-sexual reasons. For example, as long as we allow men to injure each other in sports, why should we mind when people mark their partners during sadomasochistic sex? The court's judgement in the Operation Spanner SM case (see Chapter 8) was that it was criminal to leave a mark that was more than transient or trifling in the course of sex; this could, of course, mean love-bites. Yet during the same period, the Law Commission, attempting to write a law to this effect, specifically wrote an exception into their draft bill exempting injuries in 'manly sports', even as one manly sportsman lay in intensive care after a particularly rough match. They also made an exception for discipline of children, and a case decided in the same period came to the conclusion that beating children and leaving marks lasting a full week was perfectly acceptable. Obviously, it is sex, not violence, that is generating the objections with regard to SM.

Reproduction is so central to our cultural organization that some people would rather keep the sexual focus on male arousal and orgasm, which are required for those sperm to go swimming up to the ovum in the way God intended. It is no accident that most traditional teachings and attitudes on sex concentrate entirely on erection and (male) ejaculation, as if female sexuality did not exist. To judge from much of what was written before the sexual revolution, female sexuality consisted entirely of being *able* to copulate; you'd never guess that some people turn us on and some don't, that we feel like sex sometimes and don't at other times, and that there are some ways we like sex and other ways we don't. And you'd certainly never imagine that these things differ from one woman to the next.

Because procreation was the basis for the organization of our society and the roles we were expected to play in it, and because childbearing was taken to define women, female sexuality itself essentially became a non-issue. We were expected to devote ourselves entirely to children and family; our own pleasures were irrelevant. And women's pleasures were indeed irrelevant, because they were entirely unnecessary to reproduction. Male arousal and orgasm inside a woman came to be the one and only definition of sex. And by that definition, the female body became a receptacle of men's urges – women *were* objects in sex, because we had no sexual subjectivity of any value. Male desire and satisfaction were what mattered, because only male desire and satisfaction are needed for procreation. And with reproduction the goal, there was no room for sexual activity that deviated from that focus; heterosexuality is always more privileged than homosexuality, and activities that are too clearly oriented toward pleasure must always be suspicious.

Daniel Linz and Neil Malamuth noted that fear of pornography's potential to undermine this centralization of reproductive goals is an important factor in anti-pornography approaches within the academic research sphere. In *Communication Concepts 5*, they point out that

> Zillmann and Bryant have also investigated the effects of prolonged exposure to sex displays on acceptance of traditional family values. They make the assumption that the nuclear family is vital for societal welfare. Yet, they note, the values expressed in most commercially released sex materials obviously clash with the family concept, and thus potentially undermine the traditional values that favor marriage, family and children.

Linz and Malamuth cite Zillmann's complaint to the Meese Commission that characters in pornography 'enjoy sexual stimulation for what it is' and that 'This portrayal clashes with traditional values concerning enduring relationships in which sexuality and reproduction are central.' Indeed, Zillmann's entire critique of pornography rests on an orientation towards traditional (sexist) institutions and traditional roles for women. Zillmann believes men have sex with their wives because a lack of familiarity with women's breasts makes female partners seem exciting, and if men should come to accept the female body as natural and lacking in mystery, they will lose interest in their partners and, consequently, will be unable to maintain familial commitments. This is what Zillmann means when he says pornography makes men 'desensitized'. Traditionalists prefer to see men fetishize specific parts of women's bodies because they believe that without such obsessions with those parts, reproductive sex with a familiar partner will be uninteresting to them.

Such thinkers are unable to recognize the broader erotic potential of a natural acceptance of women and sexuality, let alone the preferability of partnerships based on something less volatile than the satisfaction of uncontrollable male urges stimulated by an undue emphasis on the mystery of female organs. Sex as play between loving friends, undertaken for pleasure, is unacceptable to such people, precisely because it does not centralize reproduction. Procreation, according to their prejudice, is the only true justification for sexual pleasure (and then it only justifies men's pleasure). Only by hiding the alien and forbidden female body can sexual interest be maintained when it is reduced to a predictable fuck with a predictable partner.

Modern feminism makes a very specific criticism of this goal-oriented sexuality, and it was a focus of much feminist analysis in the 1970s. Women recognized that the perception of heterosexual intercourse alone as legitimate 'sex' had actually stripped sexuality of much of its eroticism, passion and pleasure. Traditionally, (male) 'experts' had declared that women did not have sexual fantasies, but Nancy Friday compiled a lengthy catalogue of female sexual fantasy for her 1982 book, *My Secret Garden*, exploding a heavily entrenched myth. It became abundantly clear that both fantasy and play, in great variety, are crucial to sexual desire and pleasure for many women.

But for the traditionalists, if it doesn't reproduce, it's perversion, and so everything from cunnilingus to sadomasochism is out of the question. Pornography, of course, is often used for having sex alone – masturbation – and western society has always taken a dim view of that activity.

Masturbation

Anti-pornography activists from both right and left seem to take a similar position on masturbation. They may not come right out and use the word, but what else do they mean when they insist that men won't be able to have mature, healthy relationships if they use pornography for their sexual fantasies? Surely they don't imagine that sexual fantasies created without the use of pornography are necessarily any more 'mature and healthy'? People have sexual fantasies about the things that turn them on, and those who use pornography choose materials that appeal to those same tastes. When we see materials that don't appeal to those tastes, they do not arouse us. If we have no such materials, we create the fantasies out of thin air, but they are no more likely to contain whatever maturity and realism the anti-pornographers may mean. If a man likes pornography about pliant and agreeable women, he'll fantasize the same on his own; he is not going to have fantasies about women who complain, argue and refuse him just because he has no pornography available.

It is sometimes claimed that there are studies that support the belief that people become perverted by looking at perverted pornography, but the research just doesn't bear this out. Some people quote Victor Cline, the Mormon psychologist who has asserted that people need more and more perverted material if they look at pornography, but Cline has not done empirical studies on the matter and can cite no legitimate research to support his views. In Britain, Ray Wyre of the Gracewell Clinic has been the main proponent of this theory, but Wyre has done no research either, and he persistently ignores the data on both paraphilias and sex offenders in order to continue making claims that pornography plays a causative role in creating perverts or abusers.

The Meese Commission asked Dr Edna Einsiedel to review the scientific research on pornography. She reported that she could find no evidence that seeing pornography, whether it was violent or paraphiliac, made people more interested in such materials. Donnerstein and Linz came to the same conclusion in their reviews. Marcia Pally notes that many other experts agree:

> The world's foremost researcher in this area, Dr. John Money of Johns Hopkins University, told *The New York Times* (January 23, 1990) that 'he and other researchers found no evidence that pornography causes or fosters paraphilias (sexual abnormalities) ... The majority of patients with paraphilias ... described a strict antisexual upbringing in which sex was either never mentioned or was actively repressed or defiled.'

Money predicted that 'current repressive attitudes toward sex will breed an ever-widening epidemic of aberrant sexual behaviour.'

Money calls the territory of our sexuality a 'lovemap'. In his 1986 book on the subject, he said that these lovemaps were fairly well settled by the time we are eight years old. 'Further disruption may take place during the peripubertal years,' he wrote, 'but after puberty, the lovemap, if it changes, does so chiefly by decoding what has already been encoded into it. Once a lovemap has been formed it is, like native language, extremely resistant to change.' In essence, people simply find the material that appeals to them and they stick to it.

If men are not being turned into abusers by pornography, why are people so worried about it? The refrain is heard over and over again – particularly from Labour MPs – that pornography is a substitute for relationships or otherwise interferes with them, as Robin Corbett, MP (Labour) said when interviewed for GLR (BBC Radio) by Tim Smith in July 1993. Why it should be a problem that men might use pornography as a substitute when they have no relationships is, of course, unclear; how is frustration a superior alternative? That porn interferes with relationships is no more than a delusion, yet Clare Short, another Labour MP, has even suggested that people would have no trouble having relationships if they would just stop looking at pornography – as if the rest of us miraculously have great relationships when we don't look at it. It is not my impression that it's as easy as all that just to run out and find a good relationship, let alone that it's pornography that stops people from doing so. If it were that easy, no one would ever be lonely. Relationships are a bit more complicated than that; it's a sad state of affairs when parliamentary representatives can't even work out that much.

Many people learn to masturbate long before they have had any opportunity to become engaged sexually with other people. Very young girls have been known to masturbate to orgasm before they have any idea what sex is. If private fantasy is forbidden, one is left with the conclusion that the only appropriate source of sexual release is therefore to have sex with other people. It is remarkable that politicians like Short and Corbett actually promote views like this when they would never advocate that young people should be trying to have sex with each other. Or do they honestly believe that no one naturally has sexual feelings until they are 'old enough', whenever that is? Over the last few years I've been polling some of the women I meet on speaking engagements about just when they first experienced orgasm; the answers I've received have ranged from 'as long as I can remember' and 'four' to '19' and 'never'. Should four-year-old girls be having sex with others rather than sexual fantasies? Most people tend to assume that boys become sexual around the age of 12; is it being suggested that the moment boys reach this age they should be encouraged to have sex with their associates rather than masturbating? As long as young people are given so little information about sexuality and protective measures, this kind of suggestion is hypocritical.

The law, it should be remembered, specifically forbids sexual contact to people below the age of 16. When male homosexuality was decriminalized in 1967, gay men were given the right to have sex from the age of 21. (An amendment to the Criminal Justice and Public Order Act 1994 to equalize the age of consent failed in February 1994, and a compromise amendment for 18 was passed. There has never been a consent law distinguishing lesbians from other women.) Surely no one imagines boys do not have sexual fantasies before they reach the age of consent. Yet society generally expresses horror at the idea of young people having 'relationships'. What, precisely, are they expected to do in the meantime?

Other 'perversions'

Homosexuality, sadomasochism (SM), paedophilia and other paraphilias are often cited as reasons to fear pornography. Many people believe that these alternative sexualities are learned from looking at pornography – that people may become infected with a desire for the acts they see portrayed in sexually explicit materials that they would not otherwise have been aroused by. Others believe that by representing these acts, the sexualities that are portrayed are made more acceptable to the viewer, and that if pornography about them is permitted to circulate in society, we will stop recognizing that they are harmful.

Popular writing about 'perversions' is, unfortunately, a catalogue of myth and misinformation. In 1970, Dr David Reuben's book, *Everything You Always Wanted to Know About Sex (But Were Afraid to Ask)*, purported to tell us just that – but Reuben clearly had no idea what he was talking about when it came to lesbianism, prostitution and even some aspects of 'normal' sexuality, among other things. Gays and feminists eventually had a field day tearing the book apart, but in the meantime, an astonishing number of people were taking it seriously and citing it as a source for information on unusual sexuality. It was a coursebook for students at University College Hospital until the Gay Liberation Front approached the committee and it was removed.

Rubin's book is no longer considered a reliable source of information, but now we have *The Janus Report on Sexual Behaviour*, released in 1993 and purporting to be 'the first broadscale scientific national survey since Kinsey'. It was cited approvingly in *Newsweek* and excerpted in *For Women*. Yet it contains numerous 'facts' that can immediately be identified as falsehoods by those with even a slight knowledge of these issues. For example, the authors claim that 'screaming queens' is another term for transvestites and that transvestites need to steal their feminine clothes and are likely to strangle themselves on their silk stockings. They also refer to a practice called 'brown showers', seem unable to differentiate the various paraphilias from child abuse and rape, and state that necrophiliacs are fans of 'snuff' movies. These misapprehensions are allegedly based on interviews with genuine perverts, but one quickly gets the impression that if there were such interviews, the perverts were conning the interviewers – much as hippies in the 1960s used to tell reporters that they liked to smoke LSD and shoot glue. The amount of positive publicity the 'report' has received is absolutely bizarre, in the circumstances.

Falsehoods about unusual sexualities pervade our culture to such an extent that many people simply feel no need to consult real experts – whether academics or actual practitioners – when writing about, or discussing, such sexual interests and practices. We often advocate and make laws based on no more than our own prejudices. Ignorance and fear pervade the debate on pornography in much the same way as in the debate over gay rights and the gay age of consent, and a few areas in particular are mentioned often in the context of banning 'the really bad' pornography. Under the circumstances, it seems necessary to explain the obvious.

Homosexuality

Aside from women, homosexuals probably have the most impressive history of being 'explained' by 'experts' of any single group. Writing in *The Bloodshot Pyramid*, social commentator Arthur Hlavaty recalled:

> 'Latent homosexual' was a curious concept. It would seem that, if it meant anything, it meant someone who is heterosexual, but is liable to become a homosexual, but psychiatry never stooped to anything so vulgarly empirical as seeing whether any of those so defined ever actually become homosexual.

Rather, it seemed to mean someone who acts hetero, but is 'really' 'deep down inside' homo. (In an earlier terminology, one might say that such a person had the accidents of heterosexuality, but the substance of homosexuality.)

I'd like to think that the idea of latent homosexuality is dead now. For one thing, it rests on a false concept. As Gore Vidal pointed out long ago, there are such things as heterosexual and homosexual acts; these can be operationally defined and verified. But 'a homosexual' is ... What? One who always does one kind of act? One who prefers it? One who fantasizes about that kind? There are, to be sure, people who have a definite preference or identification, and whose preference is an important fact about them, but it's still a step from that to say that people 'are' heterosexuals, homosexuals, or bisexuals. And if 'a homosexual' is meaningless – a 'semantic spook,' as Korzybski would say – then 'a latent homosexual' is doubly spooky.

But I got another insight into this recently, reading Barbara Ehrenreich's *The Worst Years of Our Lives*. ... She discusses changes in the male image, thus reminding me of the way 'latent homosexuality' was really used: for a man (it was rarely applied to women) who did not fit the psychiatric ideal for a mature husband and father, working, supporting his family, etc. One might say that the psychiatric establishment of the 50s and 60s believed that one cannot motivate men adequately without being able to tell those who do not obey that they are 'faggots.'

Definitionally, even 'homosexual acts' are problematic; it might be assumed that 'a homosexual act' is simply any sexual act between members of the same sex, but many heterosexuals – some of them, unfortunately, members of the press – have a tendency to use the term 'homosexual act' as if it refers to the act itself rather than the participants. This has led to an assumption that homosexuals participate in acts that are never performed heterosexually. This simply isn't true, of course, but the bottom line in 'homosexual acts' is that they are non-reproductive, and that is why they are truly unthinkable, even for heterosexuals, according to the moral authoritarian values that permeate society.

It should be clear to any feminist that making homosexuality acceptable is not something we have to fear – most of us devoutly wish homosexuality could be far more acceptable than it is today. It is not harmful and society in no way benefits from suppressing and persecuting gays or homosexual acts; on the contrary, it offers a challenge to traditional gender roles and has vast potential to benefit women. Moreover, we know that society's hatred of homosexuality goes hand in hand with misogyny, and we'd certainly like to see the back of *that* as soon as possible.

Some people seem to believe that a repressive, heartless state is more economically efficient, and locking up lots of people keeps order in society. But homosexuality is no more expensive than heterosexuality is to a culture; on the other hand, prosecuting people and putting them in jail costs a good deal of money. Laws restricting homosexuality are responsible for enormous public expenditure from which society gets no return.

The state, on the other hand, does indeed gain something from stigmatizing homosexuality, and benefits in numerous ways. Even men and women who have never felt the faintest desire for members of their own sex can be frightened into conformity to rigid sex roles if they can be threatened with accusations of homosexuality in a culture that suppresses and reviles it. Hlavaty suggests that this is what motivated the Joint Chiefs of Staff to oppose President Bill Clinton's original plan to allow homosexuals into the military in the US – because it's easier to make soldiers fall into line if they can be threatened with being called 'faggots' when they don't. Even without actual criminalization, negative attitudes towards homosexuals can be used as a bludgeon to suppress social activism on the part of gays – particularly gay parents who know that, legal or not, their sexuality may be used by the authorities to take their children away from them and prevent adoption and fostering.

For young people who are trying to absorb and understand their own emerging awareness of their sexuality, suppression is a useful control, not merely on sexual activity, but more importantly on gaining personal confidence and a sense of identity. The state prefers us to remain insecure and compliant as long as possible; individuals who grow up strong and confident represent a threat to authority. Sexual confusion and a sense that it may be dangerous for us if our sexuality becomes known (even to ourselves) is one thing that may keep us quiet. Gays may experience this hazard in a more direct way as they begin to sort their feelings out. But even heterosexual children who have sexual feelings in an environment where there is no acceptable means of expression, and no information about sex and relationships, may experience a great deal of confusion as well as feelings of isolation.

The fact remains that people don't lose their desires as a result of 'curative' effort – not self-control, not pressure from outside, not even, in many cases in history, threat of death. Gays who are highly motivated to be 'normal' have spent enormous sums of money on therapy, entered all sorts of experimental programmes, tried every kind of 'self-control', with the result that a few bisexuals may tend to emphasize the heterosexual side of their sexuality, but no one, ever, 'turns straight'. Even without such pressures, some bisexual men who thought of themselves as entirely gay have been known to discover that there are a few women they can feel attraction and even love for; it just hadn't found expression before. But this is not an actual change in sexuality – only an acknowledgement of the breadth of their own existing sexuality. Sadly, many people have spent years, or even their entire lives, faking conformity to a sexuality they cannot enjoy.

Some feminist women have learned, to their chagrin, that the same situation pertains when they try to reject men in favour of political lesbianism; they do not stop being attracted to men if they continue to be in circumstances where such attractions can develop. It's fair to say that we're all just attracted to the people we're attracted to.

No research has been able to tell us why, although many guesses are made. There have recently been suggestions from some quarters (principally from the National Institutes of Health in Bethesda, Maryland, and from gay American researcher Simon LeVay) that there is some biological 'cause' or influence, but the things we do know about sexuality make this doubtful. Right-wing moralists have for so long taken the position that being gay is a 'choice' – and a sinful one – that some gays seem to feel the need to demonstrate that it is biological. It seems more likely that something about our relationships in early life helps to open us up to our sexuality. It hardly matters; there is no excuse for trying to deprive human beings of the right to love the people we love, nor any justification for trying to harm others because their sexual orientation is one we don't happen to share.

Many people tend to operate on the principle that a healthy individual will develop heterosexually and without any interest in paraphilias such as SM or 'golden showers' (urinary fantasies). On the other hand, many experts on sexuality believe bisexuality is our 'natural' state and that only the warped socialization we receive in heterosexist society impels us towards a specifically heterosexual or homosexual orientation. A number of social observers have noted that homosexuals make a profound artistic contribution to society and provide important transgressive models that force us to question our assumptions about gender and roles; these would be lost if a society was created in which no one was likely to develop homosexually. The liberatory feminist view is that diversity should be accepted, and that in the non-sexist society we hope to build, our differences won't matter.

Liberating the lesbian image

Some of the more reactionary women in the feminist movement presume that women do not actually like sex and only do it under pressure from men; thus, they believe, lesbians do not actually have sex as heterosexuals understand it at all. Such women might say that relationships with men are inevitably sexist and oppressive to women. They feel that women should break with male sexuality and should live and love only with women and express their sexuality in a 'woman-identified' manner. (There is a view in some circles, ironically, that women can use dildos shaped to look like dolphins, but not shaped like male organs.) The most extreme among them have even said that orgasm is in itself an enemy of women. Reactionary 'feminists' of this type feel that the lesbians who produce the new lesbian sex magazines and are involved in more overt expressions of sexuality are 'letting the side down' by representing a sexuality that is supposed to be 'male'. They would proscribe the authentic sexuality of many women who are not content to play out the traditional, asexual image of the feminine that has been foisted on us for centuries. Women have often learned that sexual activities ranging from common heterosexual intercourse or fucking with dildos to many less common

... dildos shaped to look like dolphins ...

behaviours can be pleasurable and desirable; it is simply not true that this is 'male' sexuality, nor is it true that we would not involve ourselves in such activities if it weren't for men. The view that women are innately less sexually assertive, varied and adventurous than men is sexist and patronizing.

Another criticism of lesbian pornographic imagery evolves from the fact that representations of woman-to-woman sex in heterosexual pornography have tended to emphasize what appears to be heterosexually driven 'bisexual' behaviour: the women seem to have sex with each other only because men are absent, and are instantly diverted by the appearance of a male: thus, lesbianism appears to be treated as a poor substitute for sex with men. However, the emergence of genuine lesbian erotica not only avoids this problem, but also provides an interesting insight into the way men look at images of woman-to-woman sex. Heterosexual men do look at and enjoy the all-woman pornography; they do not seem to need reassurance that the women in the images would prefer to be having sex with men if only such men were around. It is possible that, far from being used to reaffirm the superiority of males for sex, lesbian images may be used by men to affirm a contradiction to traditional sexual mores: that women can like sex for reasons having nothing to do with the heterosexual, sexist milieu in which women must perform sexual acts with men under social and economic pressure. Between two women, we can assume that the heterosexual power relations we take for granted are absent. If women have sex with each other, they must surely be doing it because they enjoy it, rather than because they are trying to get married or feel that men require it. This makes lesbianism a powerful sexuality in its own right. Lesbian sexual imagery, then, subverts the traditional view that women are innately uninterested in sexual pleasure and necessarily 'passive'.

An interesting sidelight is that among women who enjoy pornographic materials, whether they are gay or straight, it is common to hear that gay men's porn is the best – 'the hottest porn'. It would be interesting to see the results of a serious investigation comparing the porn made by and for gay men with straight porn to find out what it is about this subgenre that gives it particular appeal to women.

The idea that women can like sex for the pleasure of it is thoroughly threatening to a society based on an economy of sexual scarcity for men. It suggests that heterosexual partnerships in which men have to negotiate with women for sex on the basis of a trade for marital respectability and harmony results from a failure on the part of society to make sex as attractive as it could be. If women actually like sex, yet seem to be dissatisfied with or even repelled by the kind of sex that is on offer, this means that our entire social structure is based on a lie. In our society, sex and affection have traditionally been divided up into sex-typed 'needs' – men need sex while women need affection, and we are supposed to trade these to each other; thus, men are expected to enter into relationships with women in order to gain sex, while women tolerate the sex in order to gain relationships. By providing sex to men, women not only gain affection and economic support, but keep male sexuality and aggression channelled into the home.

Traditional moralists often express a fear that if homosexuality became socially accepted, the race would die out; obviously, they believe homosexuality is far more attractive than heterosexuality if they think no one would ever have heterosexual sex even to procreate once the option of homosexual sex was unencumbered by social restraint. This belief actually makes sense once you accept the dictum that women dislike sex and men like it; women can find affection but avoid the obligations of unwanted sex only in partnerships with women, and men can get all the sex they want from each other without the tedium of being in affective relationships. The values of the sexual revolution overturn these beliefs, suggesting that without the sex dualism and the centralization of reproduction, all individuals could enjoy both sexual pleasure and affective relationships, regardless of the gender of the partners.

It would be nice to think that the traditionalist thinking is entirely outdated, but it still plays a strong role in forming our legislative approaches to sexual expression. Although residents of Britain can be grateful that the island does not have a powerful 'Bible-belt' lobby such as exists in the United States, it is clear that the police, many magistrates and a majority of MPs are operating from precisely this set of preconceptions when legal approaches to sexual materials and the gay age of consent are under discussion. Mary Whitehouse and the National Viewers and Listeners Association may represent the view of only a small minority of the public, but it is their view that is outlined and enforced by the law.

It should also be noted that some parts of the 'feminist' anti-pornography movement also accept the traditional division of men and women into sexual users and emotional victims. That men just want to use people as objects in sex, while it is women who want 'love', is at the foundation of some kinds of political lesbian separatist theory.

Traditional anti-pornography campaigns, of course, tend to be aimed at homosexual pornography and other gay media in a very specific way. A current trend in gay sexual material has been an attempt to eroticize safer sex, to give the use of condoms and non-penetrative sex a greater image of naturalness and sexiness. (Safer sex, it is worth noting, decentralizes intercourse and highlights the other pleasurable sexual activities that have previously been consigned to the lower reaches of either mere 'foreplay' or perversion.) The most effective of these have been highly explicit and, naturally, they have been targeted by the Obscene Publications Squad and HM Customs and Excise. The lesbian magazines, whether they are sex magazines or political, have been a focus of traditional anti-porn campaigns, and the attention of anti-pornography feminists has had a devastating effect on gay media. Some 'feminist' anti-porn campaigns have actually been aimed specifically against lesbian sex magazines. The moral right has taken credibility from anti-porn feminists to continue its attack on *all* sexual media, particularly gay and lesbian materials.

Nadine Strossen noted, in 'A feminist critique of "the" feminist critique of pornography', that censorship laws tend to backfire on stigmatized groups, and that this was particularly apparent under the 'feminist' law in Canada:

> One of the first targets of the new law was a lesbian and gay bookstore, Glad Day Bookstore, and a magazine produced by lesbians for lesbians. Not surprisingly, the police, prosecutors, and other government officials viewed this lesbian imagery as degrading. They did not so view violent, misogynistic imagery. Other actions on the part of Canadian authorities that hold censorship power reflect similar attitudes.
>
> Canada's gay and lesbian bookstores have been so conspicuously singled out under the new Canadian law that one of them initiated a lawsuit claiming that it had been subjected to governmental harassment. After the lawsuit was instituted – and, some critics charge, specifically to blunt its allegations – Canadian officials broadened their enforcement efforts to include university bookstores and radical bookstores. CensorStop, a Canadian anti-censorship coalition, has charged that the officials are 'really interested in controlling radical dissent.' Whether or not this charge is actually justified, it is indisputable that the Canadian Supreme Court's adoption of the Dworkin–MacKinnon approach has given government officials a broad, discretionary weapon with which they could target radical dissent, should they so choose.

In other words, 'feminism' has become just another excuse to attack the free expression of gays, students and radical authors – but actual misogynistic materials do not seem to be targets of the 'feminist' anti-porn law.

Sadomasochism/dominance and submission

For a long time, it was generally taken for granted that games of dominance and submission were merely stronger versions of traditional sex roles; that is, that men who are involved in SM always act out the role of dominating the female, and that women always play a submissive or passive role. It was believed that all men were (or should be) sexual dominants and all women were sexual submissives, and it was just a matter of degree. For this reason, some feminists have perceived SM as being particularly sexist and especially degrading. In *Our Blood*, Andrea Dworkin wrote:

> In pornography, sadism is the means by which men establish their dominance. Sadism is the authentic exercise of power which confirms manhood; and the first characteristic of manhood is that its existence is based on the negation of the female – manhood can only be certified by abject female degradation, a degradation never abject enough until the victim's body and will have both been destroyed.

It is true that, on the surface, some SM play quite specifically involves scenarios intended to represent humiliation. However, it is by no means the case that the dominants ('tops') are always men and the submissives ('bottoms') always women, nor that these 'scenes' represent actual, real-life torture or humiliation of the 'bottom'. They are game-playing, acting, theatre performed by consenting participants, often carefully staged at considerable expense. Moreover, roles can be very fluid, and people sometimes have been known to change from top to bottom or vice versa in the middle of a scene, or even to play both roles at once in a multi-person scene. While some people are exclusively tops or exclusively bottoms, you can't count on it. And there is no relationship between gender and the roles themselves; tops or bottoms are as likely to be men as women, and many people of either sex will switch. The most 'butch' or assertive types of women or macho-type men may be bottoms (but you can't be sure), and people who seldom demonstrate aggressive qualities may turn out to be those who like to play the dominatrix or master. Or not, as the case may be. (Most research seems to indicate that men and women are about equally interested in SM. Some research shows that women are slightly more dominant and men are slightly more submissive or masochistic. SM practitioners 'on the scene' often say that masochism or submission is more common than dominance among both sexes.)

Nor is there necessarily any relationship between SM and a belief in gender roles. In fact, some people say they are attracted to SM fantasy that appears to parallel sexist gender roles precisely because they find those attitudes so alien, threatening and repellent. Women who have been sexually assaulted have reported that they have fantasies about the assaults in which crucial details, including the very meaning of the events, are changed, thus giving them a sense of control over that which was uncontrollable; but these women certainly do not convince themselves that they enjoyed being raped or that rape is 'OK'. It does seem possible that fantasies of this type are being used to address hurtful events that occur earlier in life.

Self-help sex

The humiliation many of us feel as children, being treated as less than people, never consulted in decisions that have profound effects on us, shows up particularly strongly in people who have fantasies of infantilization, where they imagine themselves treated as babies. It may be that our treatment of children plays a much more crucial role in the development of paraphiliac sexualities than anything having to do with gender roles.

However, some women do feel that SM is useful in breaking through the restrictions on female sexuality that have made us feel we had to project a lack of eroticism in order to be treated like legitimate human beings. Middle-class women in particular are taught that there is something unsavoury about the sexually expressive woman, and that if women are to achieve in intellectual fields, we cannot be associated with sexiness or sexual activity. Under such circumstances, even having a man say you are attractive can be seen as an insult, a suggestion that you are a 'bimbo' who couldn't be trusted to interpret English literature, perform psychological experiments or run a business. Mainstream films have a long tradition of portraying women who flirt or are sexually active or unconventional as being virtually unable to make a moral decision; they are either easily led 'airheads' or very nasty people indeed, conniving bitches, working for the bad guys or even for 'the reds'. SM may be allowing some women to sidestep these conventional attitudes in order to express their sexuality.

Diversity versus coercion

Many people who are involved in SM activities are fetishists who enjoy wearing the leather, latex or frilly underwear that seem to go with related sexualities in this category. Not all fetishists have a desire to act out SM scenes; they may just be turned on by wearing leather, rubber, lingerie, etc. (And some people just think they look cool in leather and latex.) By the same token, some people who are very much interested in bondage, submission and dominance, or some form of 'discipline' (which can range from light spankings to more intense types of corporal punishment – CP – and from physical discipline to other, less easily defined punishments), may not have any desire to wear, or get their partners to wear, leather or other fetish gear. A number of people who enjoy SM scenarios actually prefer street clothes or formal wear to fetish gear. Some people are aroused by bondage, but not by CP or humiliation; others may be principally into humiliation with a bit of CP, but not bondage. Some 'sadists' and 'masochists' are only interested in the physical activities without any dominance or submission games. Some people like verbal abuse, and some don't; people have widely varying reactions to specific words and phrases. There are no guarantees.

Given the complexity of the differing types of sexuality that may be encountered on the SM scene, it is obviously necessary for prospective partners to discuss their desired activities. Scenes are highly negotiated and cannot be taken for granted. Unlike non-SM sex (called, in SM parlance, 'vanilla sex'), people can't just jump into the sack and assume that they know what is expected. Of course, neither can anyone else, but a lot of people think they can, which explains why so many people are dissatisfied with their sex lives. Many practising sadomasochists consider this an advantage over vanilla sex; in vanilla situations, people often simply assume they know what kind of sexual activity is expected and acceptable, without bothering to consult their partners. (Indeed, some women consider SM clubs or groups to be safer spaces precisely because there are fewer preconceptions in this regard.)

On the other hand, the necessity for negotiation and the possibilities for incompatibility may both seem a hindrance for some people; many of us are uncomfortable with the idea of having to explain in advance what we want, and feel discomfort if our partners do not want the same things we do. It is unlikely that people who are into SM or fetish-related sexualities are all entirely free of the social tendency to perceive other sexualities as more 'perverted' than their own, and they can never be certain that they won't be called 'perverts' when they try to explain what they like. Additionally, much sexual fantasy, even for people whose desires are not particularly unusual, operates on the assumption that a partner will *know* what is wanted, and the idea of having to discuss it may ruin that aspect of fantasy. The desire for someone who is naturally compatible is probably the most common fantasy of all.

A problem may certainly arise in the case of some men with SM sexuality that appears to parallel stereotypical sex roles: male dominants who prefer submissive women, and who believe that this is 'natural' because they have been taught all their lives that these are natural gender-typed sexualities. They may, therefore, not be able to recognize it as an individual sexuality. Such men may try to dominate female partners without realizing that their partners may not have a corresponding sexuality. This is likely to be very unpleasant for the women involved, of course. Such tendencies are actually reinforced by 'feminist' propaganda (such as that quoted from Andrea Dworkin, above) that equates sadism and dominance with male sexuality. The best way to counteract this problem is continually to make people aware that dominance and submission are individual sexualities rather than gender-linked, and that women cannot be assumed to have a submissive sexuality, nor men a dominant sexuality. (Gloria G. Brame, William D. Brame and Jon Jacobs take a more detailed look at the complexities and diversity of SM in their 1993 book, *Different Loving*.)

Women and SM

Some women – interestingly, a disproportionate number of them lesbians – have written about SM as a sexuality that can be positive and should not be stigmatized. Virtually all of the lesbian sex magazines – such as *On Our Backs*, *Bad Attitude*, *Quim*, *Outrageous Women*, *Skin on Skin* and *Wicked Women* – tend to have a great deal of SM writing and related illustration. Perhaps the most noted of the SM-positive lesbian feminist writers is Pat Califia, who has written extensively on lesbian sexuality and also produced erotic writing principally involving SM. Her book *Macho Sluts* is probably the first complete volume of specifically pornographic works of this nature by a feminist. Barbara Smith has developed a following in Britain for her fiction and non-fiction writing, which takes a positive approach to SM. Other writers, such as Sharon Green, have written fantasy stories of a more science fictional sort in which (principally heterosexual) SM scenarios are integrated into the plot. This is not something unique to women, but many people feel that the SM-oriented stories written by women are less likely to be riddled with sexual impossibilities and obnoxious sexist lecturing. It has been said by some, though, that the main difference between the lesbian erotica and pornography of the same sort written by men is that the women are better writers. (Of course, women's romance fantasy novels have always had a rich strain of SM overtones. When the editors of Virgin's Black Lace series of erotic books for women did a market survey of their readers, they found that women strongly preferred 'kinky' stories.)

In Carole Vance's *Pleasure and Danger*, Gayle Rubin discussed the way sexualities, including SM, are stratified and stigmatized, and explained why it is in the interests of women's advancement to support stigmatized sexualities. Tuppy Owens of the Outsiders, a support organization for people who are isolated for social or physical reasons, has also noted that people who are involved in sexual behaviour that is outlawed or otherwise considered bizarre nevertheless tend to stigmatize other sexualities in the same way that 'normal' society does. It is interesting that even though we believe we have stepped outside of sexist society and its expectations, we take many of its prejudices with us. Whether we are heterosexuals who have abandoned monogamy or lesbians who have turned our back on straight culture, we may still be accomplices in the social tendency to treat our own sexuality as privileged while pointing the finger at that which is different or not well understood.

Anti-SM feeling runs strong among pro-censorship feminists. There are two basic threads to this approach: one, that sadomasochism is simply sick and degrading, and that people who like it shouldn't be allowed to do it, is very much like what one expects to hear from conservatives as well; the other is that sadomasochistic fantasy is fairly common among men and women, but is created by sexism, out of our sexist gender roles, and thus we have been infected inside our own minds by it. The same prescription is offered whatever the diagnosis: suppress the fantasies, suppress related pornography, and don't engage in SM sex. Some anti-SM feminists clearly are turned on by SM and have (presumably submissive) SM fantasies, or they wouldn't assume that most people have them. They often tend to believe that if we stamp out SM porn and activities in this generation, future generations will not have such fantasies. Some say that SM fantasy is a direct emulation of sexist stereotypes, and eliminating sexism would eliminate SM. Alternatively, they will say that if we just stop thinking of them and get into good relationships, we will all stop having the fantasies. (And haven't we heard all this before, about homosexuality?)

Again, there is no evidence to support this belief. Like all other sexualities, it seems to be largely rooted in early life, and suppressing fantasies seems to create an enormous amount of frustration and pain, but certainly doesn't 'cure' SM and is more likely to lead to dysfunctional behaviour. Numerous theories abound – some of them remarkably silly (particularly those of Sigmund Freud and Jacques Lacan) – regarding the formation of fetishes and SM fantasy, but no one knows where they come from, no one knows how to get rid of them, and no one has ever demonstrated a single reason why we should try so hard to suppress them. There is no evidence whatsoever that having such fantasies, producing porn about them, or even acting them out causes any harm to society.

Universal compulsory sexuality

What most emphatically is harmful is the ludicrous belief our society seems to hold that anything not forbidden therefore becomes compulsory. 'Normal' sex is what everyone *has to* do; the rest is sick. Our refusal to recognize that there is absolutely no sexuality that is shared by all of us allows people to think they are free to put pressure on their partners to perform whatever sexual acts they can convince them are common or accepted. This has always been a problem with intercourse and heterosexuality, but feminists should not be fighting to suppress sexualities just because some people might try to force them on others; it is force and coercion, not unusual sexual practice, that is the problem. No woman wants to have heterosexuality *or* lesbianism, SM *or* vanilla sex, forced on her. Whether the sexual practice in question is considered common and acceptable or weird and perverted is entirely beside the point. It is hardly a pleasure to be forced or coerced into 'normal' sex.

By the same token, it is irrelevant whether a husband comes home with pornography and demands that his wife perform the acts represented therein. If he's making demands, she should know she has a right to refuse – and if she doesn't know that, it is the fault of a society that has persistently failed to make that message clear to people before they find themselves in relationships. Pornography is just a method of communication in such circumstances; an abusive partner can as easily use the English language to describe what he demands as he can show his partner a picture. He might also simply force it on her with direct violence, without pornography being involved at all; this would hardly be an improvement. In the same way, people can use both verbal suggestion and pornography as a way to explore their sexualities in a mutual and non-hostile way: a man might bring home a sex magazine and say to his partner, 'See if there's anything in there that interests you.' It is very possible that the woman herself has been looking for a way to bring up such subjects. (Women have also been known to bring pornography home in order to suggest sexual activities to their partners.) On the other hand, she can merely say she has no interest in the sex acts portrayed and leave it at that. This would not be degrading or humiliating simply because it involved pornography that may contain representations of 'kinky' sex.

In the traditions of a society that believed a woman's sexuality belonged to her husband, men have long felt free to force their sexual desires on their wives. Up until 1991, English law supported that belief, treating marital rape as a part of the marriage contract, rather than a crime. Brutality could be justified in such circumstances on the grounds that the husband was entitled to sex from his wife.

When the authorities decide that a particular act is sufficiently awful, they make that act illegal even in consenting circumstances, which is often the only way that a woman can get any legal redress; heterosexual anal sex is entirely illegal, and therefore a woman's consent does not let the man, even her husband, off the hook. (Of course, if she says she consented, she can be prosecuted as well.) This may seem necessary, since wives may often 'consent' to acts they really do not want, because they feel compelled to. Those of us who have been raped might as easily demand that all sex be made unlawful so that men can't escape the consequences of rape by claiming we consented; obviously, this would not be an option, but it is the basis of the reasoning some people use for making certain acts illegal.

It is because we fear that we cannot enforce our refusal in any other way that we often support the idea of making illegal those acts we think we could never enjoy ourselves. If you are disgusted by SM sex yourself and are afraid your husband will force you into it, a law against SM would be convenient if you ever want to take him to court; he can't use the excuse that you consented. (If he does, however, you might end up being prosecuted as well.) But it is worth reiterating that there is no sexual act, however common, that we should ever be forced into; people who respect each other don't use force and coercion for sexual acts in the first place, whatever those sex acts are. Laws against specific sex acts do not eliminate coercion and force, though that should be our priority.

Paedophilia

Arousing fears for our children is the most prominent method of getting restrictive and repressive legislation passed. Virtually any suggestion of sexuality or sexual facts in the context of children can get people into such a state of panic that they will throw caution to the wind, even believe the unbelievable, and ultimately support laws that have no justification at all. When all else fails, nothing succeeds like pointing a finger at paedophiles, perhaps the most despised of any single sexual identity.

A paedophile is an adult who is sexually attracted to children. Once again, there is no evidence that pornography is in any way implicated in causing paedophilia. Paedophiliac desires are not created by seeing adult pornography, nor do paedophiles usually have any great need for child porn, as most of the materials that they use as pornography are pictures that would not be perceived as porn by anyone else: photos taken from ordinary newspapers of kids playing sports or receiving prizes at school; pages from the children's section of catalogues; snapshots of kids out romping on the beach. The only way to eliminate material that is potentially arousing to paedophiles would be to ban *all* images of children. The police recently searched a man's home and, finding nothing illegal there, seized a photo of a child that he'd cut out of the *Daily Mirror*. But the children who are in these pictures are never affected by the fact that, in the privacy of their own homes, paedophiles may be using them as masturbatory materials. Most other adults would look at such pictures and perceive them as innocent, with no sexual content (and of course, paedophiles may often look at pictures of children in the same ways).

The danger of paedophile witch-hunts

Parents frequently take numerous pictures of their children, posing or playing, as keepsakes for themselves and for the children when they are grown up. The fact that paedophiles might find such pictures arousing does not mean that they are innately 'pornographic' or that other people would be turned into paedophiles by seeing them.

Unfortunately, the police are aware that paedophiles use innocent pictures of this nature, and it has become pretty chancy of late to take ordinary baby pictures of your own children and have them developed at your local chemist's shop. In a household where children have not been taught to feel embarrassed or shamed by nudity, children may run around naked at times and parents may take pictures of them doing what seem to be clever or silly things. Parents have a way of being charmed by all sorts of behaviour on the part of their offspring that may not seem so wonderful to the rest of us, but this largely accounts for the fact that so many annoying little rugrats manage to survive to adulthood. The police, however, seem remarkably disposed to see child porn in just about any photo of a child

Since most Britons would rather have the police protect them from violence, it would surely be more economical to eliminate the OPS.

Promoting the myth

Ray Wyre, whose Gracewell Institute 'treats' those accused of sex offences, often tries to support his belief that porn causes child abuse by saying that sex abusers are frequently found with child pornography, from which we may be led to believe that they have been using those awful commercial child porn photos and videos of children being raped that are always described in this kind of scaremongering. In fact, such materials are found far less frequently than such rhetoric and exaggeration would make us think. Some people write their fantasies down in their own journals, or make diary entries about sexual acts that they have with children, and some even keep photo records (polaroids) of such acts, and it is this that Wyre and the police are referring to when they say 'child porn' has been found – materials not commercially made or distributed. Many heterosexual adults record their (legal) fantasies and (legal and consensual) sexual experiences in diaries and on video in much the same way. These items would not exist if the people who make them were not already interested in the sexualities that are described or portrayed in them; the desires lead to the creation of the materials, not the other way around.

In Catherine Itzin's *Pornography: Women, violence and civil liberties*, an article by Wyre even suggests that pornography can turn someone into a paedophile:

> I recently had referred to me a social worker who had told his supervisor that he was having sexual fantasies about children. He said he didn't know where they were coming from. But I discovered that he had a big stash of pornography, a whole suitcase full, which included a pornographic magazine with one story about father–daughter incest and another about a social worker having sex with all the girls in a girls' home. ... Pornography certainly reinforces and can also create the predisposition to carry out abuse. It feeds the fantasy. And it creates distorted thinking.

Wyre never asks how or why this man had pornography of this type in the first place. It is not very common and he certainly would have had to go out of his way to acquire it. It did not fall into his lap and suddenly start him thinking about sex with children. Every genuine expert in both paedophilia and child molestation could have told him that people look at such pornography because they already have that interest, and not the other way around.

Wyre and Itzin both tend to make much of the belief that non-paedophiliac men are encouraged to develop or maintain sexual interest in children by pornography sold to 'normal' men that, they claim, is merely child pornography in disguise. In 1993 I saw a presentation by Catherine Itzin in which she held up a magazine photo of an obviously adult woman which she claimed was meant to represent a young female child. She based this assertion on the straw hat, patterned dress, white socks and shaved pubic area pictured. What she described as a 'child's straw hat' was in fact an expensive kind of fine straw hat with a wide black band, of a sort that many adult women wear. The dress was of the type associated with Laura Ashley's designs, and had a bright print of a kind I have never seen on children's clothing. And although in our generation it would have been laughably uncool for an adult woman to wear white socks, the fact is that today many young adult women do wear them and they can be considered fashionable, even with jeans or dresses. This clothing on a fully developed adult can hardly be said to constitute child porn.

That leaves the ever-contentious shaved pubic area, a pornographic convention that Itzin and others like her are unable to disassociate from images of children. For one who claims to be so expert in pornography, she seems remarkably ignorant of how pubic shaving came to be considered sexy in pornography in the first place. It had nothing to do with little girls. It was illegal to show pubic hair in nude photos, and so more and more of the hair was shaved down in order that more of the pubic area could be shown. Many men actually come to associate this shaving with *adult* sexuality precisely because of this convention. And as some of the related restrictions were lifted, pornographic photographers wanted to be able to show female genitals more explicitly, and found that pubic hair got in the way. For this reason, many of them prefer not to have pubic hair obscuring their subject.

Japanese pornography is often mistaken for child porn for this very reason. Until quite recently, pubic hair has been taboo, so the models are shaved. Japanese models may look younger than they are to the western eye, and as a result British police and other anti-porn crusaders often think they have found child pornography when they have not. (Interestingly, the emergence of erotic photographs in Japan featuring pubic hair seems to be part of the developing Japanese women's liberation movement. It is not driven by the porn industry so much as by the women themselves, mainstream actors and singers who have now decided to produce books or

It was illegal to show pubic hair in nude photos

magazines featuring themselves, unshaven, in nude erotic poses. As in the west, with its history of flappers and miniskirts, Japanese women are taking control of their sexuality by using their bodies for their own purposes, rather than conforming to the traditional feminine image of modesty and humility. The 'hair books' have proven to be enormously popular.)

But many women actually choose to shave the pubic area. Linzi Drew, perhaps Britain's most famous porn star, says that she does it specifically because she likes the feel of it – it is more 'sensual', she says. And some lesbians have said they prefer their partners to be shaved because it makes it easier to perform cunnilingus on them. (It should be lost on no one that pubic hair is much more likely to get in the way during cunnilingus than during fellatio.) None of these reasons has anything to do with children.

Although people like Catherine Itzin and Judith Reisman (see below) seem to read paedophilia into places where it is not present, it is true that there is a (relatively rare) form of pornography that portrays adult women in roles or clothing more closely associated with younger females. What anti-pornography women may overlook is that for some, it is precisely the juxtaposition of the symbols of childhood with the adult woman that may make it interesting. (I have heard prostitutes say that some clients actually request older, rather than younger women, for this purpose.) There are many possible interpretations of pornography of this type. Childhood innocence is not only associated in our society with helplessness; it also represents more authentic, uncorrupted expression, as well as selfishness – children are often more likely to say what they want, what they like and don't like, and mean what they say. Men may use images related to childhood in order to create the impression that these adult women are still capable of the fresh enthusiasm that is normally equated with children. It would be interesting to see the results of a study on this sort of question, if there was one – but I know of none that actually examines the interpretations that men place on the pornography they see and use.

The Reisman research

In 1984, Reagan-appointee Alfred Regnery commissioned a $734,371 study by Judith Reisman, who wanted to do research in support of her belief that common men's magazines like *Penthouse*, *Hustler* and *Playboy* promote child abuse. Reisman claimed that between 1954 and 1984, those three magazines published over 6,000 cartoons, photos and other illustrations of children.

Although it was obvious that the Reagan administration appeared willing to do almost anything in support of the most sexually repressive programmes, it is extraordinary that the US Department of Justice squandered such an enormous sum of money on this demonstrably ludicrous hypothesis – the Meese Commission itself did not have this kind of funding. In the end, even Regnery had to admit that it was a mistake to commission this report. It was a scientific disaster, riddled with researcher bias and baseless assumptions. The American University (AU), where Reisman's study had been academically based, actually refused to publish it when she released it, after their independent academic auditor reported on it. Dr Robert Figlio of the University of Pennsylvania told AU that, 'The term child used in the aggregate sense in this report is so inclusive and general as to be almost meaningless.' Figlio told the press, 'I wondered what kind of mind would consider the love scene from *Romeo and Juliet* to be child porn.' Pally cites this and numerous other objections to Reisman:

> Dr. Loretta Haroian, cochair of the plenary session on Child and Adolescent Sexuality at the 1984 World Congress of Sexology and one of the world's experts on childhood sexuality, said of the Reisman study:
> 'This is not science, it's vigilantism: paranoid, pseudoscientific hyperbole with a thinly veiled hidden agenda. This kind of thing doesn't help children at all. ... Her [Reisman's] study demonstrates gross negligence and, while

she seems to have spent a lot of time collecting data, her conclusions, based on the data, are completely unwarranted. The experts Reisman cites are, in fact, not experts at all but simply people who have chosen to adopt some misinformed, Disneyland conception of childhood that she has. These people are little more than censors hiding behind Christ and children.'

Despite having been given one of the largest research grants of the period, Reisman managed to distinguish herself as such an unreliable anti-pornography researcher that even the Reagan moralists were embarrassed by her. Yet some feminists persist in citing her as an authority on the harm of pornography.

The reality

Child pornography has only limited popularity to begin with, and making it is far too risky for anyone to spend much time doing so. (Indeed, the various experts have found that there was little child porn of any kind in the United States even before people started to demand a law against it, and there was virtually none left in distribution in the country by the time the anti-child porn law was passed in 1977.) The penalties for sex involving children are so high that few would court the dangers of making child porn for the tiny amounts of money that can be made on it from such a small audience. As Dian Hanson said, there is such material, but:

> very, very small quantities of it. People will say, 'You pornographers don't want to admit that child pornography is being created.' But let's look at it cost-effectively: besides the fact that most pornographers are as morally repelled by the exploitation of children as any other Americans, how many people do you know who are turned on by pre-pubescent children? There aren't very many. It's not like this is the common thing, that everybody in the U.S. is saying, 'We're turned on by pre-pubescent children but we'll take women with huge breasts, since we can't get children.' It's a very small group of people who are interested in this material, who would be consumers of this material. Meanwhile, the penalties for producing this material are immense, while the amount of money to be made by producing and selling it is infinitesimal. It's tiny. So it's not cost effective for any pornographer – for anybody who wants to make money off of pornography – to produce child pornography. It just doesn't make sense. And so it's not done. If people thought about it logically, this would occur to them. But nobody does because you can't say the words 'child pornography' without everybody screaming hysterically and rushing around hitting you.

The population of paedophiles is small, and a significant proportion of them are uninterested in intercourse. Moreover, paedophiles are not interested in films of children being raped, but rather in fantasies of *consensual* acts with children. In other words, even paedophiles would not provide much of a market for films and photos of children being sexually assaulted. Why, then, would anyone attack children on film in order to make profits? The simple fact is that there is no profit in doing so.

Child abuse

Life would be easy if child abuse was down to paedophilia – which the moral right persists in equating with homosexuality – but paedophiles represent only a very small part of the population and, moreover, have little to do with child abuse. The moral right would have us believe that 'Sixties permissiveness', homosexuals and pornography are responsible for child abuse, but most child abusers are not paedophiles at all; rather, they are the parents of the children: otherwise ordinary heterosexual adults who have never felt any sexual interest in children at all before. Religious fundamentalists who campaign against pornography would rather we ignored the facts about child abuse and instead followed their repressive agenda.

When the first outcries against domestic violence and sexual abuse were heard from feminists in America, the moral right actively prevented the passage of legislation attempting to deal with these issues because, they said, it would mean government interference with a husband's rights over his wife and the rights of parents over their children; domestic violence and child abuse, apparently, were not so terrible that a man shouldn't be able to beat his wife or rape his child when he wanted to. They changed their tune about domestic abuse only when anti-porn feminists made it possible to blame it on the very things the moral right had always opposed – the people on the sexual margins of society who have never been responsible for domestic violence and abuse: homosexuals and pornographers.

But child abuse has become a remarkably convenient cause for the moral right. It has made women fearful of allowing men to be alone with children, which means that women must return to being full-time carers and men will not be expected to be active parents. (When right-wing men talk about 'family values', they mean that *women* should do the work of the family so that men won't have to.) The American right has consistently opposed day-care centres, as well, and scares about abuse in day care have been a godsend to them. They have also promoted the canard that child abusers within the family are principally stepfathers rather than natural fathers – this being a specific criticism of another target of the right: divorce. We are consistently being led away from recognizing where the real problem lies.

Perhaps it is best to repeat here Pally's quote from Dr Henry Giaretto of the Child Sexual Abuse Treatment Program in Santa Clara:

> In contrast to common belief, a great number of men who turn to their children for sexual purposes are highly religious or morally rigid individuals who feel that this is 'less of a sin' than masturbation or seeking sexual liaisons in an outside affair.

Once again, conservative attitudes brought from childhood are most strongly implicated in the creation of abusive adults. It is not merely specious to blame pornography, but such campaigns actually help to encourage the very conditions that create sexual abusers. Using 'child porn' and 'child abuse' as their justification, the moral right, with the help of the government and the police, have promoted an atmosphere of ever-widening repression that may very well make us more hateful of our bodies, more fearful of sex, and more likely to experience sexual problems and violence.

7
Feminists versus feminists: the insult to women

It is the contention of some anti-pornography feminists that pornography is offensive to women – all women – and should be banned for this reason. This might have some validity if all women could be made to agree that they are offended by pornography, and if it could be established that we are never offended by it for sexist reasons – such as that we have been made to feel excluded from it by sexist society, for example, or that we have been taught to feel that we are supposed to be too pure for sex. But the truth is that even with all of the social factors that encourage women to feel distaste for pornography, there are many women who don't care about porn one way or another and others who actively like it. Carole Vance says she uses 'the one third rule' – that one third of women hate it, one third of women like it, and one third of women are indifferent to it. Although there is no empirical research to support this, many estimates suggest that one third of the population – half of them women – may indeed make up the core of the porn market in the US, and Vance's point is well taken; we have no evidence that disgust with pornography is so uniform among women. We cannot all be pigeonholed into one monolithic stereotype.

Pornography or erotica?

During the 1980s, the word 'pornography' was used frequently by anti-porn campaigners in the context of violent, degrading material, and many residents of Britain came to think in those terms when they heard the term. It is on this basis that it is often easy to get women to say that they find pornography degrading; using the anti-porn definition, pornography is *by definition* that which is degrading. As Gayle Rubin says in 'Misguided, dangerous and wrong':

This is argument by tautology. If pornography is defined simply as that which is inherently degrading to women, then by definition it cannot be reformed and must be extirpated. This tactic completely finesses the necessity of providing some demonstration that what is generally thought of as pornography is accurately denoted by such a definition.

However, most pornography is unlike this false representation of it, and when pollsters ask people whether they would wish to see bans on material that depicts erections and common sexual acts, the vast majority of people say they think it should not be banned and is harmless. Indeed, when in 1993 the UK government started moves to ban the satellite station showing such materials, Red Hot Television (formerly Red Hot Dutch), polls taken at the time showed that there was little support for such a ban; nevertheless, the government made it illegal for RHTV to sell the decoders for reception of the station. Most people are not aware that depictions of erections, penetration and genital contact of any kind in erotic materials are already treated as illegal.

Much as anti-pornography feminists claim they are interested only in banning the violent, degrading and 'horrible' materials, it is clear that many of them really do mean *all* pornography, ranging from pin-ups aimed at heterosexual men to lesbian erotica. When Gayle Rubin, in 'Misguided, dangerous and wrong', tried to pin down the difference between the definition of pornography and that of those items of sexual material that would not be banned – 'erotica' – she found out that their vagueness defied any useful interpretation and appeared to be no more than a cover for a campaign to get rid of all sexual entertainment materials:

> When the targets of anti-porn agitation are identified they are the things more commonly associated with the term 'pornography', i.e., X-rated videos and films, *Playboy* and *Penthouse*, the magazines sold in adult bookstores, lesbian sex magazines, gay male one-handed reading – in short, smut in the more usual sense. If pornography is that which is violent and/or intrinsically degrading to women in one sentence, it cannot be sexually explicit popular media in the next ...

Anti-censorship feminists find this definitional sleight of hand dishonest. On the one hand we are told pornography is 'violence', and on the other that even advertising and pin-ups are 'pornography'. Moreover, anti-porn activists continually repeat the complaint that porn is 'a multi-million pound industry in this country', citing figures that can only be reached in Britain if the softest of materials and literary references to sex, as well as the real estate dealings and holdings of the owners of soft-core publications (*and* the turnover from their non-sexual publications), are included in the definition of 'pornography'.

Even anti-porn feminists cannot agree with each other what 'pornography' is. Catherine Itzin of Campaign Against Pornography and Censorship (CPC) persistently makes a distinction between 'pornography' – violent, degrading and unacceptable – and 'erotica', which is the good, nice stuff we should approve. This is a popular notion among some supporters of anti-pornography ideology. But Campaign Against Pornography (CAP) isn't so sure it will accept 'erotica', either. CAP member Anne Mayne told Monique El-Faizy in an interview for the *Guardian* that she opposes this material, too. 'Who is making the erotica?' she asked. 'There is no equality at this point.'

But given that Itzin seems able to find child pornography and violence where there is none (see Chapter 6), it is clear that she would ban items that most people would find entirely inoffensive – although she would first explain why they *are* offensive. At a joint meeting on censorship between the National Council for Civil Liberties and free expression activitists Article 19, Itzin described a 'degrading' picture of a nude woman wearing an ammunition belt around her waist, 'with the bullets pointing down, inviting penetration' – an obviously invasive intention. But men also wear ammo belts with the bullets pointing down – it is how they are designed to be worn, and for very practical reasons. On such dubious deconstructions are most anti-porn evaluations based. A more straightforward interpretation of the picture might be that of a play on the contrast between the classic, feminine-looking model and the macho-aggressive symbol of the battle paraphernalia: this woman is no helpless wimp; she'll do what she wants when she wants, and no one pushes her around. She's got the ammunition, and she probably has a great big *gun* to go with it.

The photo in question comes from a slide show presentation compiled by an American group called Organizing Against Pornography. The descriptions are presented as an article in Itzin's book, *Pornography: Women, violence and civil liberties*, explaining that the slide show 'aimed to inform people about what pornography was available, what it communicated about women: to explain its meaning'. Three slides come from a notorious photo-spread in the December 1984 issue of US *Penthouse* (Itzin never differentiates this from UK *Penthouse*, although they are two entirely different magazines and the US version is not legally available in Britain). The 1984 *Penthouse* spread was uncharacteristic of the magazine; it attempted to solicit interest from the SM market, but it bore little resemblance to the materials normally sought by sadomasochists and did not appeal to them. Rather, it merely offended its regular readers. It was never repeated. The ammo belt cited above (from *Playboy*) is described as 'bondage paraphernalia', although it is in no way typical of bondage equipment. Other similarly disingenuous descriptions permeate the text. The first description is of a cosmetics ad, not pornography at all.

At the same time, the arguments about what men do with pornography seem to imply that there *is* no erotic material that would not lead to 'improper' fantasy uses. The argument is repeatedly made that men will have fantasies in which women are idealized – not only are the women in the pictures too glamorous and too much in keeping with Hollywood stereotypes, but when men read pornography, they are treated to a vision of relationships that are without ordinary human conflict: the women don't become ill, don't complain, don't have interests that are not in concord with the man's, don't tell him to brush his teeth or have a shower, and never put the toilet paper in the other way. This, in theory, sets men up for being unable to cope with the kinds of negotiation that must be made between real people, and women who are not 'ideal' come up short. Of course, such an argument assumes that men will not independently have equally idealized, unrealistic fantasies, which is itself an unrealistic expectation. (It also does not explain where women get some of our equally unrealistic ideas about relationships and men.) And would 'erotica' portray women as being more 'realistic'? In my experience, the material that is regarded as 'erotica' is often *more* idealized, soft-focus and lacking in realistic consequences than is common pornography.

However, in her book *Pornography: Men possessing women*, Andrea Dworkin says she sees no difference between 'erotica' and 'pornography'. Erotica, she says, 'is simply high-class pornography'. In this she agrees with most anti-censorship women, who would make the same point: the distinction is not one of content, but rather one of class-derived values displayed with higher-priced resources. It is not surprising that many of Dworkin's supporters believe that any sexual representation whatsoever is 'degrading' to women, as does Suzanne Kappler, who argues just this point in her book, *The Pornography of Representation*.

A fate worse than rape

Indeed, in *Intercourse*, Dworkin goes so far as to suggest that consensual, loving and pleasurable coition is thoroughly degrading for a woman. She cites Flaubert's famous fictional character with her evidence: Madame Bovary is not destroyed by a repressive society; rather, she is destroyed by having *felt* desire, and being moved by sexual pleasure during copulation. Like Jeffreys, Dworkin sees 'surrender' to desire with a man as demeaning – so much so that, because the woman is complicit in her own 'degradation', it is worse than being raped. In a forcible act of intercourse, she would at least not be *giving* herself. If she hates it, she is not possessed; if she enjoys it, on the other hand, she is lost:

> Therefore, women feel the fuck – when it works, when it overwhelms – as possession; and feel possession as deeply erotic; and value annihilation of the self in sex as proof of the man's desire or love, its awesome intensity. And therefore, being possessed is phenomenologically real for women; and sex itself is an experience of diminishing self-possession, an erosion of self.

Interestingly, the fact that men have also been known to feel overwhelmed, sometimes experiencing a loss of self, during sexual pleasure is not believed to place them on a par with 'possessed' women. The French use the phrase *'petite mort'* to describe a sense of a small 'death' during orgasm. Surely if men are so lost during sex, this cannot explain why it is so terrible for *women* to have similar experiences. Dworkin notes these things, but never quite seems to absorb, explain or contextualize them.

For Sheila Jeffreys, 'Heterosexual desire is eroticised power difference. Heterosexual desire originates in the power relationships between men and women, but can also be experienced in same sex relationships.' Under the circumstances, any heterosexual depiction of sex, or any lesbian depiction that could parallel a heterosexual depiction, would equally be part of the same degraded relationships between males and females that must, for women, be replaced by political lesbianism, as she claims to show in *Anticlimax*:

> Under male supremacy, sex consists of the eroticising of women's subordination. Women's subordination is sexy for men and for women too. For years this was a secret within women's liberation. In order to challenge men's pornography which reiterated that women enjoyed pain and humiliation, and to campaign against sexual violence in a culture which asserted that women enjoyed sexual abuse, feminists denied that women were masochists. Feminist theorists of male violence would acknowledge that women had sadomasochistic fantasies but assert that there was a huge difference between the fantasy and the reality. No women, they said, wanted abuse. The existence of s/m fantasies were not really dealt with as an issue because of its explosive potential.

Note that Jeffreys appears to believe that *all* women become sexual masochists under patriarchy. That many women have no sadomasochistic fantasies, and that many SM women are entirely uninterested in fantasizing or acting out the masochistic or passive position, elude her; such sexuality is not truly possible under patriarchy. Note also the statement, 'No women, *they said*, wanted abuse.' Is Jeffreys suggesting that this statement is debatable, that women in fact desire *actual* abuse?

The suggestion that male dominance and female submission as sexualities are so near-universal is itself pernicious. In earlier times, it was used to justify male supremacy on the basis that these feelings were said to be 'natural', but it can just as easily be used to pressure women into submissive roles because 'it's what all women secretly want', whatever the reason. Perhaps Jeffreys feels guilt about having a submissive sexuality, but she should think before trying to deal with it by projecting submission onto all women. Such common misapprehensions of female sexuality are no doubt used by coercive men to justify their behaviour. And it would be difficult for even the most non-aggressive male dominant to resist trying to press his wife into service once he was told – by self-proclaimed feminists, no less – that it is what all women, for whatever reason, desire in the back of their minds anyway. If feminists continue to stereotype female sexuality in this way, how can we expect men not to?

John Stoltenberg, who shares a home with Andrea Dworkin, has presented a convoluted view of sexual acts, even between gay partners, in which males merely assert their masculinity (and male supremacy) when they have sex, or absorb the masculinity of other males in gay sex in the 'passive' role (to fuck is to participate in male dominance; to be fucked is to accept female inferiority). There are, Stoltenberg specifies, no true male masochists, and no true female dominants. Lesbians who play the dominant role are merely trying on the male role, attempting to get closer to having the power of men; sexually submissive females cannot be genuinely consenting as they are brainwashed by sexist society. In the highest of ironies, he presents an allegedly feminist theory that women, incapable of deciding for ourselves, need men like John Stoltenberg to tell us how we should comport ourselves sexually. Men have so oppressed women that we need men to tell us what to do.

When women 'submit' to sex and 'surrender' to pleasure, then, we have aided and abetted our oppressors, actually gone willingly to the chopping block. Worse than docile cattle headed for the slaughterhouse, we go further, proceeding *eagerly* to a fate worse than death. Clearly, this is even more horrible than being forcibly raped. Under the circumstances, it is hard to see how 'erotica' involving heterosexual acts, defined by Itzin as portraying relationships 'premised on equality', could exist at all.

But once again, a tricky game has been played with us. Rape, we are consistently told, is the terror at the end of the spectrum of heterosexual relationships, the *proof* that men do not love us but merely want to exercise their power over us with violence. Rape is the bogeyman we are told to fear, in order to justify censorship, or political lesbianism, or at least feminism. And yet, the chief proponents of such anti-porn, anti-sex views have made plain that rape is perhaps the *least* oppressive of heterosexual constructions – it is pleasure, and not pain and terror, that we should fear the most. Indeed, even within a lesbian relationship, consensual pleasure might be a worse, more powerfully degrading act of *heterosexual oppression* than could the most brutal and painful rape.

Anti-censorship feminists who have ourselves been sexually assaulted cannot help but feel exploited by this trivialization of the real violence we have experienced. That we have been raped is being used to support the most abusive and dangerous theories of how society should be constructed, and yet, when the theorists who do this are given free rein, they make it clear that they see rape as something comparatively mild, hardly to be feared, when our own desire is our true worst enemy. Similarly, it has been said that merely walking into a newsagent where *Penthouse* is sold, or seeing a copy of *Bad Attitude* or *Quim*, constitutes an act of violence against women that is virtually indistinguishable from being raped. In the end, it is hard not to return the contempt that Jeffreys, Dworkin and those like them feel for us; how can we respect women who would deny each of us pleasure merely because we have felt pain?

The $ize of the problem

Much is made of the fact that pornography makes money. It is even claimed that pornography is an £8-billion industry in Britain. This figure is ludicrously high – half again as great as the worldwide figure of $8 billion that the United States government estimates, and a quarter the size of the enormous National Health budget. Certainly if the British porn industry were really that huge, it would be an economic disaster for the country should it be eliminated. Campaign Against Pornography has continually claimed in leaflets and interviews that the porn industry is bigger than the rest of media *combined*. But of course, such estimates are entirely fictional.

The claim that pornography makes these enormous sums of money – or indeed, the fact that it makes any money at all – is frequently used as a condemnation of it. For some reason, however, this same argument is never used against products that make far more money than pornography does – fashion and clothing in general, grocery stores and restaurants, and so on. No one suggests that food and clothes should be eliminated because they make money (and given the contempt women get from the fashion industry, maybe they *should*). Economically speaking, the porn industry is a poor relation to the real money-makers in our society. Yet pornography alone is attacked on the basis that some people make money on it.

This argument is simply silly coming from socialists, who presumably should have a critique of capitalism itself and not foolishly perceive porn as being the sole existing capitalist industry. In October 1993, a leaflet purporting to be from some 'Cambridge Anarchists' attacked pornography for supposedly being larger economically than 'the mainstream film, record and video industry combined' (and attacked FAC as its 'front organization'). Anarchists normally would dismiss such an argument. But even members of the Conservative Party use the 'porn makes money' charge as evidence that it should be banned. This is the same party that spent the 1980s promoting a policy of mercilessly selling off necessary utilities in the pursuit of money – the party that praised economic achievement even when it destroyed jobs, industries and the nation's stability. The Tories are not normally noted for decrying economic success.

Yet anti-porn activists persistently level the charge that opposition to censorship rests on a dedication to making money. That Britain's anti-censorship activists are by no means as moneyed as our opponents should be enough to put paid to such a ridiculous charge, but since the 'feminist' anti-porn position presumes that women are not capable of thinking for ourselves and judging the price of government censorship to be too high, they conclude that we must be 'in the pay of the pornographers' in order to be willing to fight for freedom of sexual expression. In July 1993 I debated on BBC Radio Berkshire with a member of Campaign Against Pornography whose sole argument seemed to be that Feminists Against Censorship were 'mouthpieces for the pornographers'; she implied that we were actually being paid to campaign. The truth is that no porn publisher had ever given us a penny. And, despite rumours that have dogged us since we first came together in 1989, we had no funding from any organization of any kind, with the exception that, we can gratefully say, *Gay Times* sponsored two of our leaflets, printing them at no charge to us. In January 1994 we received a private donation of £250; until then, the largest donation we had ever received was £50. None of us is paid to campaign for FAC.

Making movies for money

Candida Royalle is a porn star who decided it was time to move to the production end of the industry and make films that might be less offensive and more satisfying to women. With her own company, Femme Productions, she has attempted to portray sexuality in the context of relationships and from a woman's point of view. When she spoke about this on *The Time/The Place*, she was repeatedly interrupted by Corrine Sweet of CPC, who charged her with selling her videos *for money*. As far as Sweet was concerned, this was proof enough that Royalle could not possibly have any other motive; if she accepted money for her work, she could not also claim that she did that work to improve the product of her industry and its value to women. By doing so, Sweet as much as stated that every other woman who has a paying job is an avaricious conniver with no morality who cold-heartedly exploits her clients, employers, customers or patients without care, just to get her hands on the gold. Interestingly, the fact that nurses and teachers also do their jobs for pay is not normally used as proof that medicine and education should be eliminated. Perhaps there are thousands of women campaigning to ban scented soaps because Body Shop makes money from them, but I have not heard of such activism. Even the feminist magazine *Spare Rib*, which spent the 1980s condemning pornography, was sold for money.

It seems remarkable that women who have been surrounded by capitalism all their lives can be unaware that producing erotic materials of any kind also *costs* money; only a very rich person could afford to do it for free. *Of course* Candida Royalle sells her movies for money – how else could she afford to produce them? With the most altruistic motives in the world, there is no way she could give them away. Surely Sweet cannot be suggesting that the women who appear in the films should not expect to be paid, or that those who work on the set crew should starve rather than take remuneration, can she? Where else is the money for production and survival going to come from if Royalle does not demand payment for her products? And why on earth should women, once again, be expected to do for nothing what men are paid for? If bankers and lawyers – or indeed, the makers of non-erotic movies – are entitled to expect money in exchange for their services and products, why shouldn't women who make erotic movies expect the same? These economic arguments against pornography sound remarkably like sexist arguments against women making our own choices and being rewarded materially for our work.

The exploitation of women

It is often said that pornography exploits women, in the sense that poor women are often forced into the sex industry by economic conditions. This is, of course, true; many people take jobs that they would prefer to avoid when they are unable to find what they consider better work. Sex work is no different from factory work, in this sense; although many of us might not aspire to such jobs, they may offer hope of an income – of survival and the ability to feed our kids (or cats) – when nothing more attractive is on offer.

However, anti-porn feminists have suggested that the porn industry should be eliminated for this very reason. That sex work may not always be overwhelmingly a positive experience is not in doubt, but it *is work*, and for a woman who is in dire economic straits, surely that is better than having no money at all. Women in the Third World often leave their homes in the country in the hope of becoming successful prostitutes or porn stars precisely because they expect nothing but back-breaking labour, horrible marriages and early death from hunger and illness if they can't get into the sex industry. They are not being lured away from college educations and highly paid jobs by pornographers; they are running to a better life. Why should this option be taken away from them? Are feminists suggesting that, given a choice between starvation and a job in the sex industry, we should prefer to see women starve to death?

Middle-class western women spend very little time considering the options that are open to poor and working-class women if they don't get involved in the sex industry. In good economic times, they may be able to work behind counters or on assembly lines, possibly pay for secretarial training and work their way up to office jobs. But if this is the best that can be hoped for, a woman may decide that when nature has given her what it takes to make it in the porn industry, she might be better off appearing on page 3 and in *Penthouse* once in a while rather than working 35–40 hours a week (or more) for far less money. (Indeed, some sex workers have said they got into the industry because they found office work so demeaning and demoralizing.) In bad economic times, even those counter and factory jobs might not be available; conventional attractiveness is an asset that can promote you out of poverty, so why not use it? The truth is that even office jobs that ostensibly have nothing to do with sex make attractiveness an asset. If you're going to have to sell it anyway, you might as well get the best price. Money is power, and a job in the porn industry could be all that stands between a woman and an abusive marriage.

Of course, once a woman gets into the sex industry, her chances of getting out of it again are not as great. Part of the problem is that employers want references, and 'prostitute' or 'porn model' doesn't cut much ice on your job history. More to the point, such a background is more likely to be a dirty little secret than evidence of work experience and entrepreneurial skills. No matter how successfully you may have been able to promote yourself and make money in the sex industry, the chances are that if you do get a 'straight job', you'll be let go when word gets out that you used to be a sex worker, even if the job is one that uses the same business skills (negotiation, promotion, people-management, etc.). There is also the possibility that you've been arrested for sex work, which has a tendency to put employers off. Of course, this would be no problem at all if sex work were not highly stigmatized and in many cases illegal. Feminists actually make life worse for sex workers by continuing to promote a degraded and negative image of them and agitating for further laws against their work.

Porn as sexual violence

Members of Campaign Against Pornography and similar organizations often maintain that sexually explicit materials are a documentary of violence, made by coercing women into performing in them. The case is sometimes made that all porn showing the performance of sexual acts is made by raping women; the position is that women would not perform the acts at all, or would never perform sex acts for the camera, unless forced to do so. Moreover, some of the images in the subgenre of SM appear to include coercion or violence; this means that they are not acted out, but actually *are* coercion and violence.

Women in and out of the porn industry have pointed out that many of us enjoy heterosexual intercourse, lesbian finger-fucking, fist-fucking or using dildos, performing fellatio, giving and receiving cunnilingus, and quite a few of the other acts that women are said to be unwilling (or even unable) to perform under any circumstances. There appears to be a growing interest among women in SM – or at least overtly acting it out – particularly strong among women who have grown up during the period of the modern feminist movement (currently in their teens, twenties and early thirties). The insistence that women could not be interested in actively taking part in penetrative or paraphiliac sexualities misrepresents women by assigning us a more feminine, non-assertive sexuality that is clearly well in keeping with traditional sexism.

How, then, can women *claim* they enjoy such sexualities? One argument says that we have been brainwashed by men into believing we like penetrative sex. Heterosexual women, presumably, would give up intercourse with men altogether if society didn't keep telling them that they like it; lesbians would never be interested in penetration if the heterosexual model hadn't first been presented to them. Our own experience and knowledge – our testimony – is dismissed out of hand as having come from somewhere else: from society and men. According to Dworkin (in an interview in the *Guardian* late in 1991), the contents of lesbian sex magazines can be explained away with the assertion that sexist society causes the women who pose for these pictures and write these stories to victimize other women. The suggestion is strong that this stigmatized and powerless minority plays an important role in the oppression of women.

This is an utterly dishonest view of women. Many women have learned from sex-negative, sexist society (or, for that matter, from much reactionary feminist anti-sex ideology) that we dislike penetration; a significant number of the women in the baby-boom generation have had to struggle constantly against the belief that men were the ones who really enjoyed 'sex' – intercourse and other instrumental sexual activities. We were actively taught to feel demeaned by explicit representations of sex or even common, non-medical words for it; we were repeatedly told that it was men and only men who really liked 'perverted' sex, were into fetish gear, anal sex, and so on. Lesbians have been under particular pressure throughout the last 20 years to represent a virtually asexual, 'female' sexuality that denied any pleasure in penetration. Freud and Lacan explicitly stated that only men had fetishes. The suggestion has been strong from the very beginning, in fact, that women only lose in sexual negotiations with men. If anti-porn feminists wish to believe it, they are only doing what generations of sexists have always done. Many women have discovered that, despite what misogynistic society has said about 'the feminine', we are as capable of sexual exploration and variety as men are. We may have felt there was something wrong with us because society told us differently, but we learned to trust our own experience; anti-porn feminists would have us believe that Freud was right and our own knowledge doesn't count.

In the case of apparent coercive or violent activities in porn, these are being *acted* out, just as coercive and violent activities are in other movie genres. The insistence that any appearance of coercion in a porn movie must be *real* coercion is simply ludicrous; it is like saying that Ringo Starr was really kidnapped against his will to make *Help*, Sigourney Weaver was really terrorized and in fear for her life in the final scenes of *Alien*, and Warren Beatty actually died violently at the end of *Bonnie and Clyde*. There is far more violence and coercion depicted in mainstream film than in pornography, yet no one suggests that the likes of Paul Newman and Jodie Foster have suffered such terrible abuse in making these images that the entire film industry should be banned.

Even given these arguments, some feminists maintain that women still would not perform sexual acts in front of the camera. The assumptions here are many: that no woman actually has an exhibitionistic impulse; that women know they will be given less credibility by society if they are associated with porn and therefore would never permit such documentary materials to circulate; that women necessarily feel demeaned by the idea of strangers getting turned on while thinking about them, and would never encourage this by providing them with pornographic pictures of themselves for the purpose.

All of these statements are certainly true for a number of women, but not for all of us. Many porn models do not feel demeaned by the idea that their pictures may sexually arouse strangers; they see no harm in it. Some of them, in fact, are turned on by the idea that people are getting excited by looking at them; they often can't understand why other women get so twitchy about what they feel is a sexy experience. Women who know that they were never going to be offered 'credibility' by society don't care whether they are known to be porn models – it's what they do for a living; as long as they aren't standing in national elections (at least in Britain or North America), it doesn't matter. It is worth remembering that women themselves have stigmatized 'pretty' or big-busted women as being innately stupid; it could be overhearing comments to just such an effect that might convince a woman she'll never be given any credit for having a mind, and therefore she might as well sell her looks instead.

Women's home videos

Moreover, many women get into porn from the same impulse that motivates teenage girls to drag their boyfriends into photo-booths to get pictures taken together – they think it's romantic, they enjoy looking at them later and they like having a record of being happy. In this age of video, thousands of women have begun making tapes of their sexual activities with their lovers and husbands. Anti-porn feminists would have us believe that this is all under duress from the men involved. While I do not deny that this surely must happen from time to time, the fact is that many women not only initiate the interest in making these tapes, but they often have to convince their partners to participate. Many men feel very shy and insecure about exposing their bodies and performance to the camera's eye, and may have to talk themselves into playing along. Lesbian lovers are certainly not being coerced by mysterious men into taking private polaroids that no one else will ever see. Some women in America are so pleased with the results of their home videos – much more attractive than what can be found in porn shops, in their estimation – that they have even decided to offer such videos for sale. They are often quite deliberate in intending to improve the porn market with what they believe is a product that both men and women would find superior, something that will not contain the unrealistic and sometimes offensive distortions that come from commercial porn. More than 10,000 such tapes are now available on the porn market in the United States. Buyers say they do indeed find them more realistic, less like the glamorized actors seen in ordinary commercial pornography, and more convincing and enjoyable.

It is easier to misrepresent women's interest in pornography in Britain, where real pornographic videos are illegal. But in America, women make up about half of the porn video market. They are buying and renting films to view by themselves or with partners, and they do not much appreciate the fact that anti-porn feminists have tried to portray them as puppets and victims of pushy men. It is appalling for 'feminists' to persist in claiming that women are not making their own choices in relationships or in the porn industry; we all make different choices for different reasons, and women who have not shared our experience are not authorities on our lives. A woman who has never been in the porn industry has no business claiming that she knows more about a porn model's experience than the porn model herself does. Feminists – like black activists and gay activists – know very well the danger of letting 'objective' outsiders (men, heterosexuals, whites) claim to have greater authority than we do about our own lives.

Women as stupid children

Yet Catharine MacKinnon argued in Minneapolis, in support of the ordinance she and Andrea Dworkin had designed, that women could never make an informed choice to act in pornographic films, and that therefore any agreement to do so must be considered coercion. As feminist writer Wendy McElroy wrote in 'The unholy alliance':

> The definition of coercion was all important. The ordinance was clear. Coercion was deemed to be present even if the woman was of age, she fully understood the nature of the performance, she signed a contract and release, there were witnesses, she was under no threat, and she was fully paid. None of these factors provided evidence of consent.
>
> In essence, consent was not possible. In principle, the woman could not be treated as a consenting adult. By definition, coercion was always present in a pornographic act. MacKinnon later explained that, 'in the context of unequal power (between the sexes), one needs to think about the meaning of consent – whether it is a meaningful concept at all' (Toronto *Star*, 2/17/92). Gloria Steinem, in her introduction to Linda Lovelace's exposé *Out of Bondage* agreed: 'The question is free will: Are the subjects of pornography there by choice, or by coercion, *economic* or physical' [emphasis added].
>
> In other words, if the woman needed or wanted the money offered, this would constitute economic coercion. The politics of society made it impossible for women to fully consent to a pornographic act. Women who thought they had agreed were mistaken. Such women had been so damaged by a male dominated culture that they were not able to give true consent.

MacKinnon was relying on an argument that treated women as infants under the law, unable to make an individual choice to perform in pornography. Women worked hard for many years to gain the right to have our signatures and contracts recognized as legally binding, despite arguments that we were not competent to make and keep legal promises; MacKinnon would throw us back to the days when we were seen as too ignorant and weak-minded to make our own decisions. As McElroy says, 'It is difficult to believe that any form of pornography could be more degrading to women than this attitude.'

But taking a patronizing view of women has been elevated to a science by the anti-pornography feminists. Not only can we not make decisions that they disapprove of, but we cannot even disagree without having our intellect and our dedication to feminism dismissed. They have no willingness whatsoever to credit a woman who holds a varying opinion with having a mind of her own.

All this, in theory, is done in the name of protecting women from degradation, particularly those women who have been 'victimized by pornography' – but do abused women who 'testify' against pornography for the media, fare any better? Not at all. The feminist nannies cluster around women who describe their experiences of abuse to make sure that no one from the other side can speak to them. So certain are they that such women are incapable of handling a simple conversation with another human being who *might* not agree with everything they say – an ordinary risk of common social interaction – that they will interrupt conversation without even listening first to see if their protection is needed. In 1993 I appeared on a late-night chat show about pornography where one woman had been brought in to discuss the behaviour of her abusive husband. Afterwards in the green room, another anti-censorship woman who had appeared on the show, Tuppy Owens, asked what exactly had happened to her. While the young woman was explaining, the anti-pornography activists darted up to them and told Owens, 'Can't you see you're not wanted here?' The woman had been showing no distress, yet they were certain she wanted to be rescued. When I chatted with her about the difficulty of physically removing your belongings when you try to leave a partner you do not trust, the same women came up and demanded that I stop harassing her. They apparently believe that any woman who has been abused is no longer capable of holding an adult conversation for herself.

Andrea Dworkin and other anti-porn campaigners have stated that the women who are in pornography have all previously suffered sexual abuse. I could find no research to support this contention, but even if it were true, what would it mean? People who make such statements seem to be suggesting that choices made by women who have been abused are not sensible choices – that having suffered abuse delegitimizes their decisions. Perhaps, on the contrary, abused women who choose to appear in pornography are doing so in order to retake control of their own bodies. Certainly it should be up to them, and not others, to decide whether this is a useful way to reclaim the decision-making power over their own sexual behaviour.

Whatever happened to worker protection?

The claim of 'economic coercion' is also interesting. Women take many jobs for many reasons, but money is foremost among them. Most women, in fact, end up taking jobs that are highly demanding, are poorly paid, and obtain far less respect from society than goes to men who are in related industries, because, much as we might like to do something else, we are under the constraints of economic necessity. Many people would like to stay at home and work on personal projects or take care of their children, or at least work different hours at different locations – but the need for money defines their activities in a way nothing else does. We are all 'economically coerced' in some manner, both in the jobs we hold and in the conditions of our employment. Miners perform intensive labour under dangerous and stressful conditions, risking black lung and death in cave-ins; has it been suggested that they do it for the scenery? Many secretaries suffer insult and demoralization from employers who do not respect their work and intelligence; is this merely because they love people treating them as if they are stupid and their work requires no skills or attention? Do laundry workers inhale dry-cleaning fumes all day long because they enjoy the smell? Surely 'economic coercion' accounts for the fact that workers tolerate a variety of unpleasant working conditions – why is this only wrong when it involves pornography?

Workers tolerate a variety of unpleasant working conditions

It is also argued that women in the sex industry are sometimes (if not always) mistreated, underpaid and sexually harassed, and may find themselves in dangerous working conditions. Implicit in such a charge is the belief that women are not harassed, underpaid, exposed to danger or mistreated in any other industry. This is obvious nonsense: women died earlier this century in New York's great garment district fire before it was made illegal to lock workers into buildings, and men and women also died in a lock-up shop fire in the poultry industry during the 1980s when the Reagan administration made clear it would not enforce the law. Harassment can occur wherever men and women work together, and there is no industry where women are not economically exploited. For example, despite the popular belief in the US that female engineers can 'write their own ticket' because employers are looking for women to fill affirmative action quotas, women in the field are paid less than equally qualified men in the same jobs, even when they do more work. (I cannot help but notice that my friends who are currently suffering the most overt harassment and discrimination, to say nothing of low pay, are lesbians who work in voluntary organizations; the people who are abusing them are almost uniformly those who hold an anti-porn position.) Sex workers may face special dangers because of the stigma and illegality of their jobs, but their pain is not unique, nor are conditions of harassment and danger uniformly a threat to all of them.

In any other industry, we treat unsafe working conditions as evidence that those conditions should be changed; only when we talk about the sex industry do we hear that the industry itself and its products, rather than the unsafe conditions, should be eliminated. We may decry the materialist attitudes of the legal profession as well as sexism in the field, but we don't maintain that legal services themselves should be unavailable to the people. Even feminists who recognize the amount of discrimination and sexual harassment that goes on in office work do not insist that office *jobs* should be banned.

Perhaps it is time to ask what on earth has happened to the women's liberation movement when women who call themselves feminists speak as if the porn industry is the only one in which women experience exploitation, harassment, rape and abuse. We might also wonder what has happened to the labour movement and the party that claims to represent it when complaints about sex industry conditions evoke not a single suggestion of how to improve the safety of sex workers, but rather campaigns to eliminate their work.

Incitement to sexual hatred

Although the charges against porn that originate in America are imported into Britain as if there were no difference at all between the two countries, it should be remembered that many of the arguments are constructed under assumptions that do not and cannot hold true for Britain under the present legal system. One of these is the constraint on censorship, written into law as a right of free expression under the US Constitution, but nowhere contained in British law. The First Amendment guarantees that 'Congress shall make no law ... abridging the freedom of speech, or of the press', while British law makes clear that no such law could be written, as it would tie the hands of Parliament. American campaigners understand that even if they are successful in bringing in further curbs on pornography, the police and the courts are still under strict restraints in terms of how far they can go in enforcement and interpretation of such laws. In Britain, there are no such constraints, and there is nothing like the strong anti-censorship background that permeates the American left. (Even so, substantial violations have resulted from the anti-drug and anti-child-porn campaigns; the rights of the people are always vulnerable to manipulation.)

Without the equivalent of a First Amendment, it was relatively simple to get laws against racist speech passed in the UK in response to hateful literature that was being distributed by the fascist National Front (NF). The campaign against the NF made censorship respectable on all sides. In every forum, it was taken for granted that the need for such a law was obvious, that no one could object to such a law, and, finally, that the alleged parallels between the NF's racist speech and pornography's sexism mandated a similar law to protect women from incitement to sexual hatred.

What few people acknowledge is that the anti-race-hate content of the Public Order Act 1985 would never have been passed in the first place if the NF's literature hadn't already proven to be deeply unpopular with the majority of people in Britain – it was so blatantly vicious that even more ordinary racists were offended by it. It should also be remembered that once racist sentiments become popular, such laws are not enforced anyway. But some of us would say that the incitement to racial hatred law only sweeps the issue of racism under the carpet, and that plenty of racism, of a more subtle but effective nature, goes on all the time unremarked. Headlines in Britain's popular press use racist terms and phrases that would never appear in a major newspaper in the US, for example.

But America is in some respects a bogeyman for censorship activists in the UK. America is violent: the murder rate for an American city in a single year exceeds that for the whole of Great Britain for several years running. Even in Northern Ireland, it took more than 20 years of civil war for the number of killings to catch up with the number of *annual* murders in New York City. More rapes are reported in America, too. US crime figures are frequently cited as evidence that American freedom of the press – freedom to produce violent material and hard core pornography – leads to a violent society.

However, the people who make these claims neatly neglect to mention the other differences between the United States and Britain: in the United Kingdom, private ownership of handguns is illegal, while guns are widely available in the US; in Britain, our safety net decreases both the desire and the need for criminal activity – the UK still has a National Health Service, for example, while an uninsured American might lose her home to pay for medical costs; and finally, the American feminist movement has kept rape activism so high on the agenda that women are much more likely to report when they are raped. It is clear that British society has more to fear from emulating America's alienating contempt for the poor and unemployed than it does from freedom of the press.

Strangely enough, another difference between Britain and America is that the US in many respects practises even more overt sexual repression than is normally found in the UK. It is extremely difficult to get any positive representations of sexuality into the mass media in America. Visual portrayals of sex have not been carried in American newspapers at all or by the major networks until very recently when the moral right was outraged by the appearance of backsides (and fleeting glimpses of breasts in the dark) in television's *NYPD Blue*. For a long time, suggestions of sexuality were so limited that the word 'pregnant' could not be spoken on US television. For most of their history, the networks had a standard that said that where characters were shown to have had non-marital sex, there had to be negative consequences.

In this way, the perception of sex as unsavoury, dangerous and stupid was actively promoted. When the American equivalent of Mary Whitehouse complained in the early 1990s about all the 'sex on television', he (and it usually is a he – a variety of male conservatives ranging from then Vice President Dan Quayle to virulently anti-woman religious campaigners like Donald Wildmon) was complaining about Rosanne Barr Arnold's character, Rosanne Conner, talking to her daughter Becky about birth control. At the same time, British television audiences were able to see a production of Anne Oakley's *The Men's Room* including a scene in which the principal characters are clearly engaging in fellatio –

you didn't actually see it, but you knew it was happening. The portrayal was lustful but loving, passionate and yet consumed with an innocent playfulness that is alien to most American productions. It is unlikely that it will ever be seen on US network television. (But of course, complaints were made in Britain about the scene in *The Men's Room* – and upheld.)

Similarly, religious fundamentalists in America are still able to prevent most sex education programmes from existing at all, or from having any real content when they do. What limited sex education exists will not be attended by the children of these people anyway; they can refuse their children the opportunity to attend these classes. It is still easily possible for young American males to grow up with the worst of negative, misogynistic and proscriptive attitudes about sex and women. Although teenagers in the United Kingdom have been able to learn some sexual facts as part of their science curriculum, the government announced plans in late 1993 to bring the same error in judgement to British schools. It is no accident that America, a country that tries to keep its children from having any positive knowledge about sex, creates significantly more serial killers per head of population than any other western country. (Be that as it may, adults in America may still freely purchase adult sexual materials that cannot be sold legally in Britain.)

More to the point, racist literature in no way presents a parallel to pornography. The National Front and its allies have always been clear that they hate blacks and would be happy to see them victimized, discriminated against more openly and deported. It would be difficult to find pornography that contained such views about women. Pornography represents men and women (or men and men, or women and women, or various combinations thereof) having sex with each other, something that most of us prefer to engage in with people we like and, with any luck, love. This is a far cry from wishing to kill us all off or have us removed from the country.

The suggestion that there is some obvious connection between racist hate literature, on the one hand, and pictures of men and women having sex together, on the other, seems to be constructed as part of an argument that male sexual desire is *about* violence: that the desire for sex and the desire to harm or kill are inseparable, and that men cannot want women without subjecting us to violence. This is a wholly unrealistic view of male sexuality, portraying men as uniformly brutal, rapacious, murderous aggressors. More, it is a remarkably risky view of men to promote, as it is hardly in women's interest to convince men that they are normally monstrous in their sexual desires – and therefore freaks if they are not. It would be unsurprising if some future rapist should attempt to justify himself in court by citing the 'feminist' writings of a woman who had portrayed male sexuality in this way as if it were normal. There is no evidence that the average male's sexual fantasies, with or without pornography, involve committing mayhem against his sexual partners.

This view of male desire is insulting not only to men, but also to women. Many females have reported loving relationships that involve a great deal of sexual experimentation, even including the use of pornography. Many of us have said we have looked at pornography and not felt any sense of threat or degradation. Blacks do not report similar pleasure or lack of anger when seeing racist material. Are women so much more stupid that we can all be looking at these continuous portrayals of hatred against us, making love with men who are actually violent towards us, without noticing it? Or isn't it possible that women who enjoy pornography can tell the difference between bad relationships and good ones, hate literature and erotic materials?

Meanwhile, it is rather depressing to watch 'anti-racists' pat themselves on the back for getting the incitement to racial hatred law passed while the dialogue on racism in society has become so quiet that most white people can ignore it completely, and racism itself proceeds as usual. British racism has certainly not died out in the meantime. In fact, a unit of the Ku Klux Klan in Scotland has become surprisingly vocal.

In Article 19's *Striking a Balance*, edited by Sandra Coliver, a variety of contributors demonstrated the ways in which hate-speech laws have been used all over the world against those the law was meant to protect. In Britain, the law against incitement to racial hatred has been used to silence black activists, as the anti-hate law in Canada has been used against both blacks and women. As in Britain, so in America: campaigns to silence race hatred on campus at America's universities have not stimulated actual discussion of ways to address genuine concerns of racial minorities; on the contrary, coded racism has become increasingly acceptable at the same time.

In France, when Jean-Marie Le Pen was prosecuted for violating race-hate laws, he toned his speech down and made it appear more sensible – and was elected to the legislature. In Britain, characterizing the racial problem as a 'housing shortage' problem, the British National Party (BNP), which normally loses its election deposits, actually won a seat in September of 1993. Although not as overt as the BNP paper, the tabloids carried the same message – and, indeed, helped give the BNP position its aura of respectability.

Let us hope that feminists never accomplish so much on behalf of the fight against sexism.

The image of women

In numerous articles and speeches, Catherine Itzin has stated that in pornography, 'women are cunts'. It would be interesting to ask what, precisely, she means by this. Women in pornography are often portrayed without clothing, although not necessarily in a way that places the focus on the cunt itself. In some magazines, there are photographs in which the camera does focus quite specifically on this part of the body, sometimes with the outer labia held open so that the clitoris, inner labia and vaginal opening can be more clearly seen. In some photos and films, women are shown masturbating with the camera zoomed in as close as possible to the action. Faces, breasts, buttocks, bellies, legs, backs and full body shots are also shown. Women in films are often seen giving and receiving cunnilingus as well as performing fellatio. They are frequently shown fucking with men, or using dildos or hand-fucking in some way with women, as well as being manually manipulated or penetrated by men. They also kiss and lick other parts of their partners' bodies, and are kissed and licked in return, as well as exchanging caresses with partners. This is the content of most pornography. (There is far less concentration on genitals in most SM materials.)

In what way, then, are women 'cunts' when portrayed this way? Certainly the camera looks at cunts, in the same way that the camera looks at other parts of the body. Similarly, women in advertising could be said to be portrayed as 'hands', in the sense that they are shown using dishwashing liquids, putting plates into the dryer, handling other housekeeping implements, mopping floors, making food, and doing numerous other jobs meant to make life easier for others – the people who do not do the cooking and washing, presumably. They are 'helping hands' rather than hands with real power. However, no one complains that women are portrayed as mere 'hands' when presented in this way. Being portrayed as 'helping hands' would be superior to being portrayed as 'cunts' in this context only if one takes for granted that there is something intrinsically nasty about cunts, or having a cunt, in the first place.

Women could be seen as 'cunts' in pornographic film if one perceives women as being indistinguishable from inanimate objects and ignores the activities and uses of other parts of the body. Women might also be perceived as cunts if one assumes that, in sexual acts, women lose our individuality, our personal quirks, our differing needs and tastes, and become identical – mindless receptacles for male pleasure. That would mean that, in fact, even if we are not appearing in pornography but merely having private sex with a lover, we are always 'cunts'. Itzin's rhetoric seems to place the sexual woman into this context virtually all the time, but is that the message of pornography, or Itzin's own degraded view of women who associate themselves with sexuality – who have cunts and use them for pleasure?

In *Pornography*, Andrea Dworkin uses similarly abusive language towards sex workers. She seems to accept the Victorian perception of sexual women whole, without any taint of feminist consciousness. As Gayle Rubin notes in 'Misguided, dangerous and wrong':

> Contempt towards sex workers, especially prostitutes, is one of the most disturbing aspects of the anti-porn invective. Throughout her book, *Pornography*, Dworkin uses the stigma of prostitution to convey her opprobrium and make her argument against pornography. She says, 'Contemporary pornography strictly and literally conforms to the word's root meaning: the graphic depiction of *vile whores*, or in our language, sluts, cows (as in: *sexual cattle, sexual chattel*), *cunts*.' This is a degrading and insulting description of prostitutes. Feminists should be working to remove stigma from prostitution, not exploiting it for rhetorical gain.

Dworkin's definition of pornography as referring to 'vile whores' is often repeated by anti-porn campaigners, who seem convinced that *'porne'* actually refers to a female so low that we can barely imagine her degraded status. Feminists Against Censorship occasionally receives letters from women who seek to enlighten us on the matter, repeating Dworkin's 'vile whores' refrain and stating that the *pornea* were 'the lowest form of prostitute, literally and figuratively the cheapest, available to every man in Greece'. What fine distinction do they think separated the *pornea* from other prostitutes? We know why they were reviled by the Victorians, as any sexually expressive or active woman would have been, but in ancient Greece there were the temple prostitutes, who operated on a different basis from ordinary commercial whores. The sexual services of the *pornea*, like those of the denizens of modern brothels, were sold in direct exchange for money. In Victorian England, the only acceptable alternative to this was to exchange sexual services for marriage.

Sexist society has always found prostitutes reprehensible: a whore will have sex for money with different men, rather than selling her sexual services exclusively to one husband and then having to hope that he will spend the household money on her and her needs (and her children's needs) in useful ways. Prostitutes have an unconscionable sexual licence, which they use for their own purposes instead of the purposes of men, the family and society. Prostitutes cater to male sexual desire outright, for direct payment, rather than merely manipulating it for social respectability and family stability. We occasionally hear condemnation of pimps who may abuse the whores who work for them, but the tenor of the discussion and the resulting laws most often bring the full weight of both social hatred and legal punishment down on the female prostitutes, rather than on the male pimps or clients. No wonder so many sex workers suspect feminists of being motivated by jealousy and self-hatred.

The feminine role

Anti-pornography feminists often make the claim that sexual material casts women entirely in the feminine role, as sexual servants to men. This is a misapprehension of the role women are meant to play, sexually, in traditional sexist society. Far from being mere sexual servants to men, we are meant to be their keepers, satisfying their sexual needs only as much as we must in order to keep them in the home, away from other women, and under control.

The classic model of sexuality that was most strongly in force prior to the sexual revolution held that sex was a nasty business that men, animalistically, felt a compulsion for, but women, more pure and refined, had no taste for. Since men were easily triggered to sexual desire, wives were forced to a certain extent to tolerate such urges in their husbands, principally in order to keep those urges from manifesting, anti-socially, outside of the home. Male sexuality was seen as explosive if not carefully controlled, possibly leading to violence and criminal activity unless directed towards the appropriate female receptacle. It was considered to be unfortunate at worst if somehow male violence also had to be accepted in the home; better there than on the streets.

It was understood that men were largely unable to control themselves sexually, and thus it was the duty of women to keep all thoughts of sex, or anything that might arouse sexual thoughts, hidden and suppressed. This job was so important that any woman who failed in it deserved immediate punishment. Arousing thoughts of sex in men inappropriately

Feminists versus feminists 145

was a female sin; more, it was a major social crime. If women 'provoked' men, they deserved to be raped. This was true of even the most brutal gang rape. Women who went out at night alone deserved whatever they got – why else would they be in the streets without an escort or chaperone after dark if they were not whores?

During the period of the sexual revolution, women demanded the right to travel freely, wear revealing clothing, and socialize with men, despite our mothers' warnings. We took for granted that rape was not a normal result of such behaviour – as our experience generally proved, since we were not raped every time we did these things – and insisted that neither miniskirts nor independent behaviour could be said to promise sex or justify sexual violence. Lacking a feminist language to crystallize such thoughts, we had to brazen it out. But when a woman who wore a miniskirt, travelled alone or otherwise engaged in 'risky' behaviour actually was raped, Victorian morality – or even the morality of the Inquisition – was in full force during the rape trial. Miniskirts 'provoked' rape; travel at night, or being alone with a man, was seen to have promised sex, and thus no refusal of sexual demands by the woman was meaningful. Some judges still express such views from the bench, and it is a common theme in defence arguments.

The assumption that male misbehaviour is really down to female misbehaviour has been with us so long that we hardly question it. Even decades of anti-rape activism seem to mean nothing once the suggestion is made that, thanks to those women who take off their clothes in front of a camera, the men just cannot control themselves. Is it too much to ask feminists to realize that this is nonsense, that most men do indeed control themselves, and that neither women in miniskirts nor women in minimal underwear 'provoke' rape? It should be obvious that the 'porn causes rape' argument is nothing more than a slightly more sophisticated version of blaming (highly stigmatized, largely powerless) women for the anti-social behaviour of a minority of men.

Now, rather than saying that a woman in a miniskirt invited her own rape, we pretend that some other woman incited the rapist. A common argument against pornography says that porn 'misrepresents' women by portraying us as being willing to participate in sex for the sheer pleasure of it. The presumption, of course, is that we *cannot* participate in sex for the sheer pleasure of it, which can only lead to the conclusion that any woman who appears to do so is harming other women.

This view of female sexuality is thoroughly evil and manifestly anti-woman. Any feminist should certainly know by now that many women do enjoy sex very much, but doing it for love alone, without lust, has usually proven to be a tedious, degrading and painful event for most of us. It is shameful that self-proclaimed 'anti-sexist' men and 'feminists' can run around maintaining that women are not competent to make free choices to participate in instrumental sexual activities or pornography because we are too 'brainwashed' to understand how oppressed we are. Discouraging women from sexual exploration has been vital in making us feel we have to tolerate bad sex; we are entitled to find out what we want without having the church, our mothers, or our 'sisters' telling us what we aren't supposed to like.

Some feminists have not forgotten the misery of being expected to satisfy the needs of husbands and society because our own sexual desires were not meaningful. Why, then, should we settle for a new 'feminist' instruction to ignore our own sexual curiosity and go back to our old 'feminine' job of suppressing sexual thoughts in men? If women are to achieve any kind of freedom from oppression, it must mean that each of us owns her own body – not just her womb, but her sexuality as well. This must necessarily include the right to park our naked bodies in front of cameras if we so choose. We are not just tools from which society can build itself to its own ends; in the same way that we have argued that we do not owe unwanted pregnancies to the state or free sex to rapists, neither do we owe our sexual behaviour to society, to abstract ideals of 'the family', or to the most vocal members of the current feminist movement.

8
A dangerous game

Some feminists believe that anti-pornography feminism is a safe way to keep the arguments about sexism and violence in society going. Pornography, they believe, cannot possibly be a *necessary* part of society, and therefore banning it will do no harm. Moreover, if 'just one woman', or one child, is protected by the elimination of pornography, it is suggested, then it will all be worth it.

While it is certainly true that the feminist anti-porn movement has helped to keep mention of rape and abuse in the public eye, it is not so certain that it is by any means 'safe'. The focus on pornography as the source of harm has been so intense as to distract completely from addressing the recognized causes of women's poor position in society – such as economic inequality – and the real vulnerability of children.

No doubt many of us could live happily without ever seeing a pornographic film. On the other hand, we are not so happy about living with the effects of anti-pornography rhetoric, which at this point has so overwhelmed any opposing view that it has come to obscure the real problems involved with rape and domestic abuse, and made it difficult to address the very real effects of repressiveness that generate violence in offenders. There are many programmes that might genuinely improve life for women and children; little energy is being spent on them of late.

Some people truly believe that the feminist movement has been restored by having a new single-issue campaign to organize around. This might have been true if the issue in question was one that feminists could agree on. Given the media focus on the anti-porn movement – and, most importantly, the anti-porn feminists' representation of themselves as holding the only possible feminist position – the disastrous split the campaign has brought to feminism has not been visible to all. But that split has had profound effects, forcing many women to retreat from the movement altogether, and creating animosity between many of those who remain. Women who might have been allies in defending women's refuges, AIDS activism, child-care provision, abortion rights, lesbian mothers, family planning clinics, gay media and the like have instead become each other's opponents in this one, debatable cause. Perhaps it's time to ask if it really *has* been worth it.

A dream deferred

One of the first casualties of the anti-porn movement has been women's sense of confidence in being able to walk tall and fearlessly when we go out by ourselves. Much of the rhetoric paints a picture of streets filled with rapists poised outside our doors, waiting to assault us the moment we emerge.

It took tremendous bravery for women in the 1960s to ignore our mothers' warnings and go out on our own knowing we would be held responsible if we were attacked, and it is that very bravery that has made it possible for young women to go out in the evening today knowing they won't be blamed if someone attacks them. Women do get raped in the street from time to time, but it is hardly part of the routine of stepping out of the house, and the fact that this is recognized means that if we do get raped when we are out on our own, we are no longer likely to be asked why we didn't expect it. Yet anti-porn rhetoric makes it sound as if a woman *should* expect to be raped whenever she leaves her home. If this goes on, it won't be long before rape victims are being asked, once again, 'What were you doing out there? What did you expect?'

The talk of danger *in the street*, along with the persistent blame of pornography as a source of fear, provides neat camouflage for some more worrying facts about rape: like the fact that, although even according to the inflated statistics of anti-porn women, only 12–14 per cent of women who've been raped say pornography was involved in any way, more than *40 per cent* say that the men who raped them were their husbands. Clearly, there is something about marriage that presents hazards to women – something that is not being acknowledged in all this quibbling over pornography. The real danger is not in the street, but in the home, where traditional perceptions of marital roles – which do not come from pornography – still hold the strongest influence in allowing men to believe they can freely subject their wives to violence. Feminists have always recognized that long-held beliefs about woman's role in marriage had oppressive and dangerous effects on our lives – or at least we *did* recognize it, until it became convenient to blame it all on pornography. Feminist analysis of marriage was another immediate casualty of 'feminist' anti-porn activity.

Yet Catharine MacKinnon has said that, 'A critique of pornography is to feminism what its defense is to male supremacy.' Gayle Rubin quite rightly responded, 'I disagree. In MacKinnon's work and that of other anti-porn feminists, the critique of pornography has been substituted for a critique of male supremacy.' Nowhere is this more obvious than in the complete failure to consider previous criticisms of the role of marriage and religious 'family values' in maintaining the attitudes that promote violence against women.

The recognition that the danger of violence to women was so strong *in the home* once led us to create refuges for battered women – havens to which they could retreat when violence drove them out into the street. While the remainder of feminist attention has been directed towards pornography, those refuges have starved for funding while one woman after another, receiving no help from the law, the police and the courts, has found herself so desperate that she feels she has no other option but to kill the man who has been beating her – and, naturally, she usually goes to jail for murder. Refuge workers estimate that there are approximately three abused women seeking refuge for every one bed available in a women's shelter, but no new funding is available. The government knows that no one is looking, so no support will come from that quarter. The moral right always opposed women's refuges anyway – even the most abused wife belonged with her husband, as far as they were concerned. Thousands of women have been left with nowhere to go, thrown back into violent homes, yet anti-porn feminists in the 1980s seemed curiously unconcerned about whether 'just one' of *these* women might have been saved by more devotion to dealing with real, rather than metaphorical, violence. Or is the 'violence' of seeing a photograph of a nude women so great that it overshadows the mere triviality of being hospitalized by your husband's fists?

Fortunately, the interest in pornography may actually have played a role in reminding anti-porn women of what anti-censorship feminists already knew: that domestic violence itself is an issue, even without pornography. In January 1994, the Association of London Authorities launched the Zero Tolerance campaign against sexual violence – not a minute too soon. Although members of FAC are involved, it does seem to be driven by participation from some anti-porn women who perceive violence itself as male, and this is hinted at in some of their launch materials. Most of those do not mention pornography, but the description of Hackney Council's programmes does hint at a perceived relationship between porn and violence. Again, there is rather too much emphasis on what seems to be a near-universal tendency towards violence in males. One of the posters from the campaign says that behind successful men there are abused women, implying that no man succeeds without personally abusing a female partner; this simply is not true. And female violence is not discussed. It is worth remembering that child battering, which maims and kills thousands of children, is principally a problem of female violence – a matter that has received scant attention from anti-porn women.

Family planning, too, is someone else's problem. Once upon a time, feminists understood the direct relationship between being unable to control reproduction and the low earning power – and consequent lack of power in society – of women. The phrase 'barefoot and pregnant' was still too fresh in memory for us to pretend that unwanted pregnancy was not a serious threat to our ability to take control of our lives. We saw all too clearly the terrible price women paid – dropping out of school and jobs, and into hasty and often brutal marriages – to take reproductive freedom lightly. The availability of birth control had a profound effect in making the modern women's liberation movement possible – it gave women the opportunity to choose for ourselves whether we would have children, and when, and with whom. Marie Stopes was attacked by the Catholic church, and Margaret Sanger fought obscenity laws and went to jail, to give us this right; they knew exactly what they were doing, and we owe them a tremendous debt. But while feminists have looked elsewhere, family planning clinics have been closing down, and few activists are fighting to see that young women will still have access to protection from the unwanted pregnancies that can cut short their dreams and eliminate their freedom.

The list of feminist programmes that have been put on hold – or worse, been turned around – as a result of anti-pornography feminism is excruciatingly long. From better street lighting to equality of hiring and promotion in the workplace, little can be heard over the roar of demands for censorship. To many of us, the sound of anti-pornography 'feminism' is the sound of women being betrayed.

Most visibly, women in the sex industry are being betrayed by both the harsh language that is directed at them and the moves to create laws and social movements that would place them in further jeopardy. Anti-pornography activists are happy to exploit the danger some sex workers face if it helps to make points in favour of censorship, but they appear to care nothing for the fact that as anti-porn rhetoric heats up, so does life for sex workers. Even where pornography is entirely illegal, women get into the industry because it is a source of income – the law makes their lives more dangerous, gets them thrown in jail, makes it impossible for them to enforce contracts or press charges when they are abused or to organize for safer working conditions, but it doesn't eliminate sex work, it doesn't eliminate violence, and it certainly doesn't eliminate the dangers that come from illegality and stigma.

Anti-porn rhetoric also encourages victimization of prostitutes, making the night streets more dangerous for all women – a day may yet come when no woman can walk through the King's Cross area of London without being arrested. The English Collective of Prostitutes noted in a recent campaign that possession of condoms has lately been treated by police as evidence of prostitution – if they try to protect themselves from disease, they increase their chances of being jailed. That's quite a choice to expect a woman to make, especially in this age of AIDS. 'Feminist' anti-porn activism has encouraged this contemptuousness toward sex workers. Is this how feminists 'protect women'?

Arguments that place the blame for sexual violence on pornography merely accuse women at one remove of inciting male aggression. Sex workers need no further contempt from society, but 'feminist' anti-porn campaigns supply it anyway.

How many of our sisters – battered wives, unwillingly pregnant teenagers, AIDS-infected prostitutes – are we willing to sacrifice in order to protect 'just one woman' from pornography? Will it really be worth it? Some of us find it hard to think so.

Throwing our sisters and brothers to the wolves

Anti-censorship activists often point out that no matter what is claimed, sexual censorship virtually always ends up victimizing dissenters, sex radicals and gays while leaving the institutions of patriarchy and the fact of violence unchanged. This, of course, is what happened in Canada, where, under the new 'feminist' anti-porn law, the first 'degrading' material the enforcers noticed just happened to be a lesbian magazine in a gay bookshop. Although 'feminist' anti-porn rhetoric intended to bring in legal restraints concentrates on the degradation presumed to be found in *heterosexual* images and the implications for *heterosexual* violence, the police apparently believed that the best place to look for such content was in *gay* media sold in *gay* establishments. Why? Because it is an affront to sexual repressives that gay media and gay bookshops exist – if they can be driven out of business by using the excuse that gay material is 'degrading', that's fine with the repressives. The police and courts are not noted for giving a high priority to promoting gay rights and feminism, it should be recalled.

More recently, two feminist books specifically meant to illuminate and counter sexism, sexual violence and coercion have been stopped from entering Canada under the Dworkin–MacKinnon law: *Pornography: Men possessing women* and *Woman Hating*, both by Andrea Dworkin.

And why on earth did women who call themselves feminists flock so enthusiastically to the Meese Commission hearings on pornography? Edwin Meese and his cronies absolutely *hate* feminists, as their wing of the Republican Party made abundantly clear at their annual convention in 1992. Feminism, Republican candidate Patrick Buchanan told his political allies, is a philosophy that causes women to leave their husbands, kill their babies, turn to lesbianism, become witches and overthrow capitalism (capitalism being fundamentally the personal God of the new right extremists). Were men like this going to *help* feminists to eliminate sexism?

Clearly not. The commissioners for the Attorney General's hearings made manifest their distaste for both sex and feminism throughout the proceedings. Carole Vance noted that the phrase 'degrading to women' used by feminists became 'degrading to femininity' in their mouths. It was abundantly obvious that these people were not talking about the same thing, and yet even after hearing them define *lesbianism* as being degrading to women, Andrea Dworkin seemed to expect the right-wing men on the panel to deliver a feminist result. At one point in the proceedings a porn star got up to testify that she did not share the panel's negative view of her work, and was virtually dismissed as a tart whose word could not have any credibility.

All of this could have been predicted from the simple fact that the moral right had enthusiastically called for and supported the proceedings from the very beginning. The commission was no more likely to take a feminist view than Pope John Paul II was to advocate free abortion on demand. History in Indianapolis (see Chapter 4) would also have told feminists that they could not trust these people. Yet they came to testify and offered their support as if these anti-feminist men were indistinguishable from Gloria Steinem and Robin Morgan. The resulting Pornography Victim's

A dangerous game 153

Compensation Act 1992 did not use the 'feminist' definition of porn, but was based on the usual conservative attitudes toward sex. Yet some anti-pornography 'feminists', even in Britain, still cite the Meese Commission's official report as being reliable 'evidence' against pornography as defined by feminists.

A present to the government – on a silver platter

In the wake of anti-pornography feminism in Britain, the government has felt free to ban materials that no one has objected to: Red Hot Television was made unavailable to the public despite the fact that there was no real support for such a ban (see Chapter 7); additionally, pictures of erections and penetration are still illegal, although few people think they should be. Moreover, the nature of the arguments against porn, that spend so much verbiage defining it as violence and specifically stigmatizing SM representation, has helped the police to victimize gay men who are involved in SM sex or using fetish gear. In Operation Spanner, consensual activity was prosecuted as 'assault' and men who were harming no one (including the supposed 'victims' of the 'assaults') were given jail sentences, had their pictures published in the newspapers, lost their jobs and had their families victimized as well. No doubt the opprobrium that was heaped on these men from every quarter for their harmless activities encouraged the judges who condemned them, but it was clear from the legal opinions that what they were truly being convicted of was homosexuality. One judge even explicitly stated that he hoped a stint in jail would cause the men to turn to heterosexuality. (Feminists Against Censorship was the only feminist group to point out that the attack on SM was an attack on our right to control our bodies. Our campaign transformed much public opinion that accepted Spanner as a 'rightful' suppression of harmful conduct, and made many people recognize it as a human rights issue. For this, of course, we have been attacked as part of an 'SM mafia'.)

During the summer of 1993, FAC was notified that the police authorities had raided the home of a gay man believed to be involved in SM in the hope of finding illegal materials; when they did not, the police went to the employers of their victim and talked them into forcing him to resign. (So, having no cause to arrest him, they tried to ruin his life anyway.) Not only is this a message directed at the gay community as a whole, but a warning for all of us, regardless of our sexual practice, that the most intimate details of our personal lives have become the property of a prurient-minded and repressive police force – and that we needn't even break the law to be victimized.

Her Majesty's Customs and Excise did not always meddle in the private affairs of individuals who brought tapes with sexual material into the country for what was obviously private use, but nowadays even private tapes of yourself are up for the leering eye of Customs and will be taken away. It was disturbing enough when lesbian videos from America were seized from Jenny White, a lesbian grandmother; but even more shocking was the case of one couple who, when they returned to Britain from a stay in Australia and brought with them the videotapes they had made of their own love-making – tapes never intended to be seen by anyone else – were horrified to discover that while the staff of the Customs service and its legal paraphernalia could ogle those tapes and pass judgement on their 'indecent' nature, they themselves were no longer entitled to possess them. *Time Out*'s Catherine Pepinster interviewed one of the victims, Annie Macnamara:

> 'The thought that these people and God knows who else have been watching us making love sickens me,' said Annie. 'Do people really have any right to take a look at something which was so personal to us, and so private?'
>
> For two years, the Macnamaras have struggled to get their tapes returned. But Customs have formidable, even draconian powers. They can act as judge and jury in deciding whether to search individuals or confiscate their goods, and many policemen express envy of their powers. No Customs officer, for example, has to explain why he thinks material is obscene before he confiscates it.

We are speaking here of materials that are freely on sale and can be sent through the mails in other European and English-speaking countries. Yet in Britain, mere possession of such items is an excuse for the authorities to interfere in our intimate lives.

Exactly who is served by such invasive practices? One might almost gather that the Customs have deliberately set themselves up with their own free pornographic video service, even when it is against the will of the 'models' involved. They can also barge into people's homes and go through our private papers, dairies, home movies and photographs *and confiscate them* – and we have virtually no protection from these invasions. The power that the Customs service has acquired through our fear of pornography exploits innocent victims in a way that professional pornographers have never been able to.

The Criminal Justice and Public Order Bill 1994

Just before the holidays at the end of 1993, a new Criminal Justice Bill was introduced. Most commentators agree that the timing of the Bill was a deliberate attempt to minimize press coverage and awareness of its content. When the second reading was scheduled as early as 11 January 1994, it seemed the government was attempting to rush it through before anyone noticed. The Criminal Justice and Public Order Bill 1994 shocked those who read it; virtually every section revealed attempts by the government to give extensive powers of arrest to the police, criminalize harmless behaviours, and generally run roughshod over the civil liberties of the British people. The right to silence, right to protest, rights of travellers and gypsies and rights of privacy were being abridged so thoroughly that it was difficult to forget that the government's targets are not dissimilar to those of the Third Reich.

Most troubling for anti-censorship campaigners, of course, was Part VII of the Bill, making violations under Section 2 of the Obscene Publications Act (1959) arrestable offences. It is illegal to possess hard core pornography (material showing genital contact, erections or penetration) for gain, although, theoretically, an individual might reasonably be allowed to possess small amounts of such material for entirely private enjoyment. However, private use is not in and of itself a defence. Be that as it may, the police have always had to acquire a warrant before searching a person's home, which meant that they had to show reasonable cause for suspicion. If this is an *arrestable* offence, that means the police don't need a warrant; they can arrest you first and search your home without having to demonstrate any reason whatsoever for doing so. It is up to you to prove that you did not possess the materials 'for gain'.

As this is being written, the disposition of the Bill is not known, but many people fear that it will pass. Part VII will never even be discussed. The government has claimed it is curtailing 'pornography', which the public has been led to believe is violent and degrading material, as anti-pornography activists have defined it; but what is really being controlled is largely non-violent, inoffensive material showing common, ordinary sexual contact. Most people do not believe such materials are harmful and are not even aware that they are illegal; quite a few people who are not involved in harmful activities can easily be victimized under Britain's obscenity laws because they innocently have such material in their homes. Such a law can be selectively used to harass people who don't meet with the approval of the government or the police – gays, social activists, feminists. This is how such laws are normally used. (When the head of one anti-censorship organization, David Webb of the National Campaign for the Reform of the Obscene Publications Acts, was returning to Britain, Customs agents who saw his business card decided to search his home. This would seem to suggest that he was being legally harassed because he was an *anti-censorship campaigner*, not because there was reason to believe he had actual contraband materials for gain.)

Anti-pornography women claim their attacks on pornography are meant to protect women from 'degradation' – but instead they have made women like Annie Macnamara the victims of degradation she would never otherwise have suffered. As feminist writer Ellen Willis has wondered, 'How long will it take oppressed groups to learn that if we give the state enough rope, it will end up around our necks?'

Aid and comfort to the thought police

Throughout the women's liberation movement, it was always acknowledged that we had to be free to explore our own sexuality rather than rely on the received wisdom of a sexist culture that used our own repression to keep us under control. This necessarily meant that we would be discussing and depicting sexual issues and sex itself in a variety of ways ranging from consciousness raising to media presentation. No sooner did we start to create books, magazines and movies on such subjects than objectors came out of the woodwork to stop us. Books that specifically discussed female biology and sexuality were quickly targeted as 'obscene', as was Judy Grahn's moving lesbian poetry. The Customs service has seen to it that books, videos and comics intended to explore sexual politics are kept out of the United Kingdom whenever possible, as well as the lesbian magazines published in America and Australia. It is no longer necessary to wait for moralists on the right to launch such campaigns; the 'feminist' anti-porn movement has given them all the support that they need.

Every arm of the government that can be involved in censorship now feels free to stop sex education materials from coming into the country, harass gallery owners, snoop into our mail and, most recently, seize our computers and disks. The anti-computer porn campaign that the authorities began in 1993 is particularly frightening, since it would clearly be necessary to give the police full powers to monitor all phone lines. It's all justified on the basis of endless babble about how pornography is 'offensive' and creates 'harm' – although some people wonder whether this isn't just an effort by the police to get free access to our private communications; in America, the government has made no pretence to be concerned with pornography and has been trying to force high-tech communicators to use encryption devices that have 'back-door' codes available to federal agencies so that they could automatically spy on them. The people who actually enforce and make judgements about the 'indecent' and 'harmful' nature of pornographic materials (or those that they claim are pornographic) are those who have a disturbing tendency to find the human body and ordinary sexual practice deeply offensive in a way that most of us do not; they are deciding what we *should* be offended by, whether or not we actually are.

And we are in no position to quarrel. Videos are seized by Customs because they are 'indecent' – we can contest, and sometimes even win, if we can afford to spend the thousand or so pounds required by an attempt to retrieve our belongings. Lesbian books, videos and magazines are taken by Customs and, they claim, destroyed. The economic costs of losses of artistic property alone are enough to stop people from ever trying to import materials with any sexual content. Does this serve feminists? Hardly. Sexist men decide what we can say, and can point to 'feminist' rhetoric to stop feminist materials. Sheer economic factors keep us from being able to demand that the law serve the people instead of the other way around. No police state asks for anything more.

And what has happened to the exploration of female sexuality? With anti-porn, anti-sexual rhetoric permeating the airwaves and most high-profile feminist groups, we have been reduced to arguing over whether we should be *allowed* to define our own sexuality. Every path we might wish to investigate has been boarded up with bright 'Keep Out' signs – one would gather that anything more than holding hands is too oppressive and sexist to be considered. Women who attempt to represent their own sexuality are told that they *cannot* have such a sexuality, and it must be rejected. This criticism was used to attack Della Grace when her book of lesbian photography, *Love Bites*, was released (see Chapter 4). And every reprehensible argument that was ever made against gay rights mysteriously becomes acceptable when it is recast in this supposedly feminist mould to prohibit sexual exploration for women. Dworkin says we can't like fucking, Jeffreys says we must reject men and use other women as substitutes in nominally 'lesbian' relationships, they all say we can't wear leather or lacy underwear, and no one wants to ask women what we actually want to do. So much for the opening of possibilities and choice that women's liberation once promised.

Hypocrisy = death

The one important health matter that continues to make headlines is the AIDS crisis, which has now become a clear peril to women – particularly heterosexual women. Educational programmes and research in the gay community have demonstrated that for gay men, explicit pornographic methods are the most effective in disseminating safer sex information. For young heterosexuals, it is vital that clear, graphic materials demonstrating the proper use of condoms be openly available. Yet the anti-pornography movement has made this increasingly difficult, being more worried about the depiction of sex than the spread of a condition that brings people to an early death.

In our movies and on our television screens, we have always been able to portray the most reprehensible human behaviours. We can show war, fire-bombing, riots. We can portray crucifixion, one of the most odious forms of lethal torture that human beings have ever been guilty of. But we cannot show a condom being rolled over an erect cock. We can show a documentary segment in which a little girl is held down screaming in the dirt while the village women oversee the destruction of her genitals with a rock or piece of glass. But we cannot show the healthy genitals of a woman being kissed by a lover.

What are we telling people – including children – when we make clear that sex alone is so odious that we cannot depict it honestly, when we can see and show everything else? Are we really willing to be responsible for making even the worst violence and brutality seem less loathsome than sex – for making both sexual play and responsible contraception and prophylaxis seem more fearful than to brutalize and kill other human beings? Are feminists really willing to be party to reinforcing such notions? In America, where anti-pornography feminism has its roots, female genital mutilation is not even illegal; until very recently, there was no sign of a feminist campaign against it. Why were feminists objecting to images of sexual pleasure when they were not campaigning against the destruction of female sexuality?

With more and more women now becoming infected with AIDS, one would have thought the time for dithering over whether we can show sexuality and genitalia was long past. We have already lost numerous friends and creators to this condition – a painfully large number of them the bright young gay men of our generation. It is getting awfully late in the day, but we should be demanding honest and accurate portrayals of sexuality involving safer sex and positive sexual values, and doing our best to eradicate the sex-negative attitudes that have made the sexual destruction of women and the callous treatment of AIDS sufferers more acceptable than health, life and pleasure.

Keeping us vulnerable

The position of children and the conditions under which they are raised have always been crucial in the formation and maintenance of sexist culture. We learn power relationships early in life, within the family, and we relate to power quite specifically in terms of its manifestation in roles within the family; we negotiate our own power in relation to our respective parents, and we value each of those parents according to their relationships with power.

But anti-pornography campaigns encourage the right-wing, 'pro-family' ideologues to attack what they perceive as 'anti-family' values such as gay rights, sex education, and unconventional relationships or child-rearing methods. By becoming allied with these people, even if just on a single issue, feminists have actually encouraged the suppression of our own programmes and analysis.

Whether they come from the left or the right, campaigns to suppress sexual material contain so much 'anti-filth' and anti-sex propaganda that it becomes almost impossible to address vital issues like sex education, disease prevention and contraception for the young. Fifty years of experience in examining the causes of sexual violence, along with feminist analysis of the costs of early pregnancy for young women, have made it abundantly clear that to make any real headway in improving the position of women in society we need a broad educational campaign directed specifically at teaching sexual rights and responsibilities, as well as simple facts, to young people.

More than two decades of modern feminist activity, despite its many successes, have largely failed to change the environment in which children learn myth and lies about sex and gender, because our programmes have been kept firmly aimed at adults. Young people may see more sexy images in advertising, but informationally, their situation has not improved much. And for all the rhetoric we hear about protecting children from exploitation, hardly a soul bothers to mention children's rights or empowerment.

What few experimental programmes exist have established that children who know about sex and understand that their bodies belong to them are far more likely to be able to resist sexual abuse. We also know that such young people are less prone to accept or perpetuate later sexual violence and dangerous, unprotected sex, as long as protective measures are available to them. Yet in spite of the overwhelming evidence that these programmes can actually reduce the likelihood of harm to children and to women in society, we have expended little of our collective energy on trying to bring information and help to young people.

Puritanism and over-protectiveness have made it impossible to enact programmes that would help to arm children against abuse, early pregnancy and disease, and it is still easily possible for some families to raise their children in so much ignorance and guilt that they later explode into horrifying acts of sexual violence. The right-wing answer to problems related to sex and reproduction has always been further repression – and we can see how well that has worked.

The 'feminist' anti-pornography campaigns have actually increased the fear of exposing children to anything with sexual content. Some mothers have been accused of child abuse because their children knew the words for sexual organs, and other mothers are now afraid to inform their children about sex for just such reasons. In fact, the level of fearfulness in general has become overwhelming: one gets the impression that allowing any male to be in the unsupervised presence of a child will expose that child to sexual abuse – that's in addition to the fear that if a woman leaves her house, she herself will be assaulted in the street. The moral right could not have designed a better programme to keep women trapped in their homes.

This widespread social panic has proved to be an enormous obstruction to even the most moderate discussion of giving children enough information so that they will be able to recognize potential dangers and avoid them before they happen. Yet it is crucial that we get the facts to children early so that they can be armed against the misinformation they will be picking up in the atmosphere, in the traditional way, regardless of the law.

Ironically, public concern over child abuse is now being used as an excuse to keep young people as vulnerable as ever, and even to subject them to the most abusive behaviour, supposedly to 'protect' them. Fear of abuse is now a justification for subjecting children to invasive physical examinations by strangers, extensive interviews in which they are asked to discuss their possible involvement with sexual acts they may never have heard of before, and the most ludicrous suggestions of 'Satanic abuse'. In 1989, children in the Orkney Islands who had been abused by their father were removed from their mother's care and separated from each other indefinitely even after their father was removed from the home. Although she has been desperately trying to retrieve them, they have been told that their mother no longer wishes to see them; I find it hard to imagine what could be worse to say to a child. Four families in the Orkneys who tried to help her had their own children kidnapped, examined and questioned – kept separated for several weeks, as well as isolated from the rest of their family and neighbours – as a result. The unproven theory that all abuse victims become abusers appears to be the justification for the fact that the original children were taken from their mother and kept separate from each other under care. (The mistreatment of the other nine children whose families had come to her defence would appear to be nothing less than the most immoral political punishment.)

We are now seeing a rash of child abuse charges stemming from animosity during divorce proceedings in which a claim against the father is hoped to prevent any custody award to him. Little girls are often physically resistant to examination and sometimes have to have their legs prised apart forcibly by 'experts' who are looking for signs of abuse. When a child is screaming and in tears over such an unprecedented intrusion, you'd expect 'experts' to ask themselves just who is doing the abusing. (And if they really were experts, surely they would know that such examinations are not really useful in demonstrating most prior abuse.) In a case where someone accuses a public figure of abusing their child, they are compounding the problem by exposing that child to the glare of publicity – in the recent cases of accusations against Woody Allen and Michael Jackson, that has meant long-running international press coverage from which the children have had no protection. This kind of exposure may ultimately be more damaging to the young people involved than would the effects of what they are supposedly being 'protected' from. These children have, of course, been asked numerous embarrassing questions of a kind that many young people find frightening.

A little thought might remind us just how humiliating and appalling such interrogations might have been for us when we were young, but the new passion for ferreting out abuse seems to have made people forget they were ever children themselves. One would have thought that preventing trauma, rather than merely proving abuse, should be our priority with regard to children, but abuse investigations these days are carried out for all the world as if a child could not possibly suffer from being repeatedly badgered for hours, days, weeks or even months to 'admit' to engaging in bizarre events which the adults who ask the questions make clear are foul and ruinous (often under sleep-deprivation conditions). It has now become common to hear of children subjected to this on no evidence at all. This *is* child abuse. Does saving 'just one child' truly justify it? *Never* on these terms.

Closing our minds

When the feminist debate on pornography came to Britain, many women hoped that, however wrong-headed some of its terms were, at least the discussion of sexuality would be reopened. It may have been so in the pages of non-feminist magazines aimed at young women, but within the feminist movement, what we have seen more closely resembles a closing down of whatever debate there had been. Indeed, an important, deliberate tactic of the anti-porn movement is to refuse to debate or even admit that there is anything to discuss. Debating issues, it is said, is a 'male' strategy designed not to explore issues, but to give men the opportunity to posture and express their macho aggression verbally.

Of course, much debate does seem to suit this characterization. University debates often look as if they are set up for no other purpose than to allow students to show off their skills in oratory. It is frequently the case that the debaters have no commitment to the positions they are presenting, but are merely playing an assigned role. The design of such debates is artificial and shoehorns issues into a limited frame that doesn't allow for free discussion and open thinking. But formal debate isn't the only means to discuss issues, and anti-porn feminists refuse open-ended exploration of opposing views as well. They will not join anti-censorship feminists in joint meetings, they shout down audience speakers who disagree, and they have cleverly foreclosed on any discussion in the media by rejecting any public speaking offer that involves opposing *feminist* speakers. Their foreclosure on any mixed, non-hostile discussion has polarized the debate as effectively as the 'male' tactics they deplore.

This is certainly a clever strategy. Clare Short was happy to appear on a nightly news debate against Isabel Koprowski, then managing editor of

UK *Penthouse* and UK *Forum*, asserting that the media can only ever find 'pornographers' to speak against her, since only people with a vested economic interest could possibly question her pro-censorship position. Yet when Gloria Hunniford's show, *Gloria Live*, asked Short to appear with a member of Feminists Against Censorship in May 1991, she refused, she said, to be on 'with some vituperative feminist', and appeared alone. The tactic originated in America, of course, where Andrea Dworkin in particular has a long history of rejecting appearances with anti-censorship feminists. Similarly, when BBC World Service asked Dworkin to come in to tape a discussion with a FAC member in November 1992, during one of her visits to Britain, she refused. World Service was smarter than most broadcasters and simply kept looking until they found someone else to debate with FAC. Some universities have also taken the position that if debate is not possible, discussion led entirely by a member of FAC will do just fine. But television programmers are loathe to present issue-oriented programming in a live format that is not 'balanced', and this means that if no opposition from the anti-pornography camp can be found, the issue ends up not being discussed at all.

However, it is not always impossible to find a forum where members of Campaign Against Pornography are confronted with opposition from feminists. There are still those who assume that there *is* no such opposition, and they sometimes go out to speak expecting to find no disagreement. Their response to serious questioning of their position from feminists is, to say the least, unsettling. In some instances, supporters of CAP have been so abusive to members of FAC that our speakers feared they were in danger of physical violence. On the other hand, I have been present when we inadvertently reduced anti-porn women to tears by suggesting that some of their statements required closer scrutiny. One woman had claimed that snuff movies were freely available on the shelves of W.H. Smith's, and we naturally pointed out that it would be impossible to find snuff movies (which don't even exist) *or* hard core pornography of any kind at Smith's; she seemed unaware that obscenity laws existed at all in Britain. On another occasion, a well-known anti-porn feminist, Liz Kelly, attempted to illustrate what she apparently thought was the especially racist nature of pornography by pointing out that most of the sex workers in the world are 'non-white'. Of course, this is true, since most of the *people* in the world are not white, but in predominantly white cultures like Britain and the United States, the vast majority of women who appear in pornography are white, just as in the non-pornographic media.

Missing the point

Was Kelly trying to capitalize on our natural revulsion from racism by using an essentially racist argument that relied on the assumption that most people in the world are white? She certainly seemed to be taking it for granted that it is the fault of pornography, rather than other industries and media, that women of colour may have a harder time finding jobs *outside* of the sex industry.

It is predictable that women who cannot get other jobs will eventually find their way into sex work if that is all that remains as an area of potential earning, and that, in white racist culture, a disproportionate number of those women will be those who come from underprivileged racial groups. Moreover, the suggestion that the appearance of women of colour in pornography makes it racist underlines an astonishing failure to recognize the *real* racism we experience in media that so rarely recognize women of colour as attractive. Given that black women in Britain and America are disproportionately poor, one would expect to see a disproportionately high number of black women in pornography, and in the sex industry in general. This would say nothing about the inherent racism of pornography, but more about the racism of a culture that offers even fewer economic choices to women of colour than it does to white women.

Beautiful black women

But the truth is that the number of black women in pornography in Britain and America is disproportionately *low*. Yet black women are so invisible to these 'anti-racist' women that they don't even have an awareness of the relative absence of black women from media about 'attractive' or 'sexy' women. And as the film about prostitution, *Working Girls*, pointed out, black women, seen as less attractive, are actually less popular as prostitutes than white women are. White women in the anti-porn movement seem remarkably oblivious to both the economic and social costs other women experience as a result of being seen as less attractive by white culture.

'Good looks' get women jobs, whether they are office jobs or sex work; when your racial type is not considered attractive, it hurts you economically no matter what work you are looking for. For some women, it is precisely the fact of not being considered pretty enough for jobs that involve 'meeting the public' (which may sometimes mean representing the company, but also includes 'prestige secretaries', who are the women at the economic top of the secretarial ranks, often doing the least work, and getting the most money for it) that leads to the worst jobs, whether they be in the sex industry or outside it. In white culture, black women are less valued in the office, in popular mainstream media, and in pornography. Porn directly reflects the racism of the dominant culture in its failure to treat black women as attractive or desirable; it does not express racism in any new or special way.

Some feminists may sneer at the desire of women of colour to be seen as attractive, but perhaps they should think again about how much it costs to be so consistently in the position of being negatively compared with white women. 'Good looks' count in rape trials and sexual harassment hearings, too. When juries find women unattractive, they tend to take the position that such women *could not* have been raped. In one of my women's studies classes, a film was shown called *Prisoners Against Rape*, by a group of that name formed by convicted rapists, who spoke about their own attitudes and feelings, and some of their cases. They pointed out that common attitudes contributed to the fact that they were so often acquitted, and one (white) man mentioned that he 'actually felt sorry for' a black woman he'd raped, because during the trial it was so clear that they thought black women were ugly and should feel privileged to have the attentions of a white man. (It's no accident that a disproportionate number of men who are in British and American prisons for rape are men of colour who have raped white women, despite the fact that more white men than blacks rape interracially, most rapists are white, and the vast majority of rapes are not interracial at all.)

This view, sadly, is not confined to whites, and is in large part what was being said between the lines during the October 1991 confirmation hearings of Clarence Thomas for the position of US Supreme Court Justice when Anita Hill accused him of having sexually harassed her. Many middle-class whites were confused by apparent support for Thomas, and refusal to believe Hill, that emanated from the black community in America. Hill, perceived as a 'black-looking black woman', was not seen as being *worth* harassing. Thomas, an unusually powerful black man who even had a white wife, was perceived as someone who did not need to bother with a 'black-looking black woman'. Thomas capitalized on racist American attitudes about black women during the hearings by strongly suggesting that there was something wrong with allowing a black woman to speak, and by bringing in a witness who as much as accused Hill of having the morality of a street-corner hooker. The subliminal message was this: you don't have to listen to her – she's just another coloured whore.

He then confused white liberals further when he accused them of opposing his nomination because he was an 'uppity black' – indeed, he astonished them, because it was precisely the fact that he was *not* uppity that made him seem such an inappropriate choice to replace the manifestly, admirably 'uppity' Thurgood Marshall on the bench. But many blacks were embarrassed by this remark from Thomas, knowing full well what he was referring to: he had a white wife, a fact that meant absolutely nothing to the white liberals who were fighting to have him rejected, but does mean something to both the Ku Klux Klan and the blacks who have fallen for the devaluation of black women in American society. Perhaps it meant something to Strom Thurmond, who pretended to be standing up for blacks when he supported Thomas; he is the same man who once ran for president in the US by promising to preserve segregation. No doubt it meant something to pseudo-revolutionary Eldridge Cleaver, the author of *Soul on Ice*, who, having to explain why being a rapist whose principal victims were black women made him a revolutionary, said that he raped black women as 'practice' – for 'the real woman': the white woman. Cleaver once wrote movingly honest and personal love letters to Beverly Axelrod, a white woman; he has more recently distinguished himself by giving interviews in which he maintains that it is his role as a man to beat his (black) wife, Kathleen.

Race in space

Racism is nowhere near as blatant in British broadcast media as it is in America, where blacks make up some 12 per cent of the population but are by no means that well represented on television. On the BBC or Independent Television, characters – even leading characters – on shows may be black without comment, even in interracial couples. Way back in the mid-sixties, popular television shows had black characters in roles where race was irrelevant, including powerful individuals who were the bosses of the lead characters – and they weren't 'black', or 'African', or 'Caribbean'; they were *British*. In the late sixties in the United States, continuing black principal characters other than domestic servants were rare. One of the first appeared on *Star Trek*: Nichelle Nichols as Uhura, the communications officer on the bridge of the Starship Enterprise. The token woman and the token black had been merged into one role, of course. In some respects, this was a tremendous triumph for blacks, who had never before been seen in such a role on a prime-time series (an officer!), but Nichols nearly left the show over what was an insult to both women and blacks. The simple fact was that black women's voices were most often heard in America at the end of a phone; the black female telephone operator was virtually a stereotype, and Uhura was little more than that. Martin Luther King himself talked her into staying.

Star Trek also gave America its first televised interracial kiss when the ship's captain, James T. Kirk (William Shatner), was physically *forced* to kiss Uhura by telekinetically powered aliens (even so, the camera never saw their lips meet). Nichols was then and is still a stunning woman by anyone's standards; that no white man could be shown kissing her consensually on American television is a clear demonstration of just how pervasive racist attitudes have been. Here was one of the most beautiful women appearing on television at the time, and her love life was zero – at one point she flirts briefly with a black crewman, but he turns out to be a disguised alien salt-vampire who's setting her up to suck salt out of her blood. In three years of *Star Trek*, there was apparently no man who found her sufficiently attractive to ask her for a date – although the barbarian evil twin of Sulu (George Takei, who was not too white to notice her under very specialized conditions) did once get fresh with her in another dimension. Perhaps the show's creators were concerned not to let the only black woman in a continuing role seem too randy, but in a world where the women who are portrayed as beautiful are principally blondes and redheads, what kind of message were Americans getting from Hollywood about the physical attractiveness of black women?

Anti-porn feminists talk about the racism of pornography, but they have been curiously silent in America about the fact that women in mainstream media are only portrayed as having appeal to men when they suit a white Aryan stereotype. They seem more disturbed by the fact that *some* pornography, occasionally, contains pictures of black women than by the fact that porn may be the only place where black women are treated as genuinely desirable.

Happily, British television has handled race a lot more intelligently than the American networks, and is less likely to pander to the Ku Klux Klan's end of the spectrum. Black characters are generally treated in much the same way as they would be if played by whites, except where race itself is being treated as an issue. The science fiction spoof *Red Dwarf* is not a 'black' show, but 40 per cent of its cast is black, although only a small percentage of Britain's population is. (Perhaps it is ironic that the only female character, Holly, is just a computer with a female face – a brain without a body, you might say.) Black women are shown as desirable to white men without comment on their race. Given the shallowness of most US network programming, it is perhaps a mercy that the American programmers stay away from racial issues as much as possible, but they do sell more television programmes abroad than most countries make; they pollute the airwaves internationally, and that includes Britain.

Racism on Earth

And entertainment images, unfortunately, are not the only places where racism appears. In real life, Britain has as much to answer for as America does for the poor economic situation that plagues blacks. The welfare state keeps life from being quite so bleak for the poor in the UK as it is for underprivileged Americans, but that only means racism is sometimes more subtle. Those of us who are not quite white enough often notice it: in offices throughout London, you will see rooms full of typists where the full-time employees are white while the temps are black; race is an issue in the subtle code words in employment ads that refer to appearance and presentation, too. Feminists used to care about issues like this, but race, it seems, is now just another issue that can be used to argue for censorship; on its own, it no longer appears to interest those white feminists who claim to be 'anti-racist'. However passionately they say they care about discrimination, it is not so much that they can be moved to *do* something about it. Is it 'worth it' that black women exist under increasingly intolerable conditions – conditions that may drive them into prostitution, by the way – while feminists campaign to eliminate mere sexual images in the name of 'protecting women'?

Giving bigotry a good name

Anti-pornography rhetoric, especially when it comes from the government and the police, is rife with a pernicious anti-foreign element that should worry anti-racists a good deal. Much is made of the fact that most illegal pornographic materials that come to Britain, as well as the satellite station Red Hot Television, originate in Europe. The tabloids as well as the authorities have been known to use the phrase 'foreign filth' to explain what it is that must be stopped. There are hints that over on the continent, those people who talk in funny languages live lives of utter depravity, mired in child porn, bestiality and other un-British traditions that must be stemmed at the borders. Noted Tory anti-porn campaigners are particularly fond of the 'foreign filth' argument – no surprise when so many of them are leading Eurosceptics in any case. We might ask whether their resistance to European sexual materials is instrumental in leading them to oppose European harmony, or whether it's just another convenient excuse for keeping the borders closed.

We are left with an image of vile, bad-smelling foreigners, stinking of garlic and rubbing their hands furtively, wrapped in a conspiracy to force-feed their foul and depraved propaganda to innocent, decent Brits. Unless heroic measures are taken by the Customs service and the Obscene Publications Squad, we will soon be mired in a cesspit of fleshly corruption and crime no less squalid than the lives lived by those pathetic outsiders who did not have the good sense to be born British.

It is time for activists in the UK to ask why we are letting Alf Garnett's attitudes define our approach to the peoples of other European countries. Europe may have more liberal laws and attitudes with regard to pornography and sex, but they don't have more rape and sexism. In fact, they have lower rates of teenage pregnancy – at levels Britain can only aspire to. It seems clear that the anti-pornography argument is being used by some as yet another means to stigmatize foreigners and maintain a Fortress Britain attitude towards them, justifying continued bigotry against outsiders. There was a time when language of this type would set off alarm bells for progressives in Britain; now they are allied with the very people who rely on this kind of jingoistic jargon. Is creating an atmosphere that legitimizes nationalistic chauvinism 'worth it'?

For our own good

Because one group of women wishes to control the image of other women and our right to speak for ourselves, many feminist goals have been allowed to fade into obscurity or have been perverted altogether. When 'feminism' amounts to ignoring real violence against women, treating rape and racism as mere rhetorical weapons in the fight to ban pornography, it loses any sense of true value. When 'feminism' means joining hands with the likes of Mary Whitehouse, John Patten, Peter Lilley, Michael Hames, Jerry Falwell and Patrick Buchanan and turning our backs on reproductive freedom and gay rights, it is doing women more harm than good. When 'feminism' means stigmatizing women, ignoring real racism and sexism in the workplace, making people feel guilty about sexual fantasies, and abandoning gay rights, it is no wonder that so many women have left the movement. When 'feminism' is about exploiting the powerlessness of children rather than about doing something to give children some agency in their own lives and helping them to grow up without the repression that creates the most virulent and violent forms of sexism, then feminism might just as well be about nothing at all.

Real women – real *feminists* – have genuine concerns about the dangers of censorship and the price that real women and children, as well as gays and others outside society's privileged mainstream, are paying every day for the damage that is being done by the so-called feminist anti-pornography movement. But women who call themselves feminists choose to suppress all discussion of those concerns because they believe that as long as we disagree with them, we cannot be thinking straight, cannot be representing the real lives, real thoughts and real concerns of real women. They say they want to 'protect' us, but how do they do this? By shouting us down? By telling us we are unable to think for ourselves? Were women being 'protected from violence against women' when Chain Reaction, the SM dyke club, was invaded in 1988 by anti-SM women in ski masks who swung crowbars around, smashed up furniture and broke the leg of one woman present? Have anti-SM, anti-porn women become so lost in their rhetoric that they would commit *actual* violence against women to protect us from symbols, fantasy and metaphor? Will women kick and kill us to 'save' us from violence?

For our own good, they will treat us like mindless pawns who have no real credibility, no understanding of our own lives, and they will pretend to speak on our behalf while keeping us firmly gagged. Because they happen to share our gender, they believe they are entitled to have us declared incompetent, take over our political voices, and silence us.

The media have played right into their hands, insisting on 'balance' that the anti-porn 'feminists' will not provide, and thus keeping only their own view in the public spotlight as the 'feminist' position. But feminists still have much more to talk about than pornography: we still have street lighting, the family, gay rights, safety for sex workers, ageism, the position of lesbians in the gay community, sex education, children's empowerment, the examination of female sexuality, the health risks of hormones in our food and as treatment for menopause, battered children, racism, economic conditions, fascism and the real causes of sexual violence to discuss, to name but a few. Far from revitalizing the women's liberation movement, anti-porn 'feminism' has actually closed down debate, distracted us from or corrupted many of these issues, and victimized women who had been working and living on the fringes of society, often on behalf of feminist activism.

Has it been 'worth it'? Hell no.

9
Men against pornography: a clouded mirror

Much has been written of late about the failure of the so-called 'New Man', who was supposed to have been some sort of evolutionary improvement over Macho Man but appears to have been a bit of a disappointment, according to articles in, for example, the *Guardian*. It is implied that New Man differed from Macho Man in that he was simply not sexist, not pushy, and was able to recognize female needs and respect women as equals – and that for this very reason, women found him, in the end, unattractive. From this we are meant to infer that Macho Man is back, and that men can all breathe a sigh of relief and return to being the unreconstructed male chauvinist pigs they were before, because that's what heterosexual women *really* like.

As with so much else, this is just another example of media hype over-simplifying complex social patterns and in effect creating a complete misapprehension of the real events and reasoning behind the phenomena that we must muddle our way through. 'New Man' never really existed; feminist ideology merely made it more comfortable for middle-class men not to have to flex their muscles very much. Some males who had felt like oddballs in their native social milieux found they had been offered a niche where they could fit in. A growing number of men have come to realize that it is unrealistic to expect to be able to support, let alone find, a woman who is happy to stay at home and bake all day without having any money. Women have always preferred men who can talk and think to men who engage in the embarrassing display of trying to be 'manly'. Many men were relieved to know that they could now ask questions instead of suffering in silence, and have made use of this weird new skill called 'communication', but New Man seldom does this, preferring to trumpet his own sensitivity and elevated awareness. He uses new terms and phrases to express old thoughts in what may appear to be a more civilized and socially conscious manner. And some men – the really visible, ardently correct New Men – latched on to anti-pornography rhetoric and demonstrated that they could be even more critical of men than some of the best feminists they knew. Strangely, many women were unimpressed by men who beat their breasts and expressed their macho-aggressive character by assertively condemning pornography and male sexuality; this was interpreted to mean that heterosexual women preferred to become involved with creeps.

Although some would suggest that some sort of female masochism is responsible for the rejection of New Man, women had better reasons to find him unattractive. A cursory look at some of the things New Man was writing about pornography is enough to explain why.

A circus of contempt

In September 1990, Campaign Against Pornography and Censorship (CPC) held a conference in London entitled 'Opposing pornography: A one-day conference for men'. On behalf of CPC, Peter Baker led the meeting, which was all-male with the sole exception of the opening speaker, Catherine Itzin. There are reports that the total number in attendance at the conference was somewhere in the neighbourhood of 115. Several existing press reports from the period indicate that a number of these men were journalists rather than independent supporters, and some organizations, including Feminists Against Censorship, had sent male friends or members to report on the proceedings. Most of the reports we have collected came from people who were critical of CPC; it is unknown, therefore, how many of those attending were actually sympathetic to their views and goals.

The report to FAC described a certain amount of controversy, particularly among gay men in attendance, principally in reaction to a speech by John Stoltenberg, a self-proclaimed faggot, that blamed gay male practice (most notably SM and fist-fucking) for the spread of AIDS. Stoltenberg also described male homosexual acts as emanating from a fear and hatred of women and a desire to absorb the masculinity of other males. SM in particular, said Stoltenberg, 'helps resolve a misogynist struggle to cling to male supremacy' for gay men. At one point, according to the printed text of his speech, Stoltenberg admits that objectification would happen without pornography, but most of his discussion of porn, concentrating as it does on his evaluation of SM imagery, seems to deny this point. And the mere act of looking at pornography, regardless of its content, creates for Stoltenberg a specifically misogynist experience of separation from the female, and solidarity with other men, for the male viewer. Content, then, is irrelevant; all sexual imagery must be seen to promote misogyny and homophobia.

> A world in which pornography does not sexualize women's inferior status for men would be a world in which eroticized hostility and hierarchy would have no claim on human intimacy. And a world in which pornography did not play its seemingly intractable role in the acculturation of male sexuality – with its addiction to objectification, its dependence on domination – would be a world in which justice and human sexuality were not so mutually exclusive as they now tragically appear to be.

Pornography, he says, 'helps keep sexism sexy'. In Stoltenberg's view, it is virtually impossible for men (gay or straight) to look at pornography (gay or straight) without internalizing attitudes that are both misogynistic and homophobic. Stoltenberg has gone so far as to say that no SM act, regardless of the gender of the participants, is anything other than a reinforcement of male supremacy. Elsewhere, he has written that women cannot choose freely to participate in SM acts, even with each other. Here is the New Man, the anti-sexist man, telling us all what we are allowed to do, delegitimizing our personal decisions, our sexuality and practices, all on the basis of an unproven and insupportable theory that gives every appearance of resting on his *own* misogyny and homophobia. In this guise, the New Man is a dictator who would define our sexuality for us lest we define it first on our own terms.

Insult to injury

Another participant in the festivities was science fiction author Michael Moorcock, who has written extensively about pornography and his relationship with Andrea Dworkin. Moorcock was previously associated with an anti-censorship position, notably in his support of Manchester publishers Savoy Books, which has had continuing problems with censorious officials. Many women feel that Moorcock's own books prior to 1977 distinguished themselves by a contemptuous attitude towards women. That contempt is still evident in his more recent 'feminist' writing. He has belittled feminist attempts to explore female sexuality by

The New Man is a dictator

discussing vibrators and other sex toys, for example. And in an article called 'Who's really covering up?' reviewing a book on the porn trade, *Porn Gold*, he dismissed the testimony of female sex workers who had positive experiences in the porn trade in this way:

> [The book] contains no hint that women's sexual identities are anything but what men define. The only women quoted are those who, for whatever reasons, are happy to accept that definition. *Porn Gold* is like a 19th century examination of the slave trade where the pros and cons of the business are comfortably discussed, quoting only slave-owners or those slaves who (on American plantations, for instance) told interviewers they would be miserable if freed.

Moorcock begins with the position that women in the sex industry who disagree with his view of their experience (an experience he cannot know or share) are not credible witnesses – they are like slaves who claimed to prefer slavery.

Yet Moorcock admits that Britain's obscenity laws are unhelpful and used by the authorities politically. In 'The case against pornography' he says:

I believe that the Obscene Publications Act with its vague wording about proof being needed that something has a 'tendency to deprave and corrupt' is both ineffectual at controlling pornography and dangerous in that depravity and corruption are, after all, a matter of opinion. Whoever happens to be in power can decide what constitutes those tendencies. ... All kinds of political, social and sexual material can, and have, been defined as harmful under this definition. The activities of people like James Anderton [ex-chief constable] in Manchester, whose police force were responsible for jailing a friend of mine for selling novels which had been on public sale in this country for ten years, is a case in point.

Once, when I personally disagreed with Moorcock about the way 'feminist' anti-porn laws would be used, he informed me that I was wrong and that I 'got that from *Playboy*'. Obviously so, since women cannot think for ourselves and come to another conclusion than his. In any case, the experience in Canada has demonstrated that Moorcock was overly optimistic about the uses of 'feminist' anti-porn laws. Indeed, the anti-porn movement in Britain has been used as an excuse to strengthen sexual repression in word and law. Yet Moorcock continues to believe that his activities are in aid of an *anti-censorship* position.

Hating the (female) image in pornography

One of the papers distributed at the conference is an article photocopied from a 1977 book edited by J. Snodgrass, *For Men Against Sexism*. We can only surmise from the fact that it was distributed with the conference papers that the organizers approved of its content; it is certainly similar to much 'feminist' anti-porn writing.

Entitled 'How pornography shackles men and oppresses women', the piece, by Michael Betzold, is a mishmash of unexamined assumptions. He tells us:

> Skin flicks and porn reading matter market women as commodities, denying physical uniqueness; women are presented as 'tits and ass' with bulging breasts and painted on smiles.

This is typical of anti-porn rhetoric, but what on earth does it mean? How does pornography deny 'physical uniqueness', for example? Pornography contains lots of different pictures, sometimes single individual pin-ups, sometimes photo-spreads where the same person appears in a variety of poses in a range of pictures; sometimes several women, or women with men, or men with men; sometimes movies in which more than one person (most often of more than one gender) perform together. Non-pornographic imagery also shows pictures of different people (and things), although most commonly they are not having sex. Hard-core pornography capitalizes to a certain extent on physical difference – the fact that women come in many different shapes, sizes, colours and styles – and the fact that different men and women have different preferences. Mainstream media show far less recognition that women of varying shapes and sizes can be seen as attractive. Pornography is virtually the only medium where the variety of female genitalia is visible – hardly a *denial* of 'uniqueness'. Pornography also recognizes difference in sexuality in a way that the dominant culture does not, with subgenres that range from the coy to the explicit, the private to the public, the more common and accepted sexualities to minority tastes. It is certainly not clear what Betzold is talking about here, let alone that porn is uniquely responsible for whatever it is.

And are women presented as 'tits and ass'? In most porn, like every other genre, people are shown whole or in part, full length, active, passive, upper torso shots, head shots, shots of the hands and arms when they are doing something, and so on. When a woman is being touched on the breast – something many women do find pleasant during sexual activity – the camera may focus on that action. If people are having sex – which women may do with their cunts – the camera will also try to expose the activity. If a woman is seen from the back, or is being caressed on her backside, this too is shown to the camera. We may find it erotic to have our lovers touch or admire these parts of our bodies.

Even with our clothes on, women *have* 'tits and ass', and these are naturally visible when we appear naked. Most of us are in this condition at least once a day if not more, and the suggestion that if we are seen this way we are nothing *but* these body parts is rather curious coming from a man who purports to be against sexism. There seems to be a strong implication here that if a woman is recognized as a sexual being, she is automatically degraded. This does not bode well for a woman's right to explore her own sexuality and enjoy sexual pleasure.

Attack of the giant knockers

Most ominous of all, women in pornography appear to have 'bulging breasts'. The term 'bulge' generally refers to an item that is in a container too small for it. Sometimes we 'bulge' when our clothes are too tight for us, for example. But as used here, the suggestion is that breasts themselves, even without the constraints of clothing, are bulging unnaturally. It is hard not to infer from this that the breasts are 'too big' by some unnamed standard; big breasts are presented as some sort of deformity.

It is difficult to know what an appropriate size for a breast is, given that criticisms of pornography so frequently reiterate that the women in porn have these grotesquely swollen breasts, despite the fact that they look remarkably like the breasts women might see on ourselves or on other women in changing rooms, or among our friends when we see each other naked, or on our lovers. Breasts, in my experience, come in a variety of sizes ranging from an A cup (up to about an inch larger than the rib-cage measurement) through a probable average of about a C cup (three inches above rib measurement) and up to at least an H, as advertised in wide-range mail-order lingerie catalogues. The B and C sizes are most common in 'page 3" photos in the tabloids, although a stir was caused when Samantha Fox, who may have been a DD, appeared and generated interest from those men who still prefer somewhat larger breasts (a taste that hasn't much been catered to in the tabloids). The DD size is not all that rare, although younger women of course tend not to have reached this size yet, and thus breasts in the A–B range are more common – after all, even the most voluptuous woman must have been an A at least once in her life. Breasts are made of fat, and therefore the size of a woman's breasts may also become smaller as she diets or exercises, and larger as she gains weight. Hormonal changes resulting from pregnancy, use of the pill or simple maturation may also affect breast size. Even among women who are lean and athletic, however, breasts in the C–DD range and higher do occur frequently in nature and are not the freakish anomalies anti-porn activists portray.

Feminism, of course, once made a point of emphasizing the fact of natural differences in female anatomy, in particular as regards female breasts. Our criticism of brassieres was not a criticism of bust *size*, but rather an expression of irritation that we were expected to constrain and disguise parts of our bodies to make them appear more 'acceptable' and mask the less controlled behaviour of the natural, unsupported breast. Yet it is not uncommon to hear avowedly feminist criticisms of pornography in which demeaning and insulting remarks are made about the hideously gargantuan proportions of the relatively average (and often smaller than average) breasts that are seen in most widely available sexual materials.

Since women's breasts do often come in sizes considerably larger than those seen in most soft core pornography, how are larger-breasted women expected to feel when inundated with a barrage of these allegedly 'anti-sexist' statements about the frighteningly overwhelming obscenity of giant B and C breasts virtually leaping off the page and offending the eye of the sensitive viewer? Why is it considered acceptable to make continual assertions to the effect that merely being seen with big breasts is to be a 'bimbo'? One would gather from the numerous insulting remarks of this nature that intelligent women deliberately grow small breasts while big breasts are grown by stupid, unthinking women who have accepted sexist conditioning with cow-like docility. It is hard to remember that heredity plays any role at all.

Contrary to popular anti-porn rhetoric, our dominant culture does not in any way privilege women for having big breasts. Having a 'fuller figure' was popular back in the 1950s, but those days are long gone and slimness, even when accompanied by few visible feminine secondary sexual characteristics, has been the fashion for decades now. The popular image in fashion magazines is of a woman so thin and lacking in curves that she could easily be mistaken for a boy. One women's fashion designer in America has stated that he designs his clothes on a *male* model. Moreover, models have become such superstars in their own right that even those of us who ignore fashion magazines cannot avoid seeing these unusually slim women trotted out on chat shows as if the mere fact that they are thin enough to be models should make us fascinated by whatever they have to say. The fashions themselves are designed in such a way that a larger-breasted woman looks fat and slovenly in them, even if she is not at all fat.

Women who are perceived as being 'too fat' by this standard – which now means even those women who were once considered 'shapely' – are publicly ridiculed. Most of the adult female population is being dismissed as hideously deformed, and yet the blame is placed on pornography, the one genre where women are *allowed* to have larger – or even average – breasts without shame.

'Actual hips'

When his attractive home was used for a fashion shoot in 1993, National Public Radio commentator Andrew Ward, watching the proceedings, mused on the 'gorgeous models' for *The Washington Post*:

> The frail and starved neurotics posing on my deck did not seem to me happy nor especially bright, and yet they not only manage to sell clothes but also to make the happy, bright, beautiful young women who date my son – girls with calf muscles, bosoms, actual hips – feel terrible about the way they look.

I sometimes find my 14-year-old daughter leaning into a mirror to deplore her skin, or lowering her waistband because she thinks her legs are too long. Almost every day I have told her that she was smart and funny and a sight for sore eyes.

But I am only her father and not the world, and the world keeps telling her she isn't perfect and won't be perfect until she lines up with her dollars at the gyms and clinics and tanning salons.

The delusion that women are still being held to a 1950s standard of beauty from the neck down seems to be strong among anti-porn activists, despite the fact that it gets no support from anywhere in our present media culture. This was never more obvious than the moment when the tabloids decided to celebrate the marriage of Prince Andrew by noting with great glee that the bride, one Sarah Ferguson, had what they felt was an enormous backside. 'Fergie' had, in fact, a fairly average body, probably even small enough to fit into the less-than-average sized clothes that are available in most high street shops, which tend to stop at a 14. Whatever one may think of royalty, surely it was worth noting that the Duchess of York was by no means the most obese woman in Britain – what were the rest of us supposed to think this meant about our own bodies?

What we were supposed to think, of course, was that we should look more like the woman Fergie was implicitly being compared unfavourably to: the picture-perfect Princess Diana, a woman who was wasting away before our eyes by, according to many media reports, the clever dietary technique of vomiting her food up on a regular basis. The standard of a woman who was said to be starving to death in public was being held up before us as an ideal.

And where was New Man during all this? I do not recall hearing him leap to the defence of unfashionably fat Sarah Ferguson and the millions of women who share her dress size or wear one even larger. Was Ordinary Woman, or even Feminist Woman, waiting to hear Peter Baker's criticism of Fergie-bashing, or John Stoltenberg's outrage that a woman was being publicly humiliated merely for being shaped like a woman? If so, she waited in vain. Instead she was treated to many equally insulting smears of Fergie's figure in the supposedly more sensitive venues favoured by *Guardian* readers and New Man himself – alleged lefty sex symbol Angus Deayton (who sometimes even writes for the *Guardian*), for example, joined in the fun as host of television's *Have I Got News For You* – after all, Fergie's rear end was part of the hilarious news. Female humorists who have appeared on the show – some of whom have bigger buns than Fergie – were not asked for comment.

It should be noted here that anti-pornography women were also curiously silent on the subject of Fergie's bum. Were they, too, so cowed by the possibility of being called 'fat' that they were afraid to speak up and suffer the same treatment? Or was it simply that the fact of Fergie's public humiliation contradicted, rather than supported, their theories of how pornography creates the standard by which women are judged? Many feminists are not fans of the royals, but surely 'sisterhood' would allow – even demand – that we see past such superficial difference and feel for a woman who was being dragged through the slime for no bigger sin than looking like the rest of us.

Self-abuse

Having insulted the physical attributes of at least half the female population, Betzold then goes on to attack masturbation:

> By providing substitute gratification, [pornography] provides an excuse for men to avoid relating to women as people. It encourages unrealistic expectations: that all women will look and act like Playboy bunnies, that 'good sex' can be obtained anywhere, quickly, easily and without the hassle of expending energy on a relationship.

One might almost believe that men will give up interpersonal sex altogether once they discover they can have a 'substitute' for it in pornography. It is ironic that anti-porn speakers often promote the two entirely contradictory views that men who look at porn will pursue sex and women more aggressively, while at the same time men who look at porn will come to *prefer* masturbation as a substitute for relationships.

Many people discover masturbation without (and before) seeing pornography. For many – perhaps most – of us, it is our first type of sexual experience. Quite a few women discover that masturbation is a more effective means of achieving climax than is sexual intercourse or tolerating the clumsy fumblings of a partner. Sometimes a partner's attempts to arouse can result in pain instead; more than one woman has complained, for example, that males start poking their dry fingers into cunts in an effort to stimulate when in fact it may feel unpleasant to be penetrated at all before arousal. Fucking, while it may be fun, doesn't always achieve the kind of orgasm that is most satisfying to many women. Some heterosexual couples may rely on cunnilingus or manual manipulation in order to ensure that the woman reaches orgasm. Such methods may also have the advantage of by-passing a need for birth control or prophylaxis. Many people fantasize when they are with partners in order to help facilitate arousal and orgasm. In some cases they do this not merely to satisfy themselves, but to make sex more satisfying to partners who may feel disappointed or inadequate if they think they have failed to arouse and satisfy them fully.

Fantasy is a normal part of the human sexual repertoire, with or without partners, and is not created merely by the existence of pornography. There is no reason to believe that the private fantasies we invent in our own minds are necessarily more realistic or less idealized than what is found in porn. Indeed, many people have fantasies that are physically impossible and are not represented in pornography at all.

It is certainly true that in masturbatory fantasy we can have the most 'perfect' sex, in which all of our desires can be met on a whim and there are no practical hassles later – no arguments, no worries about pregnancy and disease, and no little human imperfections. In our fantasies, our partners can be all things to us, perfectly compatible, eagerly behaving in exactly the ways we want without our even having to discuss it with them. In our fantasies, we can go to bed with our favourite pop stars, Sophia Loren, men who never go bald and women who never have pre-menstrual syndrome – and partners who never make us sleep on the wet spot. We can even get into time machines and have affairs with Jim Morrison and Marilyn Monroe when they were still alive and at their peak. But masturbatory fantasy, with or without pornography, does not replace the relationships we desire, and I have never heard anyone except critics of pornography suggest that it does.

Most of us, whether we look at pornography or not, know that no one can be all things to us, and that even the most ideal mate will have personal problems, illnesses, irritating habits, creepy relatives and probably even some kind of sexual incompatibility. None of this means we would be willing to forgo human companionship in favour of staying at home with a copy of *Playboy*.

The morality that existed prior to the sexual revolution allowed men to assume that women, regardless of our individual tastes and needs, would simply have to conform to our husbands' sexual desires and provide what they wanted whether compatible with our own desires or not. Today, people are becoming increasingly aware that no one can have such expectations and that we must agree with our partners to do those things that appeal to all parties, but not force undesired acts on each other. In some cases, we may find that people we love very much are not entirely sexually compatible with us; that doesn't mean we cannot find mutually pleasurable ways to make love with each other, but it does mean that some parts of our sexual psyches will not be reached within the relationship. For many of us, masturbatory fantasy – sometimes with, and sometimes without, pornography – will be a way of taking up the slack in the privacy of our minds without imposing those desires on unwilling partners. Those of us who want more sex than is available know that we are better off masturbating than badgering others for it or suffering frustration; those of us who want less sex than our partners do would certainly prefer that they fantasize by themselves rather than try to get us to go along with it. There is no point in anyone suffering sexual frustration just because there is some imagined sin in masturbation. So-called 'self-abuse' has the virtue that it abuses no one.

The nuclear family as panacea

Feminists have always recognized that the nuclear family served the needs of an exploitative capitalism by making men acutely aware of their responsibility for utterly dependent wives and children. Employers have traditionally preferred to hire men who are married fathers, because they are more 'dependable', which means they are less likely to feel free to leave an unpleasant job or go out on strike when their bosses get out of line; for this reason, female independence was not desirable. Yet Betzold spits in the face of the best feminist theorists to condemn pornography, saying that: 'it provides a cheap and non-time-consuming method of "servicing" freed sexual energies so that the worker can return contentedly to a job that is anything but satisfying'. Betzold does not see the world around him, where men march off to the office to make war toys or repossess people's homes without benefit of pornography. He ignores the fact that the legislators in his country who have been the most war-mongering, the most anti-feminist, and the most just plain sexist have also been the men who most shrilly oppose pornography. He is deaf to the cries of men who loathe their jobs and everything their employers stand for and yet go in day after day, year after year, because they need the money to support the wife and kids and try to build a future for their children. Men who have no relationships – and no families and children –

are far less likely to endure such humiliation; they might be more willing to take the risks of moving to less reprehensible, if lower-paying, jobs, if it would let them live with the work they do.

Betzold sees the sexual revolution as having 'freed' those sexual energies, and porn as the napkin that soaks them up in a way that is safe for the corporate oppressors. Oddly, he seems to be implying that men whose 'freed' sexual energies are not absorbed by pornography will do something revolutionary, but many women might be able to tell him what horny men do during a sexual revolution where masturbation and pornography are considered too crass, too much a reflection of straight society, to be sufficient to satisfy their sexual whims. Betzold might even recall that part of what 'freed' men's sexual energies in the sexual revolution was the fact that so many women were on the pill and no longer had pregnancy as an excuse to avoid sex, but did not yet have an analysis of female desire and concerns to help us tell men that we didn't *need* an excuse to say 'No' when we wanted to. Many women felt that, far from being deprived of male company by pornography, they were being used as a substitute for masturbation, and would have been delighted if horny men would have stayed in their rooms with copies of *Playboy* rather than annoying those females who happened to be in physical proximity at the time. For many of us, it was a vast relief when heterosexual men discovered that women weren't willing to act as walking sex toys and that they could take responsibility for their own erections with their own hands and a convenient magazine, rather than making women deal with it every time.

The other thing that 'freed' male sexual energy was that women were willing to experiment with sex without benefit of clergy – but that didn't mean we had to have sex with every man, or even any man, who asked. This fact had a great deal to do with why women started to express annoyance with the limits of the sexual revolution in its then present form; female energy left the principally male-ruled activist groups and counterculture media behind when it evolved into the women's liberation movement.

In the 1960s, the largest single generation in history was at the age when males tend to be obsessed with sex – but they were also young enough to have few other responsibilities to keep them from joining protest movements. As those men matured and began to develop relationships that gave them other priorities, many of them left activism behind. Yet Betzold would have us believe it was pornography that destroyed the counterculture.

Sexism wears new clothes

As if he hadn't already made his contempt for the female body clear enough, Betzold must stress once again that he knows women as little more than isolated body parts: 'By unlimited exposure of breasts and cunts detached from real people, over-saturation eventually reduces to near-nothing the porn consumers' capacities to be genuinely stimulated by human beings.' If a man sees pictures of breasts and cunts, he will get used to seeing them and therefore be unable to be aroused by women. Men have to be kept fascinated by women's body parts in order to be interested in women at all, since the human female is apparently lacking in any *other* attributes that might stimulate a man once he becomes familiar with what we look like under our clothes. No wonder the family is falling apart – wives no longer get dressed in the dark, and some of them walk around the house naked. This sounds shockingly like the theories of moralists like Dolf Zillmann.

It is unfortunate that no woman was asked how much she wants to be 'loved' by a man whose interest is compelled only as long as he has no familiarity with the female body. She might have said that there is all too much of that now.

But familiarity with women's bodies and with sex in general is not an attractive prospect for Betzold, who claims that pornography 'provokes a reaction from the forces of repression. Because most porn is degrading, it justifies the Puritan's disgust with all sexuality.' Yet 'the Puritans' don't need to see much pornography. They talk about it all the time, and they surround themselves with their own hyperbole about how nasty it is – and how nasty sex is – but they don't have to spend that much time looking at it; they are already convinced that it is vile. In fact, they *know* it is, because it contains pictures of sex, and that fact alone justifies all the extreme language. It is *sex*, and not any other imagined content of pornography, that evokes their disgust. It is ludicrous for Betzold to pretend that a thing should be suppressed merely because it meets with the disapproval of people who hate the very idea of anti-sexism anyway; on that basis, the entire feminist movement would have to be eliminated (which is just the way they'd like it).

Betzold and those like him want to project their discomfort with sex onto 'the Puritans', but it is already plain enough that it is *their* disgust that is evoked by the sight of nude women, women's breasts and women's pleasure. Their fear and distaste of sexuality come through clearly when they attempt to delegitimize masturbation and disparage the ordinary bodies of real women who happen to appear in porn. Feminists won't applaud them, but 'the Puritans' will. They have always hated pornography and they have always hated the idea of women as free and equal human beings, both for the same reasons. And they know exactly what they are doing; they've been in this business for hundreds of years and if they believe that pornography contributes to the liberation of women, they are probably right. After all, the modern feminist movement did seem to gain its strength during the same period as that in which pornography became more widely available; maybe there's a reason for that.

The Puritans have, in fact, been remarkably effective in keeping sex hidden and dirty, despite the fact that most people do not believe that pictures of sex are necessarily 'obscene'. American network television has always forbidden images of reproductive organs and female breasts. What else can it mean when the agents of repression in Indiana declare that strippers and topless dancers should wear the stick-on nipple covers known as 'pasties'? As Reed Waller and Kate Worley's Omaha the Cat Dancer says in 'Tip of the Iceberg':

> They just don't realize what this does ... It's degrading ...
> Well, shit, why don't they just bypass pasties and put labels on the dancers' tits saying, 'This is dirty!'
> It's really hatred of women, you know. Labelling pieces of us as obscene.

But then, the Puritans in Her Majesty's Customs and Excise have made sure that British residents can't see what Omaha has to say about issues like this; the comic book, *Omaha the Cat Dancer*, is prevented from entering the country, to protect us from cartoon characters who talk sexual politics.

It is moralists and the agents of governments who keep sex taboo and hidden, underground, in backrooms and under the counter, but Betzold wants us to believe that pornography hides itself:

> Ultimately, pornography is anti-sex. While exploiting them, it maintains all the Puritan taboos. Special sections of bookstores are hidden from public view, require an admission price, and enforce an age requirement ... The lesson is that turn-ons are really turn-offs, so why bother with sex?

Actually, it is the law – brought to us by moralists – that enforces an age requirement to see sexual materials in the United States, and even sex education materials approved for young people cannot be seen by someone under 18 without parental permission. Yet Betzold never suggests that images of sex be brought out into public view so that this aura of tawdriness might be removed from sexuality; how can he, when he has already told us that women's bodies and sexuality *are* tawdry? So tawdry, in fact, that representations of them can be compared with real violence against black people in the United States:

> Censorship of any sort, we all agree, is reprehensible.
>
> Yet we would be appalled if movies showed blacks being lynched or castrated, Chicanos being systematically beaten and tortured, and we would quickly protest. If whole blocks of a city were given over to the sale of material directly oppressing black people, we would run the merchants out of town with little thought about their First Amendment rights. But we say nothing when the same activity goes on with women as the victims.

Here we see racist terrorism trivialized to the point where it can be equated with pictures of people having sex. Lynching, apparently, is no worse than receiving cunnilingus; performing fellatio, we must believe, is like being 'beaten and tortured'; sexual intercourse is akin to castration. For all the extreme language purporting to describe the contents of pornography that comes from its detractors, pornography does not contain such things. Violence of virtually every kind can legally be portrayed in US media, but you won't find pictures of women being tortured in America's porn shops and 'adult' movie houses.

But perhaps Betzold thinks women *are* being tortured when we have sex. After all, how can anyone enjoy anything so vile that it would disgust Puritans? New Man would have you know that we can't.

As plain as the nose on my face

Peter Baker himself has often spoken and written compellingly of the way male identity is warped in the swamp of childhood repression. In an article for Itzin's *Pornography* called 'Maintaining male power: why heterosexual men use pornography', Baker points out that boys are taught from early on to be competitive and aggressive, to eschew affectionate behaviour, and to distance themselves from the warmer aspects of emotional life. He also demonstrates fine insight into the fact that children are given no real information about sex and thus, unfortunately, pornography may be a young person's only guide to sexuality. Yet, for all this recognition of the way boys and children in general are gender-trained and kept ignorant, his criticism seems to be reserved for pornography; it is porn that is the problem, and porn that must be eliminated.

Given the other contents of his article, we might have hoped that his principal points would have been directed at less childhood sex-typing, an improvement in sex education and a broader, more positive introduction to sexuality than children are given now. It is hard to escape the feeling that Baker's critical faculties have been derailed by anti-pornography rhetoric – otherwise, he might have organized a conference promoting sex education, rather than one aimed at suppressing pornography.

Other voices

The conference pack also contains a page mentioning a picket occurring outside, with the statement that:

> According to an article in *Gay Times* The Lesbian and Gay Freedom Movement has organised this protest because the conference for men opposing pornography 'is an attempt to oppress and censor sexuality'. This is not true. CPC respects the right of LGFM to protest outside this conference but would have preferred to have been approached for a dialogue; indeed, we are now seeking an early meeting with LGFM.

According to members of the Lesbian and Gay Freedom Movement, CPC members, like CAP members, have generally avoided dialogue whenever possible and attempted no further contact with LGFM after the conference. Catherine Itzin herself is known to have said that debating issues is a 'male' tactic and therefore inappropriate for feminist-oriented programmes. This is certainly supported by FAC's experience with CPC, Itzin and CAP (see Chapter 8). For this reason, LGFM had decided that their only means of inserting dialogue into the conference was to present their own leaflet at a picket outside the meeting. Certainly, no one with opposing views was invited to speak to the conference, which LGFM believed was the only other way to bring open dialogue to those attending. Failing that, their position appeared in a leaflet, two copies of which were handed to our reporter by LGFM members, one male and one female. It is worth quoting at length.

> LGFM is campaigning for a world without male power, sexism, and sexual violence, but unlike the organisers of this conference, we totally oppose the elimination of pornography as a way forward. We believe that not all

pornography is sexist and some can be liberating. It has in no way been established that there is a link between pornography and sexual violence.

It is so easy to blame pornography for what's wrong in this society, because that is exactly what the state wants – more laws to censor and oppress us. We are living in right-wing anti-sex times, with the Government attacking anyone whose sex or sexuality challenges the nuclear family (eg. Section 28 attacks on abortion rights and artificial insemination). They would certainly support a move against pornography. Whose side are the conference organisers on?

Pornography is a complete distraction from the *real* causes of sexism and sexual violence. Sexism is mirrored in images, and *not* created by images. We want men to talk about and challenge institutionalised male power and sexism in the real world; not attack our fantasies which are completely different from what we do in our everyday lives. We want men to challenge sexism and male power in the workplace, the pub, the nuclear family, in schools; and in advertising, TV, magazines, which constantly show women in the role of servicing men, rather than as people.

We believe that a more radical approach is needed to challenge male power and sexism and sexual violence in our society. We need to attack the patriarchal institutions that will always keep men in power and oppress women and children; we need to campaign against all governments and the institutions they set up to enforce their oppressive laws like the police and the courts, and most importantly we need to challenge the nuclear family which is where most sexual violence against women and children occurs.

It is sexual oppression and lack of understanding about sex and sexuality that leads to sexual violence. We need a less sexually oppressive society where we can discuss everything and sex is no longer seen as 'naughty' nor driven underground. A society where the state no longer makes us wear clothes, nor certain types of clothes depending on our gender. We need more information about sex and sexuality around for all of us, including pictures of naked bodies and people having sex. There is nothing wrong with sexual excitement and masturbation, in itself.

It can be very liberating to read about or see pictures of other people's bodies – naked and/or having sex – particularly for lesbians and gays, as there is so little information about for us. Lesbian pornography is very difficult to get because of censorship; any new censorship laws will always be used against this sort of pornography, not against sexist images in advertisements. Pornography is especially important for people who don't want or don't have the ability for partner sex, eg, isolated, disabled, elderly, and people with HIV/AIDS.

LGFM, with an 'A' inside the gay symbol of the triangle in their logo, clearly has an anarchist analysis that is critical of the state. But perhaps more importantly, their attitude toward gays and children is one that recognizes the position our society places them in – recognition that is sadly lacking in the anti-porn arguments that criticize the bodies that appear in pornography rather than the social milieu in which they appear. In contrast to the anti-porn lobby, LGFM still sees the family, the state and pervasive images of women as servants in the general culture as the real sources of oppression. For them, challenges to a culture that institutionalizes oppression cannot be replaced by a single-issue campaign that offers censorship of pornography as a silver bullet to cure society's ills.

While much anti-porn rhetoric makes use of attitudes within the left that are critical of capitalism and male power, it is often clear, as in Betzold's article discussed above, that there is no real criticism of how the family and capitalism come together to create an environment that is hostile to female power. In order to focus on the harm of pornography, the overwhelming effect of an economy that is as a whole capitalist must be ignored, as if only pornography commits this sin. As pornography is charged with being the centre of women's oppression, the power of the state, the actions of Puritans and the dynamics of the family are acquitted of blame, mere innocent bystanders in the processes of sexism and violence.

In this context, anti-pornography activism is, at best, a red herring that makes it easy to forget how other forces in society play vital roles in harming us all.

New Man, in other words, has been fiddling while Rome is burning.

10
Feminism and the future

It is a fundamental tenet of feminism that women must be placed at economic parity with men if we are to have equal control of our lives, and thus less dependence on men. The principal reason for women's lack of economic equality is not merely sexist attitudes; it is the fact that we are held primarily responsible for taking care of children. In her ground-breaking 1970 book, *The Dialectic of Sex*, Shulamith Firestone wrote:

> Women and children are always mentioned in the same breath ('Women and children to the forts!'). The special tie women have with children is recognized by everyone. I submit, however, that the nature of this bond is no more than shared oppression. And that moreover this oppression is intertwined and mutually reinforcing in such complex ways that we will be unable to speak of the liberation of women without also discussing the liberation of children, and vice versa. The heart of woman's oppression is her childbearing and childrearing roles. And in turn children are defined in relation to this role and are psychologically formed by it; what they become as adults and the sorts of relationships they are able to form determine the society they will ultimately build.

Feminists examined the family and found it wanting. To create a non-sexist world, we must see children emerge without being part and parcel of woman's oppression, its justification, its product and its victims. Firestone, pointing out that childhood as it is currently constituted is a modern invention, entitled her chapter on the issue 'Down with childhood'.

Childhood is the part of our lives when we first learn how we relate to the world, and what we learn is that we are unpeople, with no authority even on our innermost feelings, and no power to control even our most intimate decisions. In this world, other people decide what we will wear, what we will eat, what we may do and say and not do and say. We can make friends and see them only with the consent of our elders, we may be subjected to the most humiliating patronization, and fervently wish to be adults as soon as we possibly can so we can refuse food and choose friends according to our own wishes, temperaments, tastes and needs.

In this world, we are utterly helpless and dependent, and the person we are dependent on is usually our mother. How we experience the humiliation of childhood and negotiate our freedom from it therefore occurs in relation to our mothers. Little children identify with the female (and wish to grow up to be mothers) before the age of three, but by the age of five boys, for the most part, know what they are and know that females are *not* what they wish to be. Without men in the home providing immediate role models, boys largely learn to be 'different from girls' rather than 'like men', except that they experience men principally as absent during the better part of their day. And so do girls, which may explain why some women seem to expect to spend a lot of time waiting for men to turn up.

The adult male is seldom seen in a responsible role in the home; he is more likely to turn up to eat a dinner someone else cooks and cleans up after – something like a big child who gets to go out into the world and doesn't have to clean his bedroom. Mother has to do all the housework, the kids have to follow orders, but Dad – ah, Dad has the best of both worlds. Who wouldn't want to be Dad?

The male role model, as perceived from a child's-eye view, is one that leads out of the house, away from relationships and women, and into freedom. It is for this reason that Dorothy Dinnerstein suggested in *The Mermaid and the Minotaur* that women, as primary care-takers, cannot raise boys to be anything other than, at best, men who expect women to continue to take care of them, and at worst, sexists who, deep down inside, resent, look down on and perhaps even hate women.

Others are not so certain, but most feminists would agree that as long as boys grow up seeing that men have most of the power and garner most of the respect in our society, sexism is bound to be pervasive in every area.

Institutionalizing sexism

Our society is still set up in such a way that women are likely to lose valuable tenure on the job, and therefore the earning potential that comes with it, if they stay at home with their children. If they don't stay at home, a large share of their earnings might go to paying someone who may be a stranger to take care of their children – and women generally make less than men, anyway. Many women may feel that they are going out to work solely to pay someone else to look after the children they could be looking after themselves if they didn't have to go out to work. It isn't logical for a husband, who has the potential to make more money, to stay at home with the kids while his partner tries to earn enough to support the family. On the other end of the spectrum is the single mother who has no outside job and stays at home with the children while collecting meagre state supplements – but in both cases, the children experience an absent father during most of their waking hours. At home or not, most fathers still spend far less time with their children than is necessary merely to keep a child alive. In any home where a mother stays at home at all, children are most likely to spend their formative years seeing their parents in traditional roles – the father out in the world while the mother stays at home, cleans the house and takes care of the kids. (The irony of the right-wing objection to lesbian parenting is that lesbian families are more likely to provide two active parents than are families that fit the modern, heterosexual, nuclear-family model with the male parent outside of the home during the day.)

It was always clear to feminists that for our own sakes, we must have the same career choices and opportunities that men do. This has already become much more difficult to achieve as the economy has seemed to wither. But for those of us who hoped to see future generations emerge without the sexism our own was raised in, it became obvious that our entire approach to a nuclear family in which adult roles were divided along gender lines had to be changed. Men had to be brought closer to the family while women had to develop stronger ties to the outer world.

But the position of children has to change, too. Children who are brought up to feel that they are dictated to rather than permitted to make choices are bound to have trouble learning personal responsibility. Children who feel tyrannized by adults are often likely to equate adulthood with tyrannical behaviour and try to take on that trait as soon as possible in order to resemble more closely the people who have power: tyrannical adults. And of course, if children are kept dependent, then someone – usually mother – is forced to be available to depend *on*.

Teaching sexism

Media with one message

During the 1970s, a great deal of research was directed at locating sources of sexist socialization in our culture. Feminists were less interested in reductive laboratory research than in the events and influences we are affected by in real life. Media analysis found that the messages in most fiction and advertising tended to reinforce the most sexist stereotypes. Children's books and adult media alike emphasized adventurousness in males and showed females waiting for males, waiting on males, and waiting on the sidelines. Since there was little variation in the imagery of women, we understood that the aggregate effect of such an overwhelming and uniform portrayal of women as either dependent and other-centred or (if a woman seemed to be self-motivated) evil presented us with a constant reminder that we were required to fulfil these constricted roles.

Numerous women's media projects analysed the existing representations of women, demanded change, and were instrumental in creating new, different material that subverted sexist messages. Perhaps the best known of these are the Women on Words and Images project and the work of Sandra and Daryl Bem. As a result of this kind of research and activism on the subject, the media present far more varied images of women today; no single image of a woman, no matter how offensive, can have the power to influence our expectations in the same way as when all of the images supported a belief that only one kind of woman – a woman who lived for men, home and family – was acceptable.

Subliminal sexism

Other feminists who looked at communications during the 1970s saw that children and adults are both influenced by the subliminal messages from our communications with each other. Feminist writer/researcher Wendy Martyna noted that the generic 'he' wasn't generic at all, but male-specific. Nancy Henley observed that people touch each other or not in ways that accord with status, and that women's non-verbal communication is often reinterpreted by men to have sexual content. In *Body Politics*, Henley discussed the ways in which women's clothing, touch, gaze and other behaviour were interpreted, and how female non-verbal cues differed from those of men, as well as how we may modify them in accord with female experience. She also discussed use of space and other factors that differ, or appear to differ, according to gender. It does seem that children may learn early how to see, display or reinterpret non-verbal cues to support sex-role stereotypes.

Teach your children well

Feminist social scientists looked ever deeper into the direct influences on children. Although parents and teachers usually maintain that they treat boys in the same way they treat girls, it became clear that children were receiving constant instructions in sex-role-typed behaviour. Often, the adults who did this were giving out messages that were quite the opposite of what they intended. For example, in one study by Lisa Serbin and K. Daniel O'Leary in 1975, it became obvious that teachers were actually encouraging aggressive behaviour from boys with the very methods they were using to stop the behaviour. Boys were given far more attention for aggression than girls were, and they were scolded publicly rather than in the more private way that girls usually were. When teachers stopped paying attention to the aggressive behaviour, the boys were less likely to display it. Similarly, teachers encouraged dependence in girls by paying attention to them only when they were physically near, although they paid equal attention to boys no matter how far away they were. Boys were given direct help in problem solving while girls were not given the same help, and when girls failed to complete a task, the teachers did the work for them instead of explaining how to do it.

Research of this nature by Serbin and O'Leary, Eleanor Maccoby and Carol Jacklin, Carole Joffe and many others made clear that numerous factors in the environments we create for children actually teach them how to live by sexist rules. Many people may choose to believe that testosterone or sex-linked genes make males innately more aggressive (or violent), but in this research we see not only how boys are taught to be aggressive (and otherwise 'masculine'), but that their behaviour ceases to be aggressive when adults stop teaching them that they will be rewarded for behaving in that way. (A good overview of this attempt to locate the sources of sexism, and of the related research, can be found in *The Longest War* by Carol Tavris and Carole Offir.)

Creating victims

Children are given continual messages that their bodies and lives are not their own. They are instructed to obey adults in all things, no matter how intimate – what they eat, what they wear, and even whom they associate with. Girls are often told not to touch their own genitals, and boys may be specifically directed not to handle their organs except for urinary purposes and to dress. Children in general are frequently given specific instructions against masturbation, and may be punished if they are caught doing it. It is often the case that children do not learn specific words for their organs, and many a child has grown up learning only to refer to them as 'down there'. All of these things conspire to give children the impression that these features of their bodies belong to someone other than themselves, and thus that others are entitled to make decisions over them while they themselves cannot.

Under the circumstances, it is not surprising that many children simply do not know how to resist adult sexual interference. The idea that they could have the authority to say 'no' to an adult may be completely alien. If the abuser is a parent or teacher, resistance could be unthinkable.

It seems obvious that children should be accorded more latitude in making decisions that affect them in intimate ways. But where sex is concerned, it is particularly counterproductive to teach children that individuals have no rights of control over their own organs. In this way, we set children up both for sexual abuse in childhood and for confused patterns in their adult relationships.

Programmes in the United States have found that when young people are specifically informed that they have a right to resist sexual intrusions by others, they are far more likely to be able to avoid or resist abuse. Children who have a knowledge of sex and understand their ownership of their own bodies are better able to anticipate and elude untoward behaviour from others and to say 'No' directly. The ability to say 'No' is often crucial; many adults stop their abusive behaviour as soon as the child makes clear that this behaviour is not desired. When adults are not stopped by resistance, an informed child is aware that it is the adult who is out of line. This means children are less likely to blame themselves and far more able to go to someone for help.

Even if uninformed or misinformed children are not abused in childhood, their sense of alienation from their organs can have disturbing ramifications in adulthood. If individuals cannot own and control their own organs, the sense that those organs are controlled by others, or other forces, can result in all sorts of unfortunate behaviour. Perhaps this explains some men's feelings that their organs have 'minds of their own' – that they act independently of the wishes of the men. If men have no control of their organs and the organs act on their own, males may be perceived as having less responsibility for their own sexual actions.

For women, the sense that our own sex organs are not for us leads naturally to the traditional presumption that these organs are for the use of others. Most social history supports that view, and it is understandable that, even within the feminist movement, people tend to be suspicious of women who demonstrate a desire to make their own pleasure a priority. In the larger culture, many women simply go along with what their partners do or demand because saying, 'Why should I?' just doesn't seem like an option.

It is precisely because we are kept so sexually ignorant in childhood that some of us can be so easily coerced into sexual acts we do not actually want. The real horror in the 'pornography victim' stories is not that men bring pornography home and show it to their female partners, but that these women are so uninformed about sexuality and their own rights over their bodies that they have never learned to access their own desires, let alone allow them to overrule the demands (or suggestions) of a male partner. Even a man who is not terribly coercive by nature may be inadvertently guiding his partner to perform acts that hold no interest for her – or even repel her – if she doesn't express her own desires and he always finds himself taking the lead. Many men are admittedly inept at reading body language and picking up non-verbal cues, but no man can read minds; how is a man supposed to know that his partner is uninterested in sex he suggests if she never says so and just does what he describes without inserting her own opinion?

Traditional values made female sexual ignorance necessary; if women were sexually ignorant, they didn't know enough to object. That was just as well, since they had little choice but to go along with their husbands' demands. Victorian values said that there was something disgusting and unsavoury about a woman who had her own sexual interests, anyway, so women were pretty much expected to suffer in silence rather than suggest more pleasurable approaches.

Those things, we hope, are changing – women, at least, are no longer expected to remain entirely ignorant right up to the wedding night. But, despite some small improvements, children continue to be raised in so much sexual ignorance that young people are still trying to educate themselves even while they are already engaged in sexual experimentation and relationships with others. This can sometimes seem a bit like having to play in the World Cup final or the Superbowl on the same day that you first heard about the existence of football games. Many people end up feeling more like someone else's practice materials than like lovers and friends.

Children need good, solid, honest information about sex, not over-protected ignorance. They need to understand that each of us individually owns and has responsibility for our own sexuality before they can be misled by the traditional myth and lies that permeate our culture. Only by breaking the silence can we break the pattern of distorted sexuality that is a fundamental part of our sexist society.

Creating victimizers

All feminists wish to eliminate sexual violence, but anti-pornography feminism places its focus on the elimination of pornography rather than on sexual offenders themselves. Concentrating on pornography avoids the tricky problem of dealing with the much more pervasive and intractable evils in our culture that function to oppress women and create abusers. Pornography seems scary to members of a society that treats sex as dirty and evil, so it makes an easy target. Repression, on the other hand, is all too acceptable in a society that practises it obsessively, so we are warped by that repression, formed by that repression, and harmed by that repression without ever actually seeing the way it shapes us, clings to us and suffocates us.

A society that took for granted that femaleness was not quite *humanness* operated as if women and the facts of reproduction were an unsavoury aspect of life, and therefore women were a bit of an embarrassment to the human race – our dirty little secret. It is precisely this attitude that has made it easy to treat sexuality – and sex, and therefore pornography – as something that should be kept outside of the public view. Those attitudes are certainly projected back onto women.

Looking at pornography, we can see that it makes us uncomfortable, although we may not actually see that this is because repression makes us uncomfortable about sex, and that sexism makes us afraid to relax about sex and to treat it more attractively. We can make it so stigmatized and illegal that working in the industry becomes dangerous, and then we can say that we oppose pornography because making it is dangerous, although there are many other dangerous industries we do not make calls to eliminate.

By concentrating on pornography, we can become mired in carefully chosen statistics from laboratory research that tell us little, and we can surround ourselves in rhetoric – and, most importantly, ignore the forces in society that create real dangers to us.

By looking at rapists and child abusers, on the other hand, we are forced to see the effects of our denial. We see women trapped in 'traditional' homes with 'family values' who beat their children, sometimes to death. We see fathers who have been taught from childhood to believe that both masturbation and sex outside of the family are wrong, and so use their children for sexual satisfaction rather than have an affair or even masturbate with pornography. We see men who once were boys, taught to fear sexual arousal and hate its sources – women.

Violent sex offenders are most often men who as boys had been punished for sexual expression and – disproportionately – punished for looking at pornography, although they see no more of it (and perhaps less of it) than other boys. They have learned that there was something wrong with sexually expressive women. Women who seem to be attractive or sexually active are 'asking for' violent sexual assault and 'deserve' to be raped.

John Money wrote in *Lovemaps* that:

> The taboo in our society condemns in childhood the very heterosexuality that it prescribes in adulthood. It condemns any genital manifestation of juvenile sexual rehearsal play as a sin that requires absolution or expiation. It defines some manifestations of eroticism, regardless of age, as perversions or, in lurid legalese, as abominable and unspeakable crimes against nature. They are so unspeakable that in some courtrooms the law specifies that a sexual charge need not even be stated in words.
>
> Just as they absorb their society's native language, children absorb also its sexual precepts, negative as well as positive. Even as precepts of antisexualism are in the process of vandalizing a child's lovemap, they continue to be absorbed. Lovemap defacement may be extensive, but total obliteration is unlikely.

In other words, they can't stop you from wanting to be sexually expressive, but they can really mess you up while they are trying. And by convincing children – especially young males – that sex itself is dirty or evil, they can teach them that anything that arouses sexual thoughts (such as women) is equally dirty or evil.

When Goldstein found that *all* of the rapists in his study sample had been punished for looking at pornography, while a mere 7 per cent of his cohort sample had been, that set off alarm bells for anyone who really cared about the causes of sexual violence. Being punished for looking at porn, discouraged from sexual expression, and taught conservative sexual values was seen as normal and healthy, and yet this was highly implicated in causing the development of rapists.

It was precisely this kind of revelation that formed the foundation of modern sexual progressivism. Clearly, it was vital that we change our entire way of raising children, dispense with enforced 'innocence' and instead begin giving children *positive* sexual information. Adults had to stop teaching children to feel shamed by their own bodies. Feminists who understand this kind of social science could never cave in to the anti-pornography movement, precisely because suppression of pornography is more likely to cause, rather than alleviate, the problem of sexual violence.

The territory of defaced lovemaps

Money and others have noted that repression is an ingredient in creating sexual violence. Violence in the environment, as in the case of Ted Bundy (see Chapter 5), can have similar effects. In the worst serial offenders, we usually see examples of both in an individual's early history. But it seems clear that our society's methods of raising children in sexual ignorance set people up so that even where serious violence or overt sex-negative messages may be absent, it is all too easy for us to be influenced by other sexist messages in society, to be traumatized by the introduction of sex into our lives before we've had any preparation for it, and to experience confusion when sexual feelings emerge without any positive outlets for them.

The greatest irony is that we actually believe we are protecting children by depriving them of information about sex. A common justification for censorship of pornography is that children may come to some sort of harm if their first introduction to sexuality comes in the form of confusing and perhaps inaccurate or disturbing sexual images in pornography – and yet the obvious preventative, of making sure that children are introduced to sexual information early in a more positive way, is not prescribed; in fact, the people who most strongly advocate censorship of sexual materials are often the most strongly opposed to sex education.

Unfortunately, it is these same people who control what little sex education is made available; feminists must not simply give whole-hearted support to any programme that calls itself 'sex education'. In the context of a political establishment that still cannot respect human bodies and sexuality, we must insist on producing our own sex education materials (as well as entertainment media) that present a coherent, responsible and positive approach that will not simply continue the punitive and grossly irresponsible attitudes toward sex that come from sexual conservatives.

In late 1993, the education secretary, John Patten, while announcing a move of sex education from the science curriculum to some other, more 'family values'-oriented, context, smeared the Family Planning Association for the suggestion that children as young as five years old should be given sex education. He seems to have the support of the home secretary and the prime minister. Perhaps none of these men are aware that children can be abused before they are 'old enough', in their view, to learn about sex, and maybe they even entertain the illusion that young people will refrain from sex, and from dangerous sexual practices, if they are kept ignorant. It is precisely that philosophy that has given the United States such an astonishingly high rate of teenaged and pre-teen single mothers, and while no western European country is quite as bad as America, Britain certainly has far higher teen pregnancy rates than the more liberal countries on the continent. The difference, quite simply, is in access to information and contraception; the countries that provide them early have low rates of teenage pregnancy, and the countries that restrict them to young people have higher rates of teen mothers. That same information is relevant to the spread of cervical cancer, AIDS, and other infectious disease. It makes no sense to hide this knowledge from young people.

For the children, they say, they will invoke censorship; but their interest in children does not extend to making sure they are provided with the nourishing love and attention they require to grow up alive and healthy. The children who can be seen sleeping in doorways on our high streets are not their concern, either. The children who are having children themselves, or facing death from AIDS, are not important enough to provide proper sex education and birth control for. Neither the children who will become rapists because of silence, myth and repression nor their victims are enough to move them. They exploit our horror at a small child's death with calls for more of the same, as if it ever saved the life of a Jamie Bulger or would have prevented his young killers' short but arduous climb to criminality.

But children are not served by ignorance and hysteria. Children need to be raised in the light, not kept in the dark. And we, as a society, must be prepared to face the light ourselves. We have shaded ourselves long enough in hypocrisy.

It would be a tragic mistake to continue allowing repressives to define the agenda; 15 years of anti-pornography activism by women have taken a terrible toll on the women's liberation movement and on society in general. The police have been given unconscionable levels of power, women have been frightened back into their homes, adults no longer feel free to express any interest in the welfare of children they encounter lest they are accused of being child molesters, and most of us have been encouraged to feel more shame about our bodies and the most damaging guilt over our slightest sexual fantasies. This is the very last thing feminists should ever have wanted.

If we are to prevent future violence, we must do precisely the opposite of what our 'protectors' want from us; we must be prepared to resist emotive manipulations to accept state repression. And if feminism is to have a future, it must be one of continuing to focus the light on the way society as a whole abuses us, child, woman and man. We must be prepared to question our most common assumptions, look again at our everyday sexism, and re-examine all of the roles we are expected to play. In addition to a continuing re-examination of the family and to addressing our economic situation, we must focus honestly on the sexual battleground and support all of those who are made to feel like outsiders because of our repression. In Gayle Rubin's words in 'Misguided, dangerous and wrong':

> Instead of fighting porn, feminists should oppose censorship, support the decriminalization of prostitution, call for the abolition of all obscenity laws, support the rights of sex workers, support women in management positions in the sex industry, support the availability of sexually explicit materials, support sex education for the young, affirm the rights of sexual minorities and affirm the legitimacy of human sexual diversity. Such a direction would begin to redress the mistakes of the past. It would restore feminism to a position of leadership and credibility in matters of sexual policy. And it would revive feminism as a progressive, visionary force in the domain of sexuality.

A more honest and open approach to sex for all will go a long way toward helping to reduce violence and oppression. And greater respect for children, as human beings, from the day they are born, is absolutely vital for women's equality and freedom for us all.

Or, as feminist musician Sarah Baranian once put it:

> Take down your family portrait
> And let those children be
> Hold off your fears and leave them a healthy breed
> The house is filled with hatred
> For all my mother's love
> So let them go.

References and further reading

Ageton, S.S., *Sexual Assault Among Adolescents*, Lexington Books, Lexington, MA, 1983.
Assiter, Alison and Carol, Avedon, *Bad Girls & Dirty Pictures: The challenge to reclaim feminism*, Pluto Press, London and Boulder, 1993.
Attorney General's Commission on Pornography (Meese Commission), *Attorney General's Commission on Pornography: Final Report*, US Department of Justice, Washington, DC, 1986.
Baker, Peter, 'Maintaining male power: why heterosexual men use pornography', in *Pornography: Women, Violence and Civil Liberties*, Catherine Itzin, ed., Oxford University Press, Oxford, 1992.
Barker, Martin, ed., *The Video Nasties: Freedom and censorship in the media*, Pluto Press, London and Sydney, 1984.
Baron, L., 'Pornography and gender equality: an empirical analysis', *Journal of Sex Research*, 27, 1990.
Baron, L. and Straus, M.A., 'Sexual stratification, pornography, and rape in the United States', in N.M. Malamuth and E. Donnerstein, eds, *Pornography and Sexual Aggression*, Academic Press, Orlando, 1984.
Baron, L. and Straus, M.A., 'Legitimate violence, pornography, and sexual inequality as explanations for state and regional differences in rape', manuscript, 1985.
Baron, L. and Straus, M.A., 'Rape and its relation to social disorganization, pornography, and sexual inequality in the United States', manuscript, 1986.
Bem, Sandra and Bem, Daryl, 'Case study of a nonconscious ideology: training woman to know her place', in Sue Cox, ed., *Female Psychology: The emerging self*, Science Research Associates, Chicago, 1976.
Betzold, Michael, 'How pornography shackles men and oppresses women', from J. Snodgrass, ed., *For Men Against Sexism*, in conference pack for 'Opposing Pornography: A One-day Conference for Men', held by Campaign Against Pornography and Censorship, London, September 1990.
Brame, Gloria G., Brame, William D. and Jacobs, Jon, *Different Loving: An exploration of the world of sexual dominance and submission*, Villard Books, New York, 1993.
Brown, Brian, 'Exactly what we wanted', in Martin Barker, ed., *The Video Nasties: Freedom and censorship in the media*, Pluto Press, London and Sydney, 1984.
Califia, Pat, *Macho Sluts*, Alyson Publications, Boston, 1988.
Carol, Avedon, 'Snuff: believing the worst', in Alison Assiter and Avedon Carol, eds, *Bad Girls & Dirty Pictures: The challenge to reclaim feminism*, Pluto Press, London and Boulder, 1993.
Cash, T.L., 'Mirror, mirror, on the wall ... ?: contrasts, effects and self-evaluations of physical attractiveness', *Personality and Social Psychology Bulletin*, 9, 1983.
Caught Looking, *Caught Looking: Feminism, pornography, and censorship*, Caught Looking, Inc. (Kate Ellis, Beth Jaker, Nan D. Hunter, Barbara O'Dair and Abby Tallmer,

References and further reading 203

eds), New York, 1986; third edition LongRiver Books, East Haven, 1992.

Cleaver, Eldridge, *Soul on Ice*, Dell, New York, 1968.

Clover, Carol J., *Men, Women and Chainsaws: Gender in the modern horror film*, Princeton University Press and BFI Publishing, London, 1992.

Clover, Carol J., 'Introduction', in Pamela Church Gibson and Roma Gibson, eds, *Dirty Looks: Women, pornography, power*, BFI Publishing, London, 1993.

Coliver, Sandra, ed., *Striking a Balance: Hate speech, freedom of expression and non-discrimination*, Article 19, University of Essex, 1992.

Court, John H., 'Pornography and sex-crimes: a re-evaluation in the light of recent trends around the world', *International Journal of Criminology and Penology*, 5, 1976.

Court, J.H., *Pornography: A Christian critique*, InterVarsity Christian Fellowship, Illinois, 1980.

Court, J.H., *Pornography and the Harm Condition*, Finders University of South Australia, Adelaide, 1980.

Court, J.H., 'Pornography: an update', *British Journal of Sexual Medicine*, May, 1981.

Court, J.H., testimony to New Zealand Indecent Publications Tribunal, P.J. Cartwright, Chair, Wellington, NZ, transcripts, 1990.

Cumberbatch, Guy and Howitt, Dennis, *Pornography: Impacts and influences (a review of available research evidence on the effects of pornography)*, Home Office Research and Planning Unit, London, 1990.

Dinnerstein, Dorothy, *The Mermaid and the Minotaur*, Harper Colophon, New York, 1977.

Donnerstein, E., 'Pornography: its effect on violence against women', in N.M. Malamuth and E. Donnerstein, eds, *Pornography and Sexual Aggression*, Academic Press, Orlando, 1984.

Donnerstein, Edward, testimony to the District Court of Ontario, 1989, quoted from Marcia Pally, *Sense & Censorship: The vanity of bonfires – resource materials on sexually explicit material, violent material and censorship: research and public policy implications*, Americans for Constitutional Freedom and the Freedom to Read Foundation, New York, 1991.

Donnerstein, E. and Barrett, G., 'The effects of erotic stimuli on male aggression towards females', *Journal of Personality and Social Psychology*, 36, 1978.

Donnerstein, E. and Berkowitz, L., 'Victim reactions in aggressive erotic films as a factor in violence against women', *Journal of Personality and Social Psychology*, 41, 1981.

Donnerstein, E. and Hallam, J., 'Facilitating effects of erotica on aggression against women, *Journal of Personality and Social Psychology*, 36, 1978.

Donnerstein, E. and Linz, D., 'Technique designed to mitigate the impact of mass media sexual violence on adults and adolescents', in E.R. Mulvey and J.L. Haugaard, eds, *Report of the Surgeon General's Workshop on Pornography and Public Health*, US Public Health Service and US Department of Health and Human Services, Washington, DC, 1986.

Donnerstein, Edward, Linz, Daniel and Penrod, Stephen, *The Question of Pornography: Research findings and policy implications*, Free Press, New York, 1987.

Donnerstein, E., Donnerstein, M. and Evans, R., 'Erotic stimuli and aggression: facilitation or inhibition?', *Journal of Personality and Social Psychology*, 32, 1975.

Dworkin, Andrea, *Woman Hating*, E.P. Dutton, New York 1974.

Dworkin, Andrea, *Pornography: Men possessing women*, Perigee, New York, 1981.

Dworkin, Andrea, *Our Blood*, The Women's Press, London, 1982.

Dworkin, Andrea, *Right-wing Women*, Perigee, New York, 1983.

Dworkin, Andrea, *Intercourse*, Secker & Warburg, London, 1987.

Dworkin, Andrea, *Mercy*, Secker & Warburg, London, 1990.

Dworkin, Andrea, interview by Helen Birch, 'Porn between two lovers: right or wrong?', *Guardian*, 5 December 1991.

Dworkin, Andrea and MacKinnon, Catharine A., *Pornography and Civil Rights: A new day*

for women's equality, Organizing Against Pornography, Minneapolis, 1988.
Einsiedel, Edna, 'The experimental research evidence: effects of pornography on the "average individual"', in *Attorney General's Commission on Pornography: Final Report*, US Department of Justice, Washington, DC, 1986.
El-Faizy, Monique, 'The naked and the deadly', *Guardian*, 6 December 1993.
Everywoman, Pornography and Sexual Violence: Evidence of the links, Everywoman, London, 1988.
Feminists Against Censorship, 'Ask yourself ... do you really want more censorship?', original black and white leaflet, 1989.
Feminists Against Censorship, 'Pornography: there's no simple answer', pink leaflet sponsored and printed by *Gay Times*, 1992.
Feminists Against Censorship, 'Ask yourself ... do you really want more censorship?', purple leaflet incorporating and updating text from first two leaflets, sponsored and printed by *Gay Times*, 1993.
Feminists Against Censorship, *Pornography and Feminism: The case against censorship*, Gillian Rodgerson and Elizabeth Wilson, eds, Lawrence & Wishart, London, 1991.
Feminists Against Censorship, 'The wages of anti-censorship campaigning', in Alison Assiter and Avedon Carol, eds, *Bad Girls & Dirty Pictures: The challenge to reclaim feminism*, Pluto Press, London and Boulder, 1993.
Firestone, Shulamith, *The Dialectic of Sex*, William Morrow & Company, New York, 1970.
Friday, Nancy, *My Secret Garden*, Quartet Books, London, 1982.
Gentry, Cynthia, 'Pornography and rape: an empirical analysis', *Deviant Behaviour: An Interdisciplinary Journal*, 12, 1991.
Gilman, Charlotte Perkins, *The Yellow Wallpaper*, The Feminist Press, Old Westbury, NY, 1973.
Goldstein, M.J. and Kant, H.S., *Pornography and Sexual Deviance: A report of the legal and behavioural institute*, University of California Press, Los Angeles, 1973.
Grace, Della, *Love Bites*, Gay Men's Press, London, 1991.
Griffin, Susan, *Pornography and Silence: Culture's revenge against nature*, Harper Colophon, New York, 1981.
Henley, Nancy M., *Body Politics: Power, sex, and nonverbal communication*, Spectrum/Prentice-Hall, Englewood Cliffs, NJ, 1977.
Hlavaty, Arthur, *The Bloodshot Pyramid*, 22, October/November 1993.
Janus, Samuel S. and Janus, Cynthia, *The Janus Report on Sexual Behaviour*, John Wiley & Sons, New York, Chichester, Brisbane and Singapore, 1993.
Jeffreys, Sheila, *Anticlimax*, The Women's Press, London, 1990.
Kant, H.S. and Goldstein, M.J., 'Pornography and its effects', in D. Savitz and J. Johnson, eds, *Crime in Society*, John Wiley, New York, 1978.
Kappler, Suzanne, *The Pornography of Representation*, Polity Press, Cambridge, in association with Basil Blackwell, Oxford, 1986.
Kelley, Kathryn, 'Sexual attitudes as determinants of the motivational properties of exposure to erotica', *Personality and Individual Differences*, 6, 1985.
Kelley, Kathryn, 'The effects of sexual and/or aggressive film exposure on helping, hostility, and attitudes about the sexes', *Journal of Research in Personality*, 19, 1985.
Kelley, Kathryn, 'Prosocial responding and affect induction: sex differences following exposure to sexually explicit slides', quoted in K. Kelley *et al.*,'Three faces of sexual explicitness', in D. Zillmann and J. Bryant, eds, *Pornography: Research advances and policy considerations*, Academic Press, Orlando, 1989.
Kelley, Kathryn and Byrne, D., 'Assessment of sexual responding: arousal, affect, and behavior', in J. Cacioppo and R. Petty, eds, *Social Psychophysiology: A sourcebook*, Guildford Press, New York, 1983.
Kelley, Kathryn and Musialowski, D., 'Female sexual victimization and effects of warnings about violent pornography', presented to the Eastern Psychological Association, New

York, 1986.
Kendrick, Walter, *The Secret Museum: Pornography in modern culture*, Viking, New York, 1987.
King, Alison, 'Mystery and imagination: the case of pornography effects studies', in Alison Assiter and Avedon Carol, eds, *Bad Girls & Dirty Pictures: The challenge to reclaim feminism*, Pluto Press, London and Boulder, 1993.
Koss, M., Gidycz, Christine and Wisniewski, Nadine, 'The scope of rape: incidence and prevalence of sexual aggression and victimization in a national sample of higher education students', *Journal of Consulting and Clinical Psychology*, 55, 1987.
Koss, M. and Lros, Cheryl, 'Sexual experiences survey: a research instrument investigating sexual aggression and victimization', *Journal of Consulting and Clinical Psychology*, 50, 1982.
Koss, M. and Thomas, E.D., 'Predictors of sexual aggression among a national sample of male college students', paper presented at NY Academy of Sciences Conference on Human Sexual Aggression: Current Perspectives, New York, January 1987.
Krafka, C.L., 'Sexually explicit, sexually violent, and violent media: effects of multiple naturalistic exposures and debriefing on female viewers', doctoral dissertation, Wisconsin, 1985.
Kramer, Mark, 'The mastur race', Dian Hanson interview, *Gauntlet*, 5, 1993.
Kutchinsky, B., 'The effect of easy availability of pornography on the incidence of sex crimes: the Danish experience', *Journal of Social Issues*, 29, 1973.
Kutchinsky, Berl, 'Pornography and its effects in Denmark and the United States: a rejoinder and beyond', *Comparative Social Research: An Annual*, 1985.
Lesbian and Gay Freedom Movement, untitled leaflet on pornography handed out to 'Opposing Pornography: A One-day Conference for Men', held by Campaign Against Pornography and Censorship, London, September 1990.
Linz, Daniel and Malamuth, Neil, *Communication Concepts 5: Pornography*, Sage Publications, Newbury Park, London, New Delhi, 1993.
Lynn, Barry, *Harvard Civil Rights–Civil Liberties Law Review*, 21, quoted from Marcia Pally, *Sense & Censorship: The vanity of bonfires – resource materials on sexually explicit material, violent material and censorship: research and public policy implications*, Americans for Constitutional Freedom and the Freedom to Read Foundation, New York, 1991.
MacKinnon, Catharine A., *Feminism Unmodified: Discourses on life and law*, Harvard University Press, Cambridge, MA, 1987.
MacKinnon, Catharine A., *Toward a Feminist Theory of the State*, Harvard University Press, Cambridge, MA, 1989.
MacKinnon, Catharine A., *Only Words*, Harvard University Press, Cambridge, MA, 1993.
Malamuth, N.M., 'Aggression against women: cultural and individual causes,' in N. Malamuth and E. Donnerstein, eds, *Pornography and Sexual Aggression*, Academic Press, Orlando, 1984.
Malamuth, N.M., 'Erotica, aggression and perceived appropriateness', paper presented to the 86th annual convention of the American Psychological Association, Toronto, 1978.
Malamuth, N. and Ceniti, J., 'Repeated exposure to violent and non-violent pornography: likelihood of raping ratings and laboratory aggression against women', *Aggressive Behavior*, 12, 1986.
Malamuth, N. and Check, J.V.P., 'Penile tumescence and perceptual responses to rape as a function of victim's perceived reactions', *Journal of Applied Social Psychology*, 10, 1980.
Malamuth, N. and Check, J.V.P., 'The effects of aggressive pornography on beliefs of rape myths: individual differences', *Journal of Research in Personality*, 19, 1985.
Malamuth, N. and Donnerstein, E., 'The effect of aggressive–pornographic mass media stimuli', in L. Berkowitz, ed., *Advances in Experimental Social Psychology*, 15,

Academy Press, New York, 1982.
Malamuth, N.M. and Donnerstein, E., eds, *Pornography and Sexual Aggression*, Academic Press, Orlando, 1984.
Malamuth, N., Check, J.V.P. and Briere, J., 'Sexual arousal in response to aggression: ideological, aggressive, and sexual correlates', *Journal of Personality & Social Psychology*, 50, 1986.
Malamuth, N., Haber, S. and Feshbach, S., 'Testing hypothesis regarding rape: exposure to sexual violence, sex differences and the "normality" of rapists', *Journal of Research in Personality*, 14, 1980.
McCormack, Thelma, 'Making sense of the research on pornography', Appendix I in Barda Burstyn, ed., *Women Against Censorship*, Douglas and McIntyre, Vancouver, 1985.
McDonald, James, *A Dictionary of Obscenity, Taboo and Euphemism*, Sphere Books, London, 1988.
McElroy, Wendy, 'The unholy alliance', *Liberty*, February 1993.
Milgram, Stanley, 'Behavioral studies of obedience', *Journal of Abnormal and Social Psychology*, 67, 1963.
Milgram, Stanley, 'Some conditions of obedience and disobedience to authority', *Human Relations*, 18, 1965.
Milgram, Stanley, 'Interpreting obedience: error and evidence', in A.G. Miller, ed., *The Social Psychology of Psychological Research*, Free Press, New York, 1972.
Milgram, Stanley, *Obedience to Authority: An experimental view*, Harper & Row, New York, 1974.
Millett, Kate, *Sexual Politics*, Avon Equinox Edition, New York, 1971.
Money, John, *Lovemaps: Clinical concepts of sexual/erotic health and pathology, paraphilia, and gender transposition in childhood, adolescence, and maturity*, Irvington Publishers, New York, 1986.
Moorcock, Michael, 'Who's really covering up?' and 'The case against pornography' in *Casablanca*, Victor Gollancz, London, 1989.
Morgan, Robin, ed., *Sisterhood is Powerful: An anthology of writings from the women's liberation movement*, Vintage Books (Random House), New York, 1970.
Morgan, Robin, 'Theory and practice: pornography and rape', *Going Too Far: The personal chronicle of a feminist*, Vintage Books (Random House), New York, 1978.
Mosher, D.L., 'Sex callousness toward women', *Technical Report of the Commission on Obscenity and Pornography*, 7, 1970.
Mueller, C.W. and Donnerstein, E., 'Film-facilitated arousal and prosocial behavior', *Journal of Experimental Social Psychology*, 17, 1981.
Organizing Against Pornography, slide show, ''Entertainment for men'': what it is and what it means', in Catherine Itzin, ed., *Pornography: Women, violence and civil liberties*, Oxford University Press, Oxford, 1992.
Pally, Marcia, *Sense & Censorship: The vanity of bonfires – resource materials on sexually explicit material, violent material and censorship: research and public policy implications*, Americans for Constitutional Freedom and the Freedom to Read Foundation, New York, 1991.
Palys, Ted S., 'Testing the common wisdom: the social content of pornography', *Canadian Psychology*, 27(1), 1986.
Partridge, Eric, *The Penguin Dictionary of Historical Slang*, Penguin Books, London, 1972.
Pepinster, Catherine, 'Strange customs', *Time Out*, 4–11 August 1993.
Peterson, J., Moore, K. and Furstenberg, F., 'Television viewing and early initiation of sexual intercourse: is there a link?', paper presented to American Pyschological Association, 1984.
Pollard, Nettie, 'The small matter of children', in Alison Assiter and Avedon Carol, eds, *Bad Girls & Dirty Pictures: The challenge to reclaim feminism*, Pluto Press, London and Boulder, 1993.

References and further reading 207

Przybyla, D.P., 'The facilitating effects of exposure to erotica on male pro-social behaviour', doctoral dissertation, SUNY at Albany, 1985.

Reidelbach, Maria, *Completely Mad: A history of the comic book and magazine*, Little, Brown, New York, 1991.

Rose, June, *Marie Stopes and the Sexual Revolution*, Faber and Faber, London, 1992.

Reuben, David, *Everything You Always Wanted to Know About Sex (But Were Afraid to Ask)*, W.H. Allen, London, 1970.

Rubin, Gayle, 'Thinking sex: notes for a radical theory of the politics of sexuality', in Carole S. Vance, ed., *Pleasure and Danger: Exploring female sexuality*, Routledge & Kegan Paul, Boston, London, Melbourne and Henley, 1984.

Rubin, Gayle, 'Misguided, dangerous and wrong: an analysis of anti-pornography politics', in Alison Assiter and Avedon Carol, eds, *Bad Girls & Dirty Pictures: The challenge to reclaim feminism*, Pluto Press, London and Boulder, 1993.

Russ, Joanna, 'Symposium: women in science fiction', *Khatru*, 3 and 4, 1975.

Scott, J.E. and Cuvalier, S.J., 'Sexual violence in *Playboy* magazine: a longitudinal content analysis', *Journal of Sex Research*, 23(4), 1987.

Scott, J.E. and Schwalm, L., 'Pornography and rape: an examination of adult theater rates and rape rates by state,' in J.P. Scott and T. Hirschi, eds., *Controversial Issues in Crime and Justice*, Sage Press, Beverly Hills, CA, 1988.

Scott, J.E. and Schwalm, L., 'Rape rates and the circulation rates of adult magazines', *Journal of Sex Research*, 24, 1988.

Serbin, Lisa and O'Leary, K. Daniel, 'How nursery schools teach girls to shut up', *Psychology Today*, 9, 1975.

Smith, Anna Marie, 'Outlaws as legislators: feminist anti-censorship politics and queer activism', in Victoria Harwood, David Oswell, Kay Parkinson and Anna Ward, eds, *Pleasure Principles: Politics, sexuality and ethics*, Lawrence & Wishart, London, 1993.

Stanley, Lawrence A., 'Exposing the dirty-mindedness of the guardians of our morality', *The Organ*, 12, 1993.

Sterling, Jasmine, 'Banned in Canada', editorial, *Bad Attitude*, 8, 3, 1993.

Stoltenberg, John, 'Sadomasochism: eroticized violence, eroticized powerlessness', in Robin Ruth Linden, Darlene R. Pagano, Diana E. H. Russell and Susan Leigh Starr, eds, *Against Sadomasochism*, Fog in the Well Press, San Francisco, 1982.

Stoltenberg, John, speech to 'Opposing Pornography: A One-day Conference for Men', held by Campaign Against Pornography and Censorship, London, September 1990.

Strossen, Nadine, 'A feminist critique of "the" feminist critique of pornography', *Virginia Law Review*, 79, 5, August 1993.

Tavris, Carol and Offir, Carole, *The Longest War*, Harcourt Brace Jovanovich, New York, Chicago, San Francisco and Atlanta, 1977.

Thompson, W. and Annetts, J., *Soft Core: A content analysis of legally available pornography in Great Britain 1968–90 and the implications of aggression research*, University of Reading, Reading, 1990.

Vance, Carole S., ed., *Pleasure and Danger: Exploring female sexuality*, Routledge & Kegan Paul, Boston, London, Melbourne and Henley, 1984.

Vance, Carole S., 'Negotiating sex and gender in the Attorney General's Commission on Pornography', in Lynne Segal and Mary McIntosh, eds, *Sex Exposed: Sexuality and the pornography debate*, Virago, London, 1992.

Waller, Reed and Worley, Kate, 'Tip of the iceberg' (Omaha the Cat Dancer), *Gauntlet*, 5, 1993.

Ward, Andrew, 'Perfect woman, overplanned', *The International Herald Tribune*, 10 September 1993.

Weaver, J.B., 'Effects of portrayals of female sexuality and violence against women on percentages of women', dissertation, University of Indiana, 1987.

Webster, Paula, 'Pornography and pleasure', *Heresies* (Sex Issue), 12, 1981.

Williams, Linda, *Hard Core: Power, pleasure, and the 'frenzy of the visible'*, Pandora Press, London, 1990.
Willis, Ellen, 'An unholy alliance', *Newsday*, 25 February 1992.
Women on Words and Images, *Dick and Jane as Victims: Sex stereotyping in children's readers*, Women on Words and Images, Princeton, NJ, 1972.
Women on Words and Images, *Channeling Children: Sex stereotyping on prime time TV*, Women on Words and Images, Princeton, NJ, 1975.
Wyre, Ray, 'Pornography and sexual violence: working with sex offenders', in Catherine Itzin, ed., *Pornography: Women, violence and civil liberties*, Oxford University Press, Oxford, 1992.
Zillmann, D., 'Excitation transfer in communication-mediated aggressive behaviour', *Journal of Experimental Social Psychology*, 7, 1971.
Zillmann, D., 'Victimization of women through pornography', proposal to the National Science Foundation, Indiana University, Indiana, 1984.
Zillmann, D., testimony presented to Attorney General's Commission on Pornography, 1985.
Zillmann, D., 'Effects of prolonged consumption of pornography', in D. Zillmann and J. Bryant, eds, *Pornography: Research advances and policy considerations*, Academic Press, Orlando, 1989 (originally presented to the Surgeon General's Workshop on Pornography and Public Health, 1986).
Zillmann, D. and Bryant, J., 'Pornography, sexual callousness and the trivialization of rape', *Journal of Communication*, 32, 1982.
Zillmann, D. and Bryant, J., 'Effects of massive exposure to pornography', in N. Malamuth and E. Donnerstein, eds, *Pornography and Sexual Aggression*, Academic Press, Orlando, 1984.
Zillmann, D. and Bryant, J., 'Shifting preferences in pornography consumption', *Communication Research*, 13, 1986.
Zillmann, D. and Bryant, J., 'Pornography's impact on sexual satisfaction', *Journal of Applied Social Psychology*, 18, 1988.
Zillmann, D. and Bryant, J., 'Effects of prolonged consumption of pornography on family values', *Journal of Family Issues*, 9, 1988.
Zillmann, D. and Bryant, J., *Pornography: Research advances & policy considerations*, Academic Press, Orlando, 1989.
Zillmann, D. and Sapolsky, B., 'What mediates the effect of mild erotica on annoyance and hostile behaviour in males?', *Journal of Personality and Social Psychology*, 35, 1977.
Zillmann, D. and Weaver, J.B., 'Pornography and men's sexual callousness towards women', in D. Zillmann and J. Bryant, eds, *Pornography: Research advances and policy considerations*, Academic Press, Orlando, 1989.

Further reading

National Council for Civil Liberties, *Against Censorship*, National Council for Civil Liberties, London, 1972.
Pally, Marcia, *Sex & Censorship: Reflections on forbidden mirrors and the will to censor*, Ecco Press, Hopewell, NJ, 1994.
Thompson, Bill, *Soft Core*, Cassell, London, 1994.
Thompson, Bill, *Sadomasochism*, Cassell, London, 1994.

Index

advertising, 3, 27, 121, 142, 188, 193
age of consent, 94, 95, 101
ageism, 170, 190
Ageton, Suzanne, 72
aggression, 62–4, 67, 72, 101, 151, 162, 194
AIDS, 2, 15, 148, 151, 158, 159, 172, 188, 200
Allison, Dorothy, 51
American Civil Liberties Union, 7, 54
American Hunter, The, 74
anecdotal evidence, 84
Annetts, J., 42
Aquinas, Thomas, 89
assault, 12, 28, 36, 64, 66, 77, 148, 153, 198
attitudes, 5, 9, 11, 16, 21, 27, 44, 52, 57, 61, 63, 64, 67–9, 71, 72, 74, 75, 86, 90, 93, 97, 102, 104, 119, 137, 140, 149, 153, 159, 165, 167, 169, 173, 189, 190, 197, 200
Attorney General's Commission on Pornography, *see* Meese Commission
Austin, Mark, 77
Axelrod, Beverly, 166

Bad Attitude, 46–7, 50, 106, 126
Bad Girls & Dirty Pictures, 80
Baker, Peter, 172, 179, 186, 187
Barker, Martin, 17–19, 77–9
Baron, Larry, 62, 71, 73
BBC, 45, 93, 127, 163, 166
Beatty, Warren, 132
beliefs, 1, 2, 7, 8, 17, 23, 101, 148
Bell, P.A., 62
Bem, Sandra and Daryl, 193
Betzold, Michael 175, 176, 180, 182–6, 189
Billboard Magazine, 54
Blume, Judy, 54

bondage, 105, 123, 134
Brady, Ian, 76, 77
breasts, 15, 25, 69, 70, 73, 91, 117, 139, 142, 172, 175–8, 184, 185
Bremner, Moyra, 76, 77, 81
Brown, Wendy, 54
Brute, 86
Bryant, Jennings, 23, 67–9, 90
Buchanan, Patrick, 152, 169
Bundy, Ted, 80–2, 199

Calderone, Mary S., 51
Califia, Pat, 106
callousness, 23, 67
Campaign Against Censorship, 56, 122
Campaign Against Pornography, 47, 48, 57, 76, 81, 118, 122, 126, 127, 130, 163, 172, 187
Campaign Against Pornography and Censorship, 48, 52, 56, 57, 76, 122, 128, 172, 187
Cannibal Holocaust, 80
capitalism, 127, 128, 152, 182, 189
Cash, T.L., 83
Caught Looking, 51
Chain Reaction, 170
child abuse, 21, 22, 52, 95, 112, 113, 116, 118, 119, 160–2
children, 5, 6, 9, 10, 12, 13, 15, 17–23, 25, 29, 43, 46, 55, 68, 72, 73, 78, 79, 90, 97, 104, 109–19, 134, 136, 140, 144, 147, 150, 158–62, 169, 170, 182, 186, 187, 188, 190–201
Christian right, 53
Chugg, Sam, 49
church, 4, 5, 10, 27, 49, 146, 150
civil liberties, 7, 23, 45, 52, 54, 113, 122, 155, 186
civil rights, 4, 23, 50, 53

209

Cleaver, Eldridge, 166
Cleaver, Kathleen, 166
Cline, Victor, 92
clitoridectomy, 84
clitoris, 11, 30, 32, 35, 142
Clover, Carol J., 26, 77
Comics Code Authority, 3
condoms, 102, 151, 158
Conlin, Kelli, 54
consciousness raising, 156
constitution, 138
Cook Report, The, 83
Corbett, Robin, 93
correlation, 55, 73, 74
Court, John, 74, 75
Crumb, Robert, 3
cunnilingus, 34, 86, 91, 115, 131, 142, 181, 186
cunt, 32, 33, 35, 142–3, 176, 180, 184

Daly, Mary, 27
De Crow, Karen, 54
Deayton, Angus, 179
Dialectic of Sex, The, 190
dildos, 99, 131, 142
Dinnerstein, Dorothy, 191
Dirty Looks, 26
Dispatches, 83
domestic violence, 3, 40, 85, 86, 118, 149
Donnerstein, Edward, 42, 62–4, 75, 82, 83, 92
Dworkin, Andrea, 45, 48, 50, 51, 53, 76, 83, 102, 103, 106, 123–6, 131, 134, 135, 143, 152, 157, 163, 173
Dworkin–MacKinnon legislation, 48, 51, 53, 83, 102, 152

economic coercion, 134–6
Ehrenreich, Barbara, 54
Einsiedel, Edna, 66, 67, 92
English Collective of Prostitutes, 151
Ephron, Nora, 54
erotica
   definition of, 25, 26, 46, 47, 100, 106, 121–3, 126
Everywoman, 52, 83
exploitation, 52, 112, 117, 129, 137, 160

Falwell, Jerry, 169
family, 4–6, 9, 10, 22, 27, 72, 73, 81–3, 85, 90, 96, 111, 118, 119, 144, 146, 148–50, 159, 161, 170, 182, 184, 188–90, 192, 193, 198, 200, 201

Family Planning Association, 200
fat, 177–80
FBI, 81
fellatio, 34, 46, 66, 86, 89, 115, 131, 139, 142, 186
female genital mutilation, 84, 158
Female Mission on the Fallen, 12
female response, 31, 32
Feminist Anti-Censorship Taskforce, 51
Feminists Against Censorship, 13, 51–3, 55–9, 76, 86–8, 127, 128, 143, 149, 153, 163, 172, 187
Feminists for Free Expression, 53–5
Ferguson, Sarah, 179, 180
Festival of Light, 15, 74
fetish, 105, 112, 131, 153
Field and Stream, 74
Firestone, Shulamith, 190
First Amendment, 14, 45, 138, 186
foot-binding, 84
foreplay, 102
Forum, 138, 163
Foster, Jody, 132
free expression, 4, 45, 52–4, 102, 138
freedom of expression, 7, 8, 48, 55
freedom of speech, 2, 138
freedom of the press, 2, 47, 139
Freud, Sigmund, 108, 131, 132
Friday, Nancy, 54
Friedan, Betty, 54, 59
Frodi, A., 62
fuck 32–5, 91, 124, 125

Gay Liberation Front, 15, 16, 53, 95
Gay News, 50
Gay Times, 128, 187
Gentry, Cynthia, 74
Giaretto, Henry, 22, 119
Grace, Della, 58, 157
Grahn, Judy, 156
Green, Sharon, 106
Guardian, the, 122, 131, 171, 179
Guns and Ammo, 74

Hames, Michael, 21, 169
Hanson, Dian, 112, 117
Hard Core, 31, 42, 80,
Have I Got News For You, 179
Henley, Nancy, 193
Hepburn, Audrey, 25
Hill, Anita, 165
Hindley, Myra, 76
Hitler, Adolf, 2, 4

Index 211

Hlavaty, Arthur D., 95
Hunniford, Gloria, 163
Hustler, 116

I Spit On Your Grave, 18, 77, 78, 80
Indianapolis, 50, 51, 152
Isaacs, Susan, 54
ITC survey, 16, 17
Itzin, Catherine, 48, 49, 76, 113–15, 122, 126, 142, 143, 172, 186, 187

Jacklin, Carol, 194
Jeffreys, Sheila, 48, 124–6, 157
Joffe, Carole, 194
Jong, Erica, 54
Joy of Cooking, The, 86
Juliette, 76, 77
Justine, 76, 77

Kelley, Kathryn, 64, 71
Kelly, Liz, 163
Kincaid, Jamaica, 54
King, Alison, 71
Kinsey Institute, 95
Koprowski, Isabel, 162
Koss, Mary, 66
Krafka, Carol, 82
Kutchinsky, Berl, 74

Lacan, Jacques, 108, 131
legislation, 13, 14, 17, 18, 46, 48, 51, 53–4, 118
lesbians, 99–102, 106, 124, 126, 130, 131, 133, 151, 152, 157, 188, 192
Lesbian and Gay Freedom Movement, 187–9
lesbian separatism, 52, 101
Levin, Judith, 54
Lewis, Dorothy, 81
likelihood to rape, 64–7
Linz, Daniel, 42, 63, 68, 83, 90–2
Lovelace, Linda, 134
Lynn, Barry, 23
Lyon, Phyllis, 54

Maccoby, Eleanor, 194
MacKinnon, Catharine, 45, 48, 50, 51, 53, 83, 102, 134, 149, 152
Mad Magazine, 3
Malamuth, Neil, 65, 68, 90, 91
marriage, 10, 29, 30, 68, 90, 109, 130, 143, 148, 149, 179
Martin, Del, 54

Martyna, Wendy, 193
masturbation, 22, 34, 41, 62, 89, 91–4, 119, 142, 180, 182, 183, 185, 188, 195, 198
Mayfair, 86
McElroy, Wendy, 134
Meese Commission, 5, 50, 66, 67, 80, 83, 87, 91, 92, 116, 152, 153
Merck, Mandy, 53
Milgram, Stanley, 60, 61
Millett, Kate, 51, 59, 75
Minneapolis Hearings on Pornography, 53, 83, 134
Money, Dr John, 92–3, 198–9
monogamy, 107
Moors Murders, 76, 77
moral right, 4, 6, 15, 23, 37, 50, 68, 81, 89, 102, 118, 119, 139, 149, 152, 160
Morgan, Robin, 27, 44, 45, 152
Mosher, D.L., 62
motherhood, 135, 161, 191, 192, 201
Ms. Magazine, 45, 50, 66
Ms. Magazine Campus Project on Sexual Assault, 66
Mueller, C.W., 64

National Council for Civil Liberties, 52, 56, 122
National Organization for Women, 54
National Viewers and Listeners Association, 12
Nead, Lynda, 26
Nelson, Pamela B., 3
New Man, 171–87, 189
Newman, Paul, 132
Newmann, Eric, 33
newsagents, 47
Nichols, Nichelle, 166, 167
Norman, John, 106
nuclear family, 90, 182, 188, 192

O'Leary, K. Daniel, 194
O'Sullivan, Sue, 53, 59
objectification, 172, 173
Obscene Publications Acts, 12, 13, 19, 25, 155, 156, 175
Obscene Publications Squad, 21, 102, 112, 113, 169
obscenity, 1, 2, 12–15, 25, 32, 45, 50, 55, 112, 150, 155, 163, 174, 178, 201
Offir, Carole, 194
Omaha the Cat Dancer, 185
Omnibus, 45, 83
On Our Backs, 106

oppression, 2, 6, 7, 44, 45, 126, 131, 146, 188–90, 201
orgasm, 29, 31, 32, 34, 89, 90, 93, 99, 124, 180, 181
orgasmic, 11
Orkney Islands, 161
Orlando, Joe, 3
Outrageous Women, 106
Outsiders, 107, 133, 169, 201
Owens, Tuppy, 107, 135
Oz, 14

paedophilia, 20, 94, 109, 110, 113, 115, 118
page 3, 26, 47, 129, 177
Pally, Marcia, 22, 37, 63, 73, 81, 92, 116, 119
Paltrow, Lynn M., 54
Parliament, 28, 47, 66, 138
patriarchy, 125, 151
Penrod, Steven, 63, 83
Penthouse, 43, 116, 121, 122, 126, 129, 163
permissive, 6, 12, 42
perversion, 20, 21, 89, 91, 102
Pinzler, Isabelle Katz, 54
Playboy, 25, 43, 48, 73, 86, 116, 121, 123, 175, 180, 181, 183
pleasure, 5, 6, 30, 32, 34, 35, 49, 51, 58, 84, 85, 90, 91, 100, 101, 107, 108, 124–6, 131, 141, 143, 145, 158, 159, 176, 184, 196
Pleasure and Danger, 51, 107
political lesbianism, 48, 98, 124, 126
political lesbians, 51, 101
Pollard, Nettie, 15, 53, 59
porn shops, 39, 41, 43, 45, 46, 133, 186
'Pornography: there's no simple answer', 86
Primarolo, Dawn, 45
Princess Diana, 179
pro-social, 64
prostitution, 9–12, 14, 24–5, 39, 49, 87, 94, 129–30, 143–4, 151, 164, 168, 201
Przybyla, D.P., 64
Puritanism, 160, 184–6, 189

Quim, 33, 58, 106, 126

race, 101, 138, 141, 166–8, 197
racism, 138, 141, 164–70
rape, 5–7, 10, 28, 33, 36–8, 40, 44, 49, 52, 63–7, 71–8, 80, 87, 88, 95, 104, 109, 118, 123, 126, 137, 139, 145, 147, 148, 161, 165, 169

rape myth, 75
rape rates, 37
rapists, 77
Razzle, 25
Red Dwarf, 167
Red Hot Television, 121
Regnery, Alfred, 116
Reidelbach, Maria, 3
Reisman, Judith, 115–17
religious right, 4
reproduction, 4, 11, 89–91, 101, 150, 160, 197
research, 5, 16, 17, 20, 21, 27, 41, 42, 48, 52, 55, 60–4, 66, 67, 69, 70–3, 78, 79, 81, 82, 84, 90, 92, 98, 103, 116, 117, 120, 135, 158, 193, 194, 198
Reuben, David, 94
Rich, Adrienne, 54, 59
Robinson, Tom, 50
Rodgerson, Gillian, 53, 59
Rogers, Barbara, 52
romance, 29, 107
Royalle, Candida, 128
Rubin, Gayle, 4, 40, 87, 94, 95, 107, 120, 121, 143, 149, 201
Russ, Joanna, 3
Russell, Diana, 44

Sade, Marquis de, 76, 77
sadomasochism, 13, 91, 94, 103, 107
 see also SM
safer sex, 57, 102, 158, 159
Sanger, Margaret, 11, 150
Sapolsky, B., 62
Satanic abuse, 161
Schwalm, Loretta, 74
Scott, Joseph, 74
Segal, Lynne, 53, 59, 88
self-abuse, 180
Senate Bill 1521, 54, 55
Serbin, Lisa, 194
serial killers, 76, 80, 81
sex dualism, 101
sex shops, 14, 39, 46
sex workers, 88, 130
sexology, 116
sexual coercion, 86
sexual freedom, 10, 47, 68
Sexual Politics, 40
sexual revolution, 36, 38, 90, 101, 144, 145, 181, 183
Shatner, William, 167
Short, Clare, 47, 93, 162

Siemann, Catherine, 54
Sisterhood is Powerful, 27
Sixties permissiveness, 15, 37, 118
SM, 13, 23, 41, 42, 44, 46, 66, 86, 89, 90, 94, 98, 103–9, 122, 125, 130, 131, 142, 153, 170, 172, 173
  see also sadomasochism
Smith, Anna Marie, 57–9
Smith, Barbara, 106
Smith, Tim, 93
Snodgrass, J., 175
snuff, 57, 79, 80, 95, 163
social worker, 113
socialization, 84, 98, 193
sociology, 61
soft core, 26, 29, 43, 47, 122, 177
Soft-Core, 42
Spare Rib, 50, 128
Stanley, Lawrence, 111
Star Trek, 166, 167
Starr, Ringo, 132
Steinem, Gloria, 134, 152
stereotype, 52, 82, 120, 125, 167
stigma, 40, 56, 137, 143, 151
Stoltenberg, John, 125, 172, 173, 179
Stopes, Marie, 11, 49, 150
Strauss, M.A., 73
Strossen, Nadine, 7, 54, 102
studies, 31, 41, 51, 54, 55, 59–64, 67, 71, 73, 92
Sun, the, 4, 38, 77
Supreme Court, 53, 102, 165
suttee, 84
Sweet, Corrine, 128

Take Back the Night, 38, 39
Takei, George, 167
Tanay, Emanuel, 82
Tavris, Carol, 194
testimony, 5, 66, 83, 84, 87, 88, 131, 174
Thatcher, Margaret, 14, 17, 18
The Time/The Place, 49, 128
Thomas, Clarence, 165, 166

Thompson, Bill, 42
Thurmond, Strom, 166
transsexual, 41
Twiggy, 25

Vance, Carole S., 51, 87, 88, 107, 120, 152
victim testimony, 83, 87, 88
Vidal, Gore, 96
video, 17–20, 45, 65, 77–80, 113, 127, 133, 154
video nasties, 17, 18, 20, 77–80
vocabulary, 32, 35

W.H. Smith, 163
Waller, Reed, 185
Weaver, Sigourney, 132
Webster, Paula, 87
Weisstein, Naomi, 27
West and Wilde, 58
White, L.A., 62
Whitehouse, Mary, 12, 15, 16, 81, 101, 139, 169
Wicked Women, 106
Wildmon, Donald, 139
Williams Committee, 14, 74
Williams, Linda, 14, 31, 42, 74, 80
Willis, Ellen, 156
Wilson, Elizabeth, 53, 59
Wolfenden Report, 14
Women Against Pornography, 76, 87
Women Against Violence Against Women, 38
Women Against Violence in Pornography and Media, 87
Woodhull, Victoria, 11
Worley, Kate, 185
Wyre, Ray, 92, 113, 114

Yale University Child Study Center, 81

Zillmann, Dolf, 23, 62, 67–9, 71, 90, 91, 184